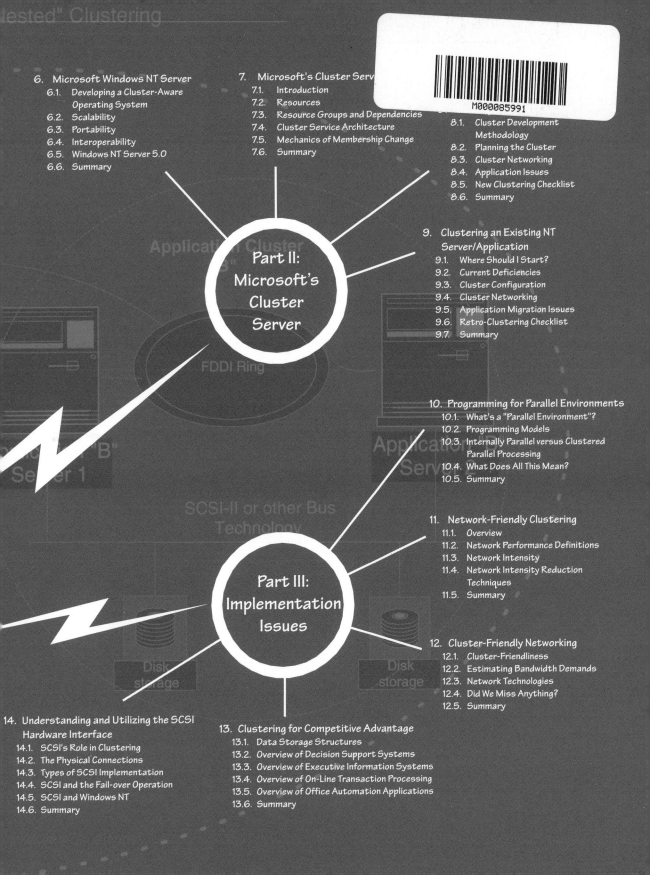

Part II: Microsoft's Cluster Server

Part III: Implementation Issues

Part II:
Microsoft's Cluster Server

Part III:
Implementation Issues

Windows NT® Clustering Blueprints

Mark A. Sportack

SAMS
PUBLISHING

201 West 103rd Street
Indianapolis, IN 46290

To my precious wife, Karen. I will spend the rest of my life trying to repay you for your love, support, and patience. Thank you for helping me throughout this endeavor.
To my son Adam, and daughter Jennifer. My life would be incomplete without you. — Mark

Copyright © 1997 by Sams Publishing

International Standard Book Number: 0-672-31135-6

Library of Congress Catalog Card Number: 97-67490

2000   99   98   97   4   3   2   1

Interpretation of the printing code: the rightmost double-digit number is the year of the book's printing; the rightmost single-digit, the number of the book's printing. For example, a printing code of 97-1 shows that the first printing of the book occurred in 1997.

Composed in Bembo and MCPdigital by Macmillan Computer Publishing

Printed in the United States of America

Trademarks

President	Richard K. Swadley
Publisher and Director of Acquistions	Jordan Gold
Director of Product Development	Dean Miller
Managing Editor	Jodi Jensen
Indexing Manager	Johnna L. VanHoose
Director of Marketing	Kelli S. Spencer
Product Marketing Manager	Wendy Gilbride
Marketing Coordinator	Linda B. Beckwith

Acquisitions Editor
Cari Skaggs

Development Editor
Jeff Koch

Production Editor
Tom Dinse

Copy Editor
Bart Reed

Indexer
Ben Slen

Technical Reviewer
Steven Tallon

Editorial Coordinators
Mandie Rowell
Katie Wise

Technical Edit Coordinator
Lynette Quinn

Editorial Assistants
Carol Ackerman
Andi Richter
Rhonda Tinch-Mize
Karen Williams

Cover Designer
Karen Ruggles

Book Designer
Gary Adair

Copy Writer
David Reichwein

Production Team Supervisor
Brad Chinn

Production
Jennifer Dierdorff
Michael Henry
Cyndi Davis-Hubler
Ayanna Lacey

Overview

Contents

III Implementation Issues

Acknowledgments

I would like to extend my thanks to:

- my boss, Portia Johnson, for her continued support of this amusing avocation;

- Michael G. Parfett, my corporate sponsor;

- Brian Sullivan for his invaluable technical insight and guidance;

- my friends and co-workers Stan Griff, Dave Kurtiak, and Rex Avery, for their insight, assistance, reference materials, and inability to escape whenever I needed someone to talk to;

- and to Cari Skaggs, Jeff Koch, Tom Dinse, and everyone at Sams for making this book possible.

— *Mark Sportack*

About the Author

Mark A. Sportack

Mark A. Sportack is an Information Technology (IT) professional with over 14 years experience in progressive levels of responsibility, and in many facets of IT. His experience includes project management, forecasting and managing multi-million dollar capital budgets, short and long range IT infrastructure planning, systems and applications design and development, directing implementation teams, and managing both technology and technical personnel. He is currently employed by AT&T and is responsible for technology planning and strategy in support of the Consumer Marketing Division (CMD).

James L. Mohler

James L. Mohler is an assistant professor in the Department of Technical Graphics at Purdue University. He has written several books about multimedia and hypermedia development including *Advanced Graphics and Page Design, Laura Lemay's Web Workshop on Graphics and Page Design, Teach Yourself How to Become a Webmaster in 14 Days,* and *The Professional Web Reference for Graphics, Animation, and Multimedia,* published by Macmillan Computer Publishing. Professor Mohler also serves as an active columnist for *Web Publisher* magazine, published by *Informant Communications Group.* You can contact James via snail mail at the Department of Technical Graphics, Purdue University, 1419 Knoy Hall, West Lafayette, IN 47907-1419 or via e-mail at jlmohler@tech.purdue.edu.

Tell Us What You Think!

As a reader, you are the most important critic and commentator of our books. We value your opinion and want to know what we're doing right, what we could do better, what areas you'd like to see us publish in, and any other words of wisdom you're willing to pass our way. You can help us make strong books that meet your needs and give you the computer guidance you require.

Do you have access to the World Wide Web? Then check out our site at http://www.mcp.com.

> **NOTE** If you have a technical question about this book, call the technical support line at 317-581-3833 or send e-mail to support@mcp.com.

As the team leader of the group that created this book, I welcome your comments. You can fax, e-mail, or write me directly to let me know what you did or didn't like about this book—as well as what we can do to make our books stronger. Here's the information:

Fax: 317-581-4669
E-mail: opsys_mgr@sams.mcp.com
Mail: Dean Miller
          Comments Department
          Sams Publishing
          201 W. 103rd Street
          Indianapolis, IN 46290

Introduction

Client/Server Is Dead!...

The client/server craze of the early 1990s is dead. This craze epitomized the anti-big-iron rebellion and generated countless attempts at *rightsizing* applications. Rightsizing is the term for porting an application to a distributed mid-range server from a mainframe. Ostensibly, a mainframe was much more expensive than a client/server solution.

This rebellion quickly stalled, and it became apparent that, even if adequate processing power for an application could be applied in a mid-range server, servers couldn't hope to match the reliability of a mainframe. Mainframes reside in data centers. Their power is highly filtered and their environment carefully controlled to ensure ideal temperature and humidity ranges. Mid-range servers distributed throughout user premises couldn't hope to match this. Consequently, many rightsizing initiatives found that any anticipated savings quickly fell victim to the losses incurred by downtime. In the end, distributed servers were, for the most part, only used to support distributed processing of low priority applications.

...Long Live the Cluster!

The client/server craze is about to be rejuvenated thanks to a new application of an old concept: clusters. Clustering, as a concept, dates back to the 1970s. At its inception, it was a highly specialized, data center-grade, niche technology. Over the years, clusters have become increasingly general purpose in nature. Clustered solutions have been available on Reduced Instruction Set Computing (RISC) platforms with UNIX operating systems for several years.

The evolution of clusters has taken them in two distinctly divergent directions. One branch focuses on providing highly scalable computing platforms. The other focuses on providing high availability and reliability. In tandem, these functional branches have the potential to ameliorate the problems that plagued early rightsizing initiatives. They can't duplicate the pampered computing environment of a data center, but they can provide the reliability and scalability that is essential to the distribution of mission critical applications.

Both branches of contemporary clusters have benefited from implementation on increasingly affordable platforms. Today, clusters can be developed in mainframes, massively parallel processors, symmetrical multiprocessors, and even uniprocessors. Integral to this variety of platforms is the variety of processors that can be used to develop clustered solutions. Up until recently, the only microprocessors that were used to support clustering were expensive, high-powered, proprietary chips. This automatically rendered clusters a fairly expensive and proprietary niche technology. This is about to change.

Microsoft is developing support for clusters in its Windows NT operating system in the form of control software. Even better, Microsoft is championing the development of open standard Application Programming Interfaces (APIs) that will facilitate the development of platform-independent, cluster-aware applications. These developments will position clusters as a viable solution for low-and mid-range servers, and leverage the extensive investments companies have already made in x86 architectures, Windows operating systems, and related training.

This degree of support for high reliability clusters on low-and mid-range servers will re-validate the client/server model. Adding high reliability to a relatively low-cost platform once again makes it feasible to consider the client/server model for more than just office automation applications. Mission critical applications will finally become legitimate candidates for distributed clustering.

It will be a while before all the essential ingredients are available and mature. These include hardware, operating systems, cluster management software, application software, and subsystem software components like Relational Database Management Systems (RDMS). They will become generally available slowly, but steadily. Once they are available, they will continue to be refined and provided with increased functionality and capacity. Once they are in place and mature, distributed clusters may well present the ultimate challenge to mainframe computing: they will offer inexpensive, yet highly scalable and highly available distributed computing.

In the meantime, take advantage of the capabilities that this nascent technology set provides. Develop the basic architectures that will enable you to begin clustering ever more important and resource-intensive applications. This book provides you with everything you need to start clustering your Windows NT applications.

Conventions in This Book

This book uses the following conventions.

Program names are indicated in all uppercase.

Screen messages and commands are shown in a monospaced type style like the command below:

```
ROUTE PRINT
```

Discussions of commands sometimes include variables that are shown in *italicized monospace*. You should substitute your command or statement where an italicized command or statement is shown.

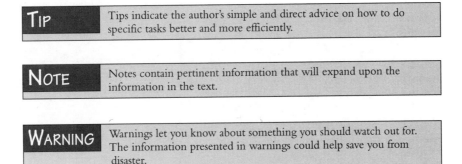

TIP Tips indicate the author's simple and direct advice on how to do specific tasks better and more efficiently.

NOTE Notes contain pertinent information that will expand upon the information in the text.

WARNING Warnings let you know about something you should watch out for. The information presented in warnings could help save you from disaster.

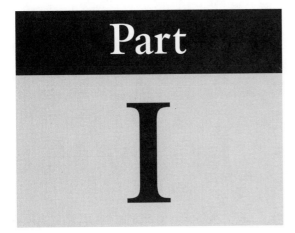

Part

I

Overview of Clustering

Chapter

1

Introduction to Clustering

Clustering has been evolving for over twenty years. During that time, it has embodied many different forms and has been applied to solve many different problems. Only recently has it become viable in low-end computing architectures through support by Microsoft's Windows NT.

This chapter describes the historical evolution of clustering, and introduces its contemporary forms and performance characteristics. These basic topics provide the context for much of the remainder of this book.

1.1. Evolution of Clustering

Believe it or not, Microsoft didn't invent clusters. The concept dates back to the 1970s when IBM implemented some aspects of clustering in its mainframe products. The first real cluster product appeared in 1982 when the Digital Equipment Company (DEC) introduced its VAXCluster. The VAXCluster offered more economical computing by uncoupling the input/output (I/O) devices from any single CPU. Instead, all CPUs could access the devices and their contents via a star topology bus and coupling device. Figure 1.1 illustrates the original VAXCluster. This simple form of clustering is still useful today, although modern cluster products go far beyond simple device sharing.

From this rather humble beginning, clustering has developed into a confusion of parallel computing that almost defies definition. Numerous factors contribute to this. First, there is no standard for "clustering" computers. Clusters can be implemented in many different ways. They can be designed and engineered to solve many different business problems, using numerous topologies in the process.

In addition, there is no standard platform on which to build a cluster. Uniprocessor and multiprocessor machines from all vendors can be mixed and matched in clusters as well. Even the choice of microprocessor is not limited. You can build clusters using either *Reduced Instruction Set Computing* (RISC), *Complex Instruction Set Computing* (CISC), or even *Very Large Instruction Word* (VLIW) processors.

UNIX-based clustering products for RISC processors have been available for years. Recently, the introduction of products based on the *Wintel* platform has been generating considerable excitement in the marketplace. Given the relatively low cost of x86 CISC microprocessors and the popularity of Microsoft Windows operating systems, clustering software for this platform can greatly reduce the cost of acquiring and operating a cluster without compromising scalability, availability, or functionality. More importantly, this combination of operating system and microprocessor opens up a whole new market: distributed client/server architectures can now provide applications with the reliability of a mainframe!

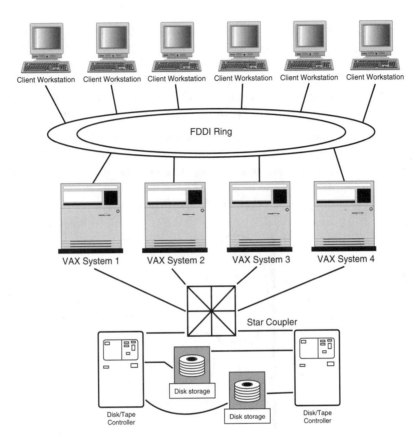

Figure 1.1.
Typical VAXCluster configuration.

Client Workstation   Client Workstation   Client Workstation   Client Workstation   Client Workstation   Client Workstation

FDDI Ring

VAX System 1   VAX System 2   VAX System 3   VAX System 4

Star Coupler

Disk storage

Disk storage

Disk/Tape Controller   Disk/Tape Controller

Introduction to Clustering

1.2. Clusters Defined

Over the years clustering technologies have slowly but steadily progressed. Originally a mainframe technology, clusters were later embraced by UNIX operating systems on mid-range computers. Today, both Novell and Microsoft are developing Application Programming Interfaces (APIs), cluster management software, and operating system support for clusters for Intel x86 architecture. As a result, clusters are now positioned for general acceptance at all levels of the computing infrastructure: mainframe, mid-range, and low-end.

More important is the development of cluster-awareness features for the Microsoft NT operating system. This graphically based operating system has become ubiquitous in the low-end server market. These technological innovations, however significant, only add to the challenge of establishing a coherent definition for a "cluster."

Despite its lengthy heritage and current market position, clustering remains a poorly defined aspect of parallel computing. The chameleon-like nature of clustering defies easy definition. A good but necessarily nonspecific definition of "cluster" is a loosely coupled set of computers that function as a single computer. Thus, it qualifies as a branch of parallel computing. Specifically, clusters are a distributed form of parallel computing. Implementations and topologies of clustering vary significantly with the degree of parallelism and the function, physical platform, operating system, network, and so on, employed.

Clusters are frequently confused with two other forms of parallel computing: *Symmetric Multiprocessors* (SMPs) and *Massively Parallel Processors* (MPPs). As Figure 1.2 illustrates, clusters demonstrate a significant overlap with both SMPs and MPPs. This is to be expected given that they are all forms of parallel computing, but they are not completely interchangeable.

Figure 1.2.

Functional overlap with SMPs and MPPs.

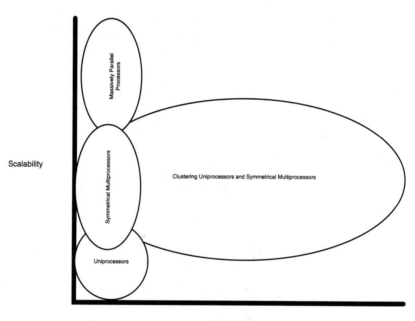

Figure 1.2 shows the partial overlap of clustered computers with uniprocessors, Symmetric Multiprocessors, and Massively Parallel Processors relative to each one's tradeoffs between scalability and availability. Clusters are capable of broader simultaneous support for scalability and availability.

Despite their similar functions, there is one important architectural distinction between clusters and both SMPs and MPPs: clusters are distributed. SMPs and MPPs are self-contained within a single computer. Therefore, even though they can redistribute workloads internally in the event of a CPU failure, they are vulnerable to downtime from failures in other parts of the computer. Clusters are more dependable because they have fewer single points of failure. They distribute the processing across multiple separate computers that are networked together.

System architects who are considering clusters must also decide whether one of the myriad commercial cluster products will meet their needs, or if they need to cobble their own cluster with a pastiche of hardware, software, and networking products. The availability of "canned" cluster solutions adds to the confusion about what clustering means because of their great dissimilarities. Vendors are intentionally trying to differentiate their clustered solutions in the marketplace either by focusing on specific niches or through feature or performance-based competition. This is evident from the lack of mutual support among competing products. Evidence of this is found in the products being championed by Microsoft (Cluster Server) and Novell (Wolf Mountain), respectively.

The physical separation and redundancy of computers within a cluster lends itself to architectural creativity. Clusters can be implemented in so many different ways, and for so many different purposes, that one would be hard pressed to find anything in common among some types of clusters.

In short, there is no single, coherent definition for "clustering." It is, rather, a generic concept for configuring multiple computers to perform the same set of tasks. Consequently, many people use clusters and cluster products every day without recognizing them for what they are.

There are two primary levels of clustering. The more mature of the two is server clustering. The other level is known as workstation clustering.

1.2.1. Workstation Clusters

In this scenario, client-level workstations are linked together to emulate the processing power of a much larger machine. This configuration is much less mature, and it suffers from the fact that I/O and networks are much slower than CPUs and system buses.

The workstations clustered in Figure 1.3 ship I/O requests to each other to minimize the number of wasted CPU cycles. In combination, they have the computational capability of a much larger and more expensive computer.

This configuration remains more of an experimental curiosity than a practical technique. It is presented here solely to demonstrate the fluidity of form that characterizes distributed parallelism (clustering).

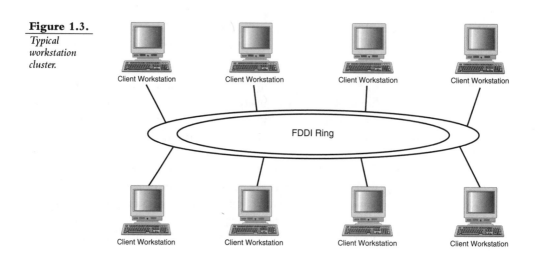

1.3. Server Clusters

In a server cluster, the linked computers are multiuser servers that support applications. In combination, they can provide either fault-tolerant redundancy for each other, load balancing, or emulation of a much more powerful and expensive computer. Regardless of which level a cluster is implemented on, ideally this loose confederation would be addressed, managed, and used as a single logical entity.

The typical server cluster illustrated in Figure 1.4 provides automatic load balancing and fault tolerance in support of a common application set. The non-clustered alternative to this configuration would be a single, larger, and more expensive computer that could not provide the fault tolerance or load balancing of this solution.

It is important to note that server clustering is much more than just logically linked hardware. The key to making a cluster work lies in the cluster management software and the operating system. These two must work together to provide the functionality that is expected of the cluster.

Server clusters have become specialized along two distinct functional paths: reliability and scalability. Clusters designed for reliability take advantage of the distributed redundancy of computer systems in the clusters to ensure that no single hardware or software failure brings the clustered application down. Conceivably, this method can achieve 100% uptime.

Clusters designed for scalability seek to increase the computational capacity of a clustered application in response to growth in the application's use.

Figure 1.4.
*Typical server
cluster.*

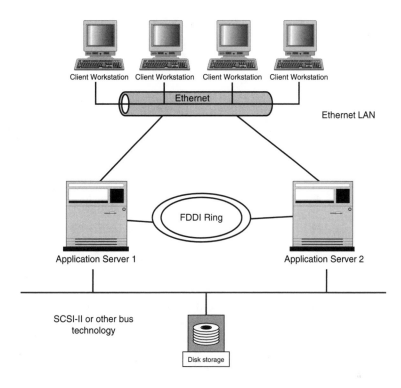

1.3.1. Clustering for Availability

Clusters that are engineered for availability are frequently called *fail-over* clusters because, in the event of a system-level failure of one of the clustered nodes, all processing that would have been sent its way is shifted over to another node in the cluster.

In a fail-over cluster, two or more servers function as back-up servers for each other. This can be implemented in a number of ways. The two most important categories of fail-over cluster topologies are *shared disk* and *shared nothing*.

A shared disk fail-over cluster features two or more nodes that split the processing requirements of a single application. If one of the nodes fails, the surviving nodes assume its processing load. This is illustrated in Figure 1.5.

In a shared nothing, fail-over cluster, two or more otherwise unrelated servers function as back up servers for each other. This requires mechanisms to ensure that each server contains current application software and data for each other, as well as the appropriate cluster management software to monitor each other's status.

Figure 1.5.
Shared disk, fail-over clustering.

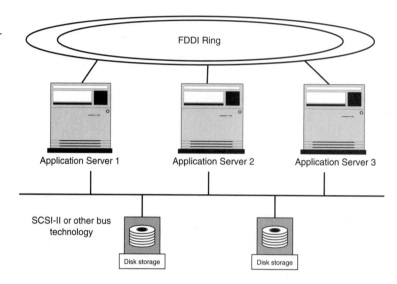

In Figure 1.6, the two processors are completely unrelated. That is, they "share nothing." Nevertheless, they provide a back-up platform for each other in the event of a failure.

Figure 1.6.
Shared nothing, fail-over clustering.

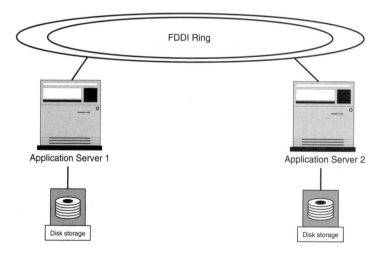

1.3.2. Clustering for Scalability

Scalability is the capability to add system resources such as RAM, CPUs, storage facilities, and so on, to an existing system. To a limited extent, almost every system is capable of internal scalability. The limit is usually imposed by some physical limitation of the computer—for example, the number of expansion slots. The only systems that can't be scaled internally are those that are already at their maximum capacity.

Clusters enhance this basic internal scalability of a computer system by providing alternative means of adding capacity—by providing external scalability. When each computer in a cluster has been fully configured, the capacity of the cluster can be scaled even further by adding additional computers to it.

In a symmetric multiprocessor, the operating system is "aware" of the presence of the processors and automatically distributes tasks among them as evenly as possible. These CPUs share RAM, storage facilities, and other machine resources. When a CPU fails, the operating system automatically recovers from the failure by identifying the failed CPU as out of service and distributing tasks among the surviving CPUs. However, when one of the shared system resources fails, it is much more difficult, if not impossible, for the operating system to recover. The entire machine might stop working.

This fundamental limitation of SMPs is overcome when SMPs are clustered. Ideally, the SMP's architecture would be used to provide scalable performance optimization for its applications. Reliability would then be provided via clustering of SMPs. This combination provides a degree of reliability and scalability that can rival mainframe performance.

The key to successfully implementing either scalable or reliable clusters can be found by extending this comparison with SMPs. Just as the SMP requires an operating system that is aware of the multiple processors, and also requires an application that can be processed in parallel, the cluster imposes similar requirements. A cluster's operating system must be aware of the other computers in the cluster. It must constantly stay up-to-date on their operational status and capabilities.

Similarly, a clustered application should also be aware that it is executing in a cluster. Otherwise, the application might not understand attempts by the cluster-aware operating system to use cluster-level services. The outcome probably would not be fun.

Both scalable and reliable clusters will be discussed in much more detail in the next two chapters. More detail on programming issues that are unique to clusters is provided in Chapter 10, "Programming for Parallel Environments."

1.4. Parallel Computing versus Clustered Computing

Because clustering is a branch of parallel computing, you should understand both the similarities and differences between them. *Parallel computing* is the integration of multiple central processing units (CPUs) in a single computer. These processors work in parallel to process instructions. Parallel processors can be purchased with as few as two CPUs, or as many as thousands of CPUs, in a single machine.

Figures 1.7 and 1.8 illustrate both the differences and similarities between parallel processors and clusters.

Figure 1.7.

The architecture of a parallel processing computer.

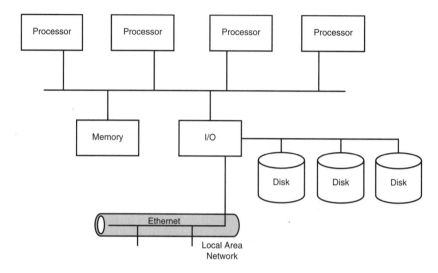

In Figure 1.7, four CPUs are strapped together to a common I/O, RAM, and System Bus. A parallel processing computer excels at satisfying CPU–intensive applications. In this example, a single chassis provides four times the processing power of a uniprocessor with a comparable CPU.

Figure 1.8 provides the same amount of processing power in a clustered configuration. Although there are many subtle differences between these two configurations, an obvious difference is the presence of two machines instead of a single one. That increases the *Operations, Administration, and Maintenance* (OA&M) support required by the clustered configuration for the same amount of processing power.

The generic diagram in Figure 1.8 shows four CPUs split between two dual-processor machines. These two computers are strapped together logically via control software that continuously monitors the status of each computer in the cluster.

Balancing this incremental increase in support costs is the performance delta. Although processing power has remained constant, the amount of competition for I/O, RAM, and other system internal resources has changed. The clustered solution cuts this in half by distributing the load approximately equally between two systems. Depending on the application's demand for resources, this may or may not affect performance.

Figure 1.8.
*The architecture
of a parallel
processing cluster.*

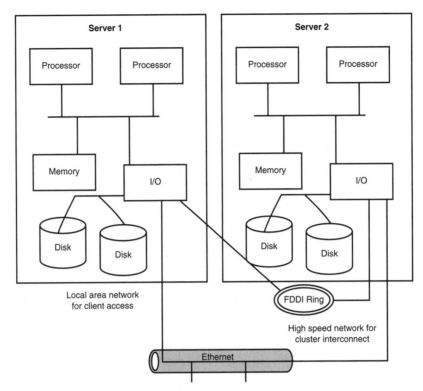

One the other side of the equation, additional processing power is required to coordinate activities between the two clustered servers. This is done via highly specialized cluster control software. Another possible negative factor—depending on how the cluster is arranged—might be the need to ship I/O requests between the two machines. I/O is already the most expensive operation in terms of resource intensity of all computational tasks. Shipping I/O across an external network only makes the task more expensive.

These run-time performance variables must be the subject of due diligence when you're designing a clustered platform for an application.

1.5. What's in It for Me?

At first glance these concepts might seem counterintuitive. Logic dictates that many computers are more expensive to maintain than a single computer. The logistics of coordinating the processing of an application's instructions and data across multiple machines can also be intimidating. The next logical question to ask is "What's in it for me? Why should I take on all that extra work?"

The answer is simple. Contemporary clusters are a radical departure from tradi-tional computing paradigms. They cannot be assessed by traditional beliefs. When you get beyond the paradigm shift, the benefits of clustered solutions become apparent.

Clusters have the potential to provide levels of availability in a distributed computing platform that were previously attainable only in data centers. Availabil-ity can be kept high because of the redundancy of Central Processing Units (CPUs), storage facilities, I/O mechanisms, and even application software.

Building a cluster out of low-cost computing components (x86 processors and NT, for example) can skew the economics of conventional computing. Inexpen-sive clusters can provide an adequate amount of computational capability and reliability for any application at a much lower cost than can a data center/ mainframe solution.

This is the crux of clustering's appeal. The client/server phenomena that charac-terized the early 1990s spawned countless "rightsizing" initiatives that were all but doomed to fail. *Rightsizing,* the term for porting a mainframe application to a distributed mid-range or low-end server, quickly ran into a constraining factor: reliability. Distributed servers, regardless of their processing power, couldn't match the reliability and, consequently, the availability of a mainframe.

A large contributor to the mainframe's reliability was the heavily conditioned and controlled environment that they typically reside in. Data center power is, typically, highly filtered and the environment carefully controlled to ensure ideal temperature and humidity ranges. These are tough conditions to simulate and maintain in buildings designed for users rather than computers. Humans, after all, can tolerate some fluctuation without incurring permanent physical damage. Consequently, many rightsizing initiatives found that any cost savings were negated by increased downtime. In the end, distributed servers were for the most part only used to support distributed processing of low priority, noncritical applications like office automation tools.

Clusters, through the coordination and distribution of processing across multiple computers, might hold the key to providing inexpensive mainframelike reliability in a distributed environment.

1.6. Recent Technological Developments

Clusters are steadily becoming more common outside the data center. This progression began with larger mid-range servers that featured RISC processors and UNIX operating systems. Typically, these clusters were designed to provide reliability through a mechanism known as *fail-over*. Fail-over clusters can contain computer systems that support a common application and provide load balancing of processing demands during normal operations. In the event of a failure, the surviving computers, or nodes, automatically compensate for the lost machine in the cluster.

An alternative approach that has been used in fail-over clustering is to loosely couple two completely unrelated computer systems. This is more cost-effective than maintaining a hot stand-by machine because all the machines are actively supporting applications.

Regardless of which approach was used, the early UNIX-based cluster products suffered from a lack of industry-standard APIs. This automatically categorized them as proprietary, single-vendor solutions. Not surprisingly, these cluster products remained fairly expensive and were regarded as niche technologies.

Recently, technological developments have focused on further extending clusters into what had previously been the relatively unsophisticated domain of client/ server applications. Clustering can provide client/server applications with cost-effective scalability and, more importantly, reliability. These features were previously only available at great cost at this level of IT architecture.

Extending clustering technologies to this arena is not a simple or trivial extension of previous efforts. The client/server domain is populated with a heterogeneous mix of hardware and operating systems. Single-vendor solutions that were acceptable in data centers or with mid-range to large UNIX/RISC platforms are unacceptable at this level. Customers require an open, low-cost, cluster solution.

Driving this extension of clustering to low-cost computing architectures is Microsoft's development of native support in the NT operating system. Microsoft has complemented this by developing open, industry-standard cluster APIs. Several companies have announced their intentions, or released beta software, to implement clustered solutions on the CISC-based x86 microprocessor with an NT operating system.

1.7. Future Technological Developments

Within the next year, open standard APIs, control software, and operating systems will mature, enabling "open" clusters to be implemented in the NT environment. Marketing coalitions are forming that will develop standardized APIs for cluster products, enabling development of "open" cluster control software that won't be tied to any specific physical platform. Available cluster products will most likely undergo incremental improvements. Initially, such products will only support fail-over and be limited to two node clusters, but this number will gradually increase. Over time, these nascent cluster products will include meaningful scalability features.

These developments will position clusters as a viable solution for low- and mid-range servers, but they are not enough to guarantee successful clustering. It will be at least a year, and maybe longer, before all the essential ingredients are available and mature. These ingredients include hardware, operating systems, cluster management software, application software, and subsystem software components such as Relational Database Management Systems (RDMS). Once in place, distributed clustered systems could present the ultimate challenge to mainframe computing: They will offer inexpensive, yet highly scalable and highly available distributed computing. However, until they are all developed and generally available, would-be cluster architects could find themselves frustrated by the limits of the available products.

One of the issues that must be resolved in the coming months involves the Application Programming Interface (API). APIs are rapidly becoming the "open" world's equivalent of a proprietary technology. There are two sets currently competing for mind share, if not market share, of the NT cluster market. The danger from this is that commercially available cluster support software might only support a limited subset of the available APIs. Until the API issue is resolved, cluster solutions could continue to be single-vendor solutions, at least in the UNIX/RISC arena.

The next feature of clustering that will likely become important in the not-too-distant future is commercially available applications. Until applications are designed to be "cluster-aware," there is a finite limit on the degree to which they can benefit from a clustered platform. For example, a noncluster-aware application running on top of a cluster-aware operating system like NT will not understand cluster services. Attempts by the operating system to use one or more of those services might be either ignored or misinterpreted by the application. In either case, the cluster probably won't function as expected.

1.8. Summary

The evolution of clusters has taken two distinct and divergent directions, with both branches being driven steadily down on the cost/performance curve. One branch focuses on providing highly scalable computing platforms, the other on providing high availability and reliability. In tandem, they have the potential to ameliorate the problems that plagued early rightsizing initiatives. Although they can't duplicate the pampered computing environment of a data center, they can provide the reliability and scalability that is essential to the distribution of mission critical applications.

Both branches of contemporary clusters have benefited from increasingly afford-able platforms. Today, clusters can be developed in mainframes, massively parallel processors, symmetrical multiprocessors, and even uniprocessors. Integral to this variety of platforms is the variety of processors that can be used to develop clustered solutions.

Until recently, the only microprocessors that were used to support clustering were expensive, high powered, proprietary chips. This automatically rendered clusters a fairly expensive and proprietary niche technology. That is about to change.

Support for highly reliable clusters on low- and mid-range servers will validate the client/server model for more than just office automation applications. Mission critical applications will be valid candidates for distributed clustering.

To effectively implement clustered solutions, you need to understand the concept of clustering, including an understanding of its capabilities and its strengths and weaknesses. This understanding will provide the foundation for building your NT cluster.

Introduction to
Clustering

Chapter

2

Clustering for Availability

One of the two main goals of clustering is to increase the availability of the application residing on the cluster. The other goal, reliability of a computer system, is a much more complex goal that encompasses far more than simple availability. High availability is strictly a state of readiness. High reliability requires that the system, including all its hardware and software subsystems, performs as expected. Although your goal for any cluster should be high reliability, a necessary prerequisite is a highly available platform. This chapter focuses on using clusters as a highly available platform for applications that must be highly reliable.

2.1. What Is "Availability"?

At its simplest, an available computing system is one that is ready to accept (and able to process) requests. A highly available system, however, is not necessarily a reliable one. It would have to be available only during those times when it is needed. Therefore, for the purposes of this book, a highly available system is one that does not suffer service-impacting downtime during usage periods.

Reliability is much more difficult to define. It is one of those funny terms—everyone understands it intuitively, yet they can seldom agree on a precise definition. This is especially true in distributed computing. Reliability in a computer system means that the system is ready and able to accept and process requests. However, reliability goes much further: a reliable system can process each request without failure.

Numerous factors can render a system unavailable, without the system necessarily being unreliable. For example, backing up data might require exclusive access to that data. This would make the system temporarily unavailable for client use. However, if the application's production schedule were such that the client didn't require its use from 10 p.m. until 4 a.m., the system could be taken offline for backups and other maintenance tasks without adversely affecting its availability. In addition, such off-hours, proactive maintenance improves the system's reliability.

Backups, routine preventive maintenance, software upgrades, and a host of other activities all contribute to a system's overall reliability. In scenarios in which a single host supports an application, these activities will result in downtime. The effect can be mitigated by scheduling and controlling downtime to minimize its impact on the application's user community.

2.1.1. Traditional Availability

Traditionally, availability has been engineered into computer systems through redundancy. Critical components whose *mean-time between failure* (MTBF) is demonstrably less than others in the system are duplicated within the system. Redundant power supplies, hard drives, even CPUs, are all used to increase the availability of computer systems. This does not increase any of the components' MTBF ratings. Instead, this internal redundancy eliminates *single points of failure* (SPOF).

A somewhat more extreme approach to eliminating SPOFs is to install a completely redundant computer system. This system, known as a hot standby machine, is idle until the primary system experiences a failure. Figure 2.1 illustrates such a system.

Figure 2.1.
Availability via a traditional hot standby machine.

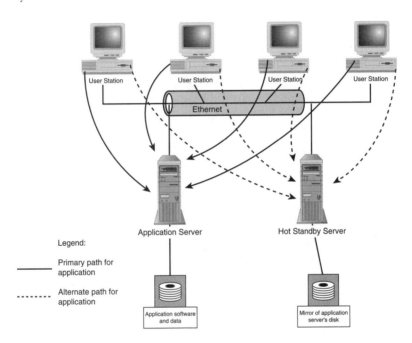

This approach, though functional, tends to be fairly expensive. Depending upon how the standby machine is configured, this approach can be expected to double the system's cost. Maintenance and operations costs are also likely to increase relative to the cost of supporting a single machine. The support costs increase from continuously updating the data stored on the standby machine. Any changes to the versions of application software and operating system on the primary system would also have to be duplicated on the standby.

For all these increased costs, hot standby solutions deliver surprisingly little. The application's performance remains constant when compared to a single system solution. This isn't surprising because the application runs on only one machine at a time. The second system is used only when the first one fails or is intentionally taken offline.

The limitations of a hot standby become obvious to the user community during a failure. The two machines do not communicate with each other, and they possess no mechanisms to automatically recover from a failure. When the primary system "dies," the users experience a lapse in service and are forced to manually log onto the alternate system. Any data that was in memory, and any instructions being executed, are lost.

2.1.2. Clustered Availability

In many ways, clusters are a new and improved version of the old hot standby redundancy approach. Clustered systems can actually improve total system performance by simultaneously using all available clustered systems. Each machine, or *node*, communicates with each of the other machines in the cluster. Workloads can be balanced, and failures can be managed gracefully.

They can also offer highly available platforms for applications by eliminating any single points of failure that may exist. For example, symmetrical multiprocessors (SMPs) offer greater availability than uniprocessors because of the redundancy inherent in their processing architecture. Unfortunately, SMPs still contain many other single points of failure. Memory, I/O, even the motherboard, can each bring the entire system down in the event of a failure. Clusters resolve this fundamental weakness by providing redundancy at the system level. Entire computer systems, whether uniprocessor or multiprocessor, are loosely coupled. This coupling provides more than adequate redundancy to eliminate any single points of failure.

The topology of a highly available cluster depends on the specific source of downtime that is being engineered out of existence. Some of these sources include routine hardware or software maintenance, backups, minor hardware or software failures, major hardware or software failures, and even disasters. They can all result in downtime for a clustered application.

Given that there is no consensus on the proper way to design or use a cluster, it is not surprising that numerous topologies have appeared. The strengths and weaknesses of some of these potential cluster topologies become apparent when those topologies are examined. Such an understanding is essential if you are to develop effective clustered computing solutions.

Clusters that are engineered specifically for high availability are frequently called *fail-over* clusters because, in the event of a system-level failure of one of the clustered nodes, all of the processing it would have done is shifted, or *failed over*, to another node in the cluster. This can be implemented in a myriad of ways. The two basic fail-over cluster topologies are shared disk and shared nothing.

2.2. Shared Disk, Fail-Over Clusters

Generally, shared disk clustering excels at satisfying I/O-intensive requirements, maximizing total system performance and load balancing. This approach is often used in conjunction with other mechanisms that auto-recover from failures within the cluster.

A shared disk, fail-over cluster features two or more nodes that split the processing requirements of a single application. If one node fails, the surviving nodes assume its processing load. This is illustrated in Figure 2.2.

Figure 2.2.
Shared disk, fail-over clustering.

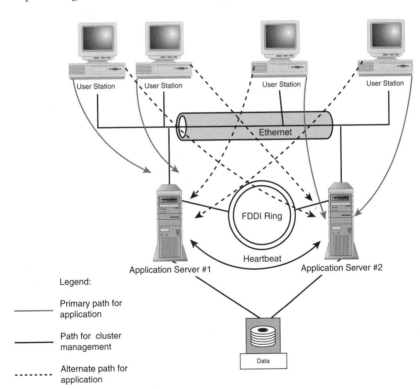

2.2.1. How Can I Support Applications in These Clusters?

The basic shared disk, fail-over topology supports applications in a number of ways. The two most significant are dynamic load-balancing and non-load-balancing application clusters.

Load-balancing application fail-over clusters feature either a single application or multiple smaller applications in which the workload is shared by all the hosts in the cluster. Intracluster communications are essential to ensuring that the load is somewhat balanced between the hosts. Communication is also necessary to coordinate and manage access to the shared disks and data. This variant is illustrated in Figure 2.3.

Figure 2.3.
Load-balancing, shared disk, fail-over clustering.

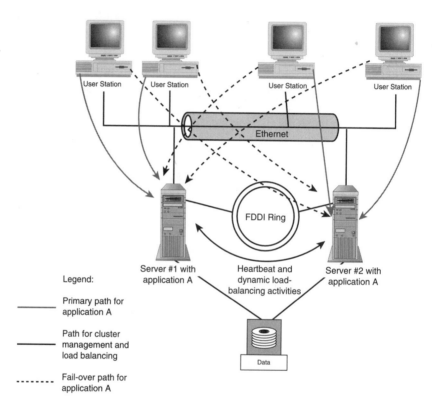

This approach can support multiple applications in the cluster. The critical distinction between this and non-load-balancing clustering is that the applications are processed communally by the cluster's nodes, rather than individually. In the event of a failure in this type of cluster, the failed machine is taken out of the cluster management software's pool of available resources. The surviving hosts then assume an increased share of the overall workload to compensate for their lost peer.

Non-load-balancing fail-over clusters do not process applications communally. Rather, each application has a primary host that is responsible for all of its processing. The only thing shared by hosts in this cluster is the disk arrays. In the event of a failure, the failed processor's workload is shunted over to a predetermined backup processor in the cluster. This technique is illustrated in Figure 2.4.

Figure 2.4.

Non-load-balancing, shared disk, fail-over clustering.

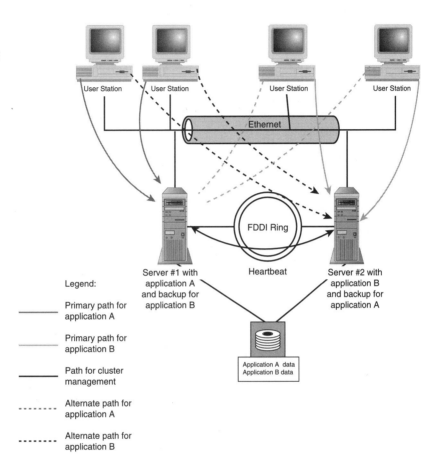

In all of these scenarios, intracluster communications are essential to conduct a fail-over.

2.2.2. Disk Sharing Issues

One virtue of sharing disks is that there is no need to duplicate the data stores. All hosts in a cluster have equal access to all of the data stored on the shared disks. This obviates the need to perform disk mirroring or other techniques that would otherwise be necessary to maintain synchronicity between multiple data stores. Such techniques may be deployed among the shared disks, but they are not vital to the cluster's capability to fail-over.

Clusters that share disks, and their contents, are directly descended from the original VAXClusters that were illustrated in Figure 1.1. Unlike the hosts in that figure, these hosts are dedicated to the same task and must coordinate access to and modification of the data. This requires interhost communication that can be satisfied via a Local Area Network (LAN). Because a cluster is likely to be serviced by two or more LANs, one of which is highly specialized and dedicated to intra-cluster communications, a more specific term for the specialized LAN is needed. For the remainder of this book, the term *Cluster Area Network* (CAN) will be used to identify the specific portion of a cluster's networking that is used solely for intracluster communications. LAN will still be used to describe the networking that connects the clustered hosts to users, routers, or other hosts outside the cluster.

Intracluster communications are used for a few different reasons that vary based on the cluster product. Hosts can share status information that is used for load balancing, replicating application states, or initiating the fail-over sequence. This group of functions is loosely categorized as *cluster management*. For more information about cluster management, refer to section 2.4, "Cluster Management."

Another potential use for a cluster area network is to coordinate I/O sharing. Some mechanism is needed to manage and coordinate accessing, modifying, and deleting data resident on shared disks. This is known as *access management*. For more information about access management, refer to section 2.5, "Data Access Management in a Cluster."

2.2.3. What's the Right Shared Disk Cluster Size?

The ideal configuration for a shared disk, fail-over cluster is one that contains three clustered hosts. The size and internal configuration of these hosts is unimportant, provided that they are similar enough to be capable of assuming the processing load for each other.

The significance of three node clusters is fairly simple. In a two-node cluster only a single failure can be accommodated. Once the first machine fails, the second machine becomes responsible for all the work. This machine, and more specifically its non-redundant components, becomes a single point of failure. The clustered application is then vulnerable to the very thing that the cluster was designed to prevent. This vulnerability persists until the failed machine can be restored to service.

In a three-node cluster, up to two failures can occur before the entire cluster is vulnerable to a single point of failure. The concept of multiple fail-overs is known as *cascading*. Beyond three nodes, the logistics and addressing of sharing disks becomes onerous and may even become counterproductive.

A more subtle problem with supporting more than two cascaded fail-overs is that the average workload supported by any node must decrease. In a two-node cluster with both nodes equivalent, each host can approach 50% resource utilization and still have enough capacity to back each other up in the event of a failure. In a three-node cluster with cascading fail-over, each host can approach only 33% resource utilization. Exceeding this threshold comes at the risk of not being able to support the second fail-over. Logically, this shouldn't be a big risk, but the ultimate determination of how much risk is acceptable is unique to each cluster and situation.

2.2.4. What's the Catch?

Generally, shared disk clusters are the least scalable of all clusters. There are several factors that contribute to this.

- The first factor constraining shared disk cluster scalability is the complex coordination required to share disks and their contents. This chore becomes increasingly complex as more computers are added to the cluster.

- Another limitation is that it may not be feasible to share disks over great distances. Channel extension technologies that can network geographically dispersed disk drives for sharing exist, but they can be expensive to implement and operate. Geographic dispersion of the data also complicates and increases the time required to coordinate access to the data, adversely affecting the clustered application's overall performance.

- Sharing disks automatically limits the topological variation that can be used to develop specialized clusters for specific business requirements. For example, the system illustrated in Figure 2.1 uses a shared SCSI-II bus to link the clustered nodes to the disks. Maintaining acceptable levels of bus throughput requires the physical specification of the SCSI-II bus to impose some stringent distance limitations. Consequently, the disks and clustered hosts must be within fairly close proximity of each other.

> **NOTE** Shared disk clusters that use SCSI bus technologies are usually limited to one-room configurations. Some topological variation is possible within this physical limitation by varying the ways that the disks are shared. For example, a single SCSI-II bus can be used to interconnect a cluster, with each node serving as a termination point. Alternatively, multiple redundant SCSI buses can be used. For more information on SCSI technologies, please refer to Appendix A, "Technical Glossary."

Shared disk clusters are generally the least expensive to implement and the easiest to operate. These benefits are blunted somewhat by the technique's limitations. Nevertheless, a shared disk cluster can do wonders for improving an application's platform availability without requiring tremendous investment or effort to build and operate.

Clustering for Availability

2.3. Shared Nothing, Fail-Over Clusters

The second cluster architecture is known as *shared nothing* clustering. This type of cluster, despite its oxymoronic name, is much more scalable and has greater potential for delivering fault tolerance and auto-recovery from failures than shared disk clusters.

In a shared nothing, fail-over cluster, two or more otherwise unrelated servers function as backup servers for each other. This requires mechanisms to ensure that each server contains the same application software and data as the other, as well as the appropriate cluster management software to monitor the other's status. This type of system is illustrated in Figure 2.5.

Figure 2.5.
Shared nothing clustering.

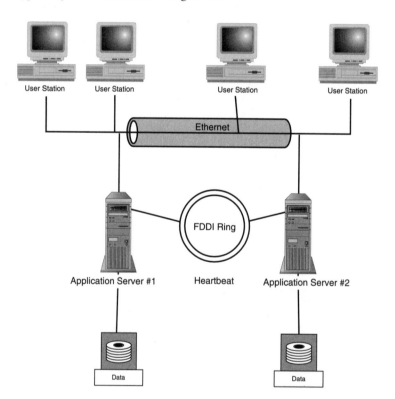

The basic shared nothing topology shown in Figure 2.5 can be implemented in a wide range of variations, and tailored to either reliability or scalability. The variants that provide reliability functions are described in this section. You learn about highly scalable shared nothing clusters in Chapter 3, "Clustering for Scalability."

2.3.1. Topological Variation

Shared nothing clusters eliminate shared drives as a single point of failure by maximizing redundancy. In addition, they are extremely flexible and permit architectural innovation. However, this degree of redundancy increases both the cost and complexity of building and operating a cluster. This type of cluster can be built in two major topologies: close proximity and geographically dispersed.

In Figure 2.6, the basic shared nothing cluster is used in a close proximity, fail-over scenario. The two processors are completely unrelated—they "share nothing." Nevertheless, they provide a backup platform for each other in the event of a failure. Thus, despite their name, they both contain cluster management software and share a cluster area network. These mechanisms enable them to continuously monitor each other's health to see if a fail-over is necessary. The polling mechanism they use to monitor each other is often called a *heartbeat*.

Figure 2.6.
Close proximity, shared nothing, fail-over clustering.

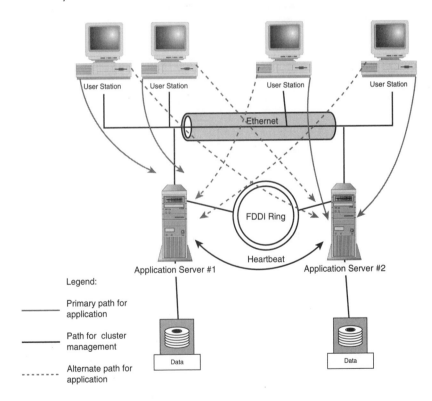

The close proximity, shared nothing cluster topology does not impose any restrictions on how close the clustered nodes need to be. These limitations would be a function of the communications technologies used to connect the cluster nodes.

Shared nothing clustering also enables clusters to be distributed geographically, permitting greater availability by creating options for disaster recovery. Figure 2.7 illustrates the same shared nothing, fail-over cluster that was presented in Figure 2.6, but implemented in a geographically dispersed manner. It is also possible for the hosts in this figure to be clusters, rather than individual computers.

Figure 2.7.

Geographically dispersed, shared nothing clustering.

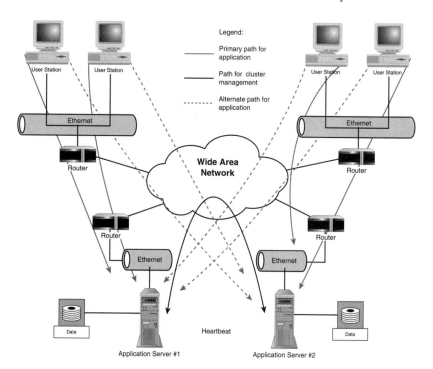

Geographically dispersing shared nothing clusters provides a degree of availability that is impossible to achieve with any system, clustered or not, that is wholly contained in a single location. Disasters, natural or otherwise, severely affect relatively small geographic areas. Spreading the clustered nodes across as large an area as possible minimizes the chance that a single disaster will completely halt a clustered application's processing.

The availability of a geographically distributed cluster comes at the cost of performance. Wide area network (WAN) facilities will almost certainly be slower than any local area network (LAN) technology. Attempts to use geographically dispersed clustered hosts for single application dynamic load balancing are doomed, because the participating hosts may need to ship I/O requests to other computers within the cluster.

For example, if Server #1 in Figure 2.7 receives a request from a client for data that resides on Server #2's disk, it must ship the I/O request across the relatively low bandwidth wide area network to Server #2 for fulfillment. This is substantially slower than retrieving data from a local disk drive.

This poor performance is probably sufficient to warrant limiting this clustered arrangement to batch processing, disaster recovery, or other applications that are tolerant of long waits for I/O requests.

2.3.2. How Can I Support Applications in These Clusters?

Shared nothing application support topologies can be varied further. The two basic functional varieties are static load-balancing and non-load-balancing clusters. Static load-balancing clusters typically support common applications. Non-load-balancing clusters can support completely unrelated applications.

Load-balancing, shared nothing, fail-over clusters feature either a single application or multiple smaller applications whose workload is shared by all the hosts in the cluster. Unlike shared disk clusters, there can be a significant performance degradation associated with dynamic load balancing in shared nothing clusters. Each node in the cluster has its own disks and probably its own data stores. Each properly designed node will receive requests for processing locally resident data. Dynamic load balancing all but precludes this from happening consistently. In a dynamic load-balancing cluster, the nodes will ship each other requests for processing based solely upon their respective workloads. Consequently, shared nothing clusters are better suited to static load balancing.

In a static load-balancing cluster, intracluster communications are not essential to load balancing. Load balancing is done in a static manner: Users are given the IP or other WAN address of one specific node. This simple, static mechanism provides a rudimentary form of load balancing across the cluster's nodes. Though not nearly as efficient as dynamic load balancing, this is the best that can be done in a shared nothing cluster.

Intracluster communications in shared nothing clusters are primarily concerned with monitoring the health of the clustered nodes and, when necessary, conducting a fail-over. This is illustrated in Figure 2.8.

Non-load-balancing, shared nothing clusters are typically constructed using completely unrelated applications and processors. They are linked together with a cluster area network and common cluster management software, but this is the extent of their relationship. If one node fails, the surviving nodes assume responsibility for the failed node's work. Figure 2.9 illustrates this form of cluster. Clustered nodes in this scenario are literally only emergency backups for each other.

Clustering for Availability

Figure 2.8.
*Static load-
balancing, shared
nothing, fail-over
clustering.*

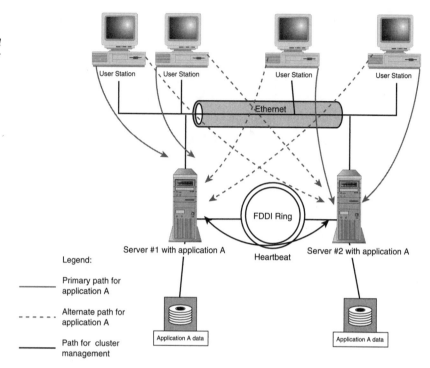

Legend:

——— Primary path for
application A

- - - - Alternate path for
application A

━━━ Path for cluster
management

Figure 2.9.
*Non-load-
balancing, shared
nothing, fail-over
clustering.*

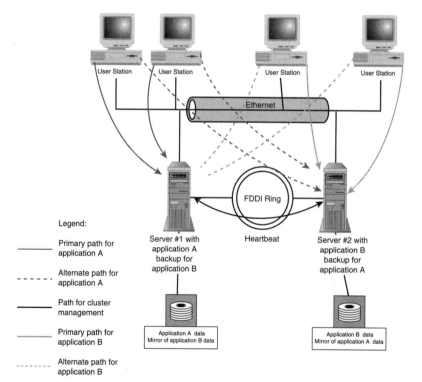

Legend:

——— Primary path for
application A

- - - - Alternate path for
application A

━━━ Path for cluster
management

——— Primary path for
application B

- - - - Alternate path for
application B

Both types of shared nothing clusters depicted in Figures 2.8 and 2.9 can be either close proximity or geographically dispersed.

2.3.3. Shared Nothing Issues

The shared nothing approach to clustering eliminates the scalability problems faced by shared disk clusters. Each computer in the cluster has one or more disks. There are no logistical complexities to be addressed when scaling upward, because competition for the same data on the same disks does not exist.

This configuration does present other issues, however. In the event of a fail-over, the surviving nodes in the cluster take over the stricken node's work load. Regardless of the topological or functional variant, nodes in a shared nothing cluster must maintain up-to-date copies of each other's executable software and data. These are the issues that must be addressed:

- Static load-balancing, shared nothing cluster nodes must determine whether the client request for data can be resolved locally, or whether it requires an I/O request of another host in the cluster. If an I/O request must be shipped, the shipping node must determine which node owns the data and is, consequently, the addressee of the request. This process depends on how the application and its database subsystem were designed and implemented, as well as on the mechanics of the cluster management software. If at all possible, shipping I/O requests should be eliminated through the clustered application's architecture and design. Otherwise, users may find themselves intermittently experiencing the performance penalties associated with shipping I/O requests.

- Non-load-balancing clusters, particularly those whose nodes support completely self-contained applications, can be difficult to implement in a fail-over cluster. The first logistical nightmare is keeping up-to-date copies of data distributed among the nodes. If the cluster architect elects to do batch transfers, a window exists for data to be lost in the event of a failure. Performing live updates of multiple databases can be network intensive, to say the least!

- In the event of a fail-over, the actual mechanics of how the switch to the alternate system occurs will vary based on the cluster management product. Some products provide for the backup node to begin listening for packets that are addressed to the stricken node. Others are a bit less sophisticated, and require users to recognize that a failure has occurred and to log on to the alternate host.

Ideally, clustered nodes are able to sense the failure, replicate the existing application and data states on the failing node, and automatically bring active users and their processing requests to the backup node. Making this happen in a shared nothing cluster requires that due diligence be paid to maintaining current copies of application software and data at each node, having cluster-aware operating systems at each node, and having cluster management software that supports these fail-over functions. Finally, the application itself must be cluster aware and respond to requests by the operating system or cluster management product to begin the fail-over process.

2.3.4. What's the Catch?

Balanced against their potential to achieve scalability and availability, shared nothing clusters may compromise application performance if they're not carefully designed and implemented. The issues outlined in section 2.3.3 must be understood and the clusters developed accordingly.

Done properly, the shared nothing cluster will be slightly more expensive to implement than a shared disk configuration, but will overcome the problems inherent in shared disk clusters. This form of cluster is much more scaleable and can be much more robust because of its increased redundancy of online storage devices and their controllers.

These benefits come at the expense of complex application architectures. Applications must be specifically designed to function in a shared nothing environment. Their data stores, if not locally resident, will be painful to access.

Maintaining the currency of application software and, more importantly, the data, is critical to the success of a shared nothing, fail-over cluster. If a failure occurs and either the application software or data is out of synch with the primary host, unpredictable results and lost data will result.

This series of trade-offs between reliability, scalability, and runtime performance must be carefully considered before you implement a shared nothing cluster. The logistics of maintaining a current copy of both software and data in shared nothing clusters are daunting. If these details can be worked out, this form of clustering offers the highest possible combination of reliability and scalability.

2.4. Cluster Management

Clusters, as topologically versatile as they may be, aren't all that different from each other in their hardware components. It's their management software that differentiates clusters functionally: Two topologically identical clusters may be very different functionally, simply because they use different cluster management software packages.

When you're selecting management software for your NT cluster, functionality should be one of your key metrics. For example, if your NT cluster supports only a single application, it's essential that the cluster management software support load balancing in addition to fail-over recovery. If the cluster supports multiple applications, each on its own dedicated processor in the cluster, then load balancing is a moot issue.

Regardless of whether one or more applications are supported in the cluster, the management software must be adept at replicating application states in the event of a fail-over. This can be difficult to assess because successful state replication requires the cooperation of the operating system, cluster management software, and the application itself. Because each of these software components may come from different vendors, reaching a definitive conclusion about the abilities or limitations of any fail-over management product may be impossible.

Cluster management products for Windows NT are examined in more detail in Chapter 6, "Windows NT Server," and Chapter 7, "Microsoft's Cluster Server."

2.5. Data Access Management in a Cluster

Parallel operating environments, regardless of whether they are internal, external, symmetric, or asymmetric, must resolve the problem of communal data access. Uniprocessors don't face this problem. There is only one CPU, so there is no competition for a common data set. In parallel environments, there are multiple CPUs competing for access to a common set of data. This creates the need to manage access to files.

Several companies have introduced cluster management products, and more are being announced weekly. Each product appears to be intentionally different from its potential competitors, complicating the already onerous task of designing cluster architecture.

2.5.1. Shared Disk Clusters

The need to manage processor access to data occurs on two different levels in a shared disk cluster:

- First, if the cluster is composed of multiprocessors, there is an internal access management issue to contend with. This internal competition for resources is managed by the operating system. Because Microsoft Windows NT Server is designed to be aware of multiple CPUs, this shouldn't be a problem. Multi-CPU competition for a common data set is illustrated in Figure 2.10. These CPUs rely on database management software to arbitrate potential conflicts.

Clustering for Availability

■ Second, access to the data must be managed across all the hosts in the cluster that may be competing for the same data. This requires both an operating system that is aware of the cluster, and cluster management software. Windows NT Server is being refreshed, in support of the Wolfpack initiative, to add cluster awareness. The real issue is cluster management software. Fortunately, the NT Server environment has been gradually adding the capabilities that it needs to support clusters since Release 3.51. By Release 5.0, it will be capable of supporting numerous cluster management products, both existing and planned. Thus, the biggest challenge will be selecting a cluster management product.

Shared disk clustered hosts access the disks directly, without a physical disk access management device such as that used in the original VAXClusters. Disk access management is still critical to the cluster's successful operation, but is performed in the application layer rather than embodied in a physical device.

Figure 2.10.
Multiple CPUs require a mechanism to regulate access to common data stores.

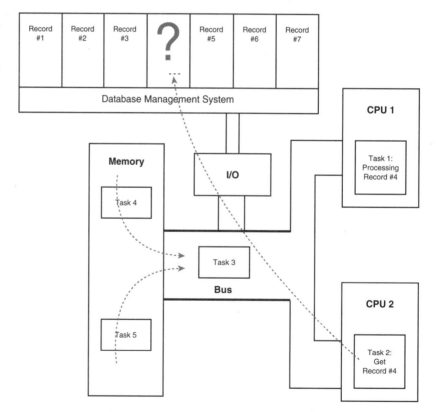

Records that are in use are locked and remain unavailable to other CPUs until they are unlocked. Only unlocked records may be accessed and modified. When a CPU receives an instruction that needs data that is already in use and locked, that instruction is sent to a memory buffer. It remains in that buffer until the necessary data is unlocked. At this point, the instruction is sent back to the CPU for completion. Figure 2.11 illustrates locking records that are in use.

Figure 2.11.
The database management system locks records that are in use.

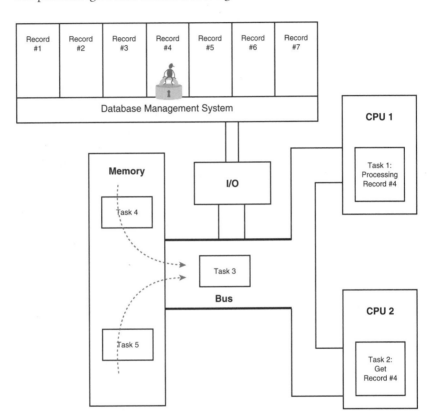

Although Figures 2.10 and 2.11 illustrate data access management in a symmetric multiprocessor, the concept is directly applicable to all parallel processing environments. The presence of multiple CPUs absolutely requires some mechanism to arbitrate access to shared data. Failure to implement such a mechanism may have unpredictable, if not disastrous, results. At best, the data will quickly become corrupted and unreliable. At worst, the application may unexpectedly terminate if it can't resolve the conflict for data access. This termination may result in the loss of any additional data that was in memory and being processed.

2.5.2. **Shared Nothing Clusters**

In a shared nothing cluster, competition for data is a bit more limited than it is in shared disk clusters. Each computer in the cluster has its own disks and, theoretically, its own data. Any load balancing will be done statically, so the potential for generating I/O shipping requests is minimized. Thus, the need for data access management in a shared nothing cluster is reduced to regulating the competitive requests for data by the CPUs contained inside each clustered node. This regulation is easily handled by the multitasking Windows NT Server operating system and commercially available database management software packages.

2.6. Which One Is the Right One?

Right about now you are probably wondering which, if any, of these high reliability cluster approaches is right for you. If you work in a strictly Microsoft shop, the answer is probably fairly straightforward. Microsoft's cluster products are built around NT Server and feature a shared disk fail-over topology. Your choices are then limited to processing platforms that support NT Server. These include the Intel x86 processors, the DEC Alpha processors, MIPS RISC processors.

However, if you are using NT Server as a platform for cluster management products from other companies, your answer might take more careful consideration. When you're evaluating cluster management products, it is important to have a clear understanding of the clustered application's reliability and performance requirements. You can then determine the degree to which any cluster management product is able to satisfy those requirements.

As evidenced throughout this chapter, there is wide variation in fail-over clusters. Many clusters are nearly identical from a topological perspective. The important differences are a function of their cluster management software. Each management product will probably offer a different combination of protection and performance. These must be evaluated carefully against the applications' resource and performance requirements.

2.7. Summary

Clusters, despite having been around for over 20 years, are just starting to enter a phase of rapid growth. Only time will tell if the marketplace drives clusters and cluster management products towards consistency and standardization, or if competition will result in ever increasing disparities in the function and performance of the different vendors' products.

One thing is certain: The development of cluster support in the NT Server operating system will bring this technique into the mainstream. The basic topologies and approaches presented in this chapter will provide a solid foundation for your NT Server-based clusters.

Chapter

3

Clustering for Scalability

Scalable clusters could become the Grail of distributed parallel computing. Unlike clustering for high reliability through redundancy and topological variation, scalability is a much more complex goal. Achieving massive scalability might not be possible with today's technology.

This chapter defines scalability, examines its implications for clustering, and identifies the chronic performance bottlenecks that impede scalability in today's systems. It also covers new and emerging technologies that can eliminate many of these bottlenecks, and presents specific recommendations for developing clusters that can be readily scaled.

3.1. Introduction

Scalability refers to the capability to expand a system. Unlike availability in clusters, scalability is not a function of topological variation. Rather, scalability is the product of the physical platform's overall design. It has two distinct components: capacity and performance.

Capacity scalability is the capability to add system resources such as RAM, CPUs, storage facilities, and so on, to an existing system or cluster. As explained in Chapter 1, "Introduction to Clustering," scalability comes in many forms. Computer systems tend to be internally scalable—up to the limit of their fixed capacity.

Clusters composed of either uniprocessor or multiprocessor systems can be both internally scalable and externally scalable. External scalability means adding additional self-contained resources (additional computer systems) to the cluster.

Yet even this cluster-level scalability has capacity limits. Most cluster management products, whether planned or available, have finite limits on the extent to which the cluster can scale. These limits, though rooted in software, are no different in their effects on the internal scalability of a computer system's hardware than are architectural limits. They are simply different expressions of capacity limitations. Capacity limits are imposed by the inefficiencies of the technologies forming either a system or cluster. In other words, capacity limitations tend to be a function of performance limitations.

This chapter explores some of the more critical aspects of massive scalability and the emerging standards, technologies, and architectures that can make massively scalable clusters a reality.

3.2. Exploring System Bottlenecks

Every computer system contains fundamental performance constrictions known as *bottlenecks*. The problem with bottlenecks is that they are relative: what constitutes a problematic performance constriction for one application might not be problematic for another application. Figure 3.1 illustrates the conceptual relationship between an application's performance requirements and the system's capacity to satisfy those requirements.

Figure 3.1.

Conceptual view of a system bottleneck.

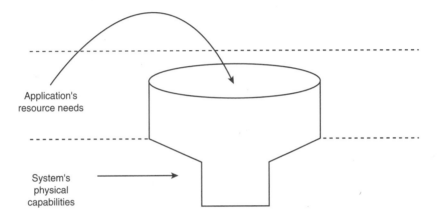

Application's
resource needs

System's
physical
capabilities

The bottleneck illustrated in Figure 3.1 can represent any one of a computer system's physical resources: CPU, memory, I/O, and so on. Consequently, a system's performance is likely to contain a series of bottlenecks.

Historically, one of the biggest limitations on computing performance for all application types has been *input/output* (I/O) technologies. Because there are enormous disparities between the speeds of I/O technologies and CPUs, I/O is the most expensive function a computer can perform. The reason for this is the amount of CPU cycles that are, or can be, wasted just waiting for the I/O request to complete.

Many workarounds to common bottlenecks have been developed, including paging, multiprogramming, and multithreading. These techniques minimize the effects of performance disparities without really addressing them. Each technique's effectiveness varies with the application type. Different applications have different degrees of hardware intensity. Scientific applications, for example, tend to be more CPU-intensive than anything else. Therefore a processing platform built for the scientific community should be optimized for CPU-intensive operations.

Clustering for Scalability

NOTE   Paging, multiprogramming, and multithreading are different techniques for using the finite resources of a system more effectively. Although each has a common goal, they take very different approaches.

Paging involves the temporary swapping of memory-resident data and/or instructions to a disk cache. Ostensibly, this occurs because the paged matter was in a wait state, or a higher priority instruction came along. Either way, the operating system cached it to disk to make better use of the CPU's time. Because of the speed mismatch between memory and disk drives, excessive paging can actually decrease system performance.

Multiprogramming, also known as multitasking, is a commonly used technique that enables two or more different applications to execute simultaneously. This is possible because of the speed mismatches that exist between the CPU, memory, and the various I/O devices. In its simplest form, while one program's instruction is awaiting the completion of an I/O request, it is preempted by an instruction from the other program. For more information on multiprogramming, please refer to Chapter 10, "Programming for Parallel Environments."

Multithreading is multitasking, but within a single program.

Business applications—Executive Information Systems (EIS), for example—tend to be more disk- and I/O-intensive. Other decision support systems, including data mining and warehousing, can be both I/O- and CPU-intensive. The point is that workarounds are not panaceas. They can provide relief only if they are well matched to the needs of the application, and if they help to mask the limitations of the hardware from that application.

Extending this logic reveals the quandary: hardware platforms are frequently generic, with limited potential for customization. Thus, developing a cluster platform that is capable of massive scalability requires a system whose basic components are as closely matched as possible.

Massive scalability requires that performance bottlenecks be significantly reduced or eliminated. Figure 3.2 illustrates conceptually a computer system that is constructed by a perfectly matched set of technologies. Each component is capable of the same level of performance as every other component in the system; consequently, there are no bottlenecks.

Unfortunately, the constitution of a perfect system depends on its intended function. A perfect system for an I/O-intensive application might be absolutely punishing to a CPU-intensive application. Thus, a universally perfect system, with no bottlenecks, might not ever be commercially available or affordable.

Given this caveat, the single greatest performance bottleneck in most systems is its I/O mechanism. Several concepts are emerging that promise to improve the scalability of clusters either by avoiding the I/O bus entirely or by at least changing the paradigm for accommodating I/O requests. These concepts establish new input/output models and are presented in the rest of this section.

Figure 3.2.
*Conceptual view
of a perfect
system with no
bottlenecks.*

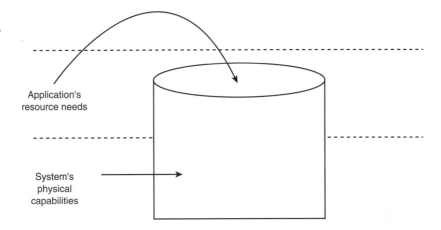

Application's
resource needs

System's
physical
capabilities

3.2.1. No Remote Memory Access (NORMA)

The *No Remote Memory Access*, or NORMA, I/O model is the conventional form of memory access that most people are familiar with. In fact, this model might be so familiar that it is taken for granted. NORMA requires that all requests for access to memory originate locally and pass through the local I/O bus. Figure 3.3 illustrates this model.

Figure 3.3.
*The NORMA
I/O model.*

Clustering for Scalability

Traditional LANs use the NORMA I/O model. They access the I/O bus through a *network interface card* (NIC). The NIC is responsible for translating between two different data transport formats: the bus and the LAN frames.

3.2.2. Non-Uniform Memory Access (NUMA)

Non-Uniform Memory Access, or NUMA, is a hybridized I/O model. It still requires requests for memory access to pass through the I/O bus, but this is satisfied in a non-uniform manner. It is non-uniform because requests for memory access do not have to originate locally and, therefore, require a non-uniform amount of time to satisfy. An external switching mechanism enables remote hosts—other cluster nodes—to directly address and access the memory resources of any given host.

Figure 3.4 illustrates the NUMA model.

Figure 3.4.
NUMA provides for direct memory access by foreign hosts.

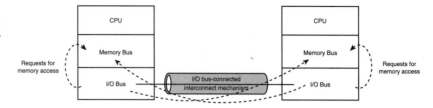

Specific examples of technologies that use the NUMA model are ServerNet and PCI-SCI. Each of these technologies is described in more detail in this chapter.

3.2.3. Cache Coherent Non-Uniform Memory Access (ccNUMA)

Cache Coherent Non-Uniform Memory Access is also referred to as ccNUMA. It is a bit more avant-garde than both NORMA and NUMA because it is a direct memory access methodology. ccNUMA bypasses the I/O bus entirely.

Figure 3.5 illustrates the direct memory access of the ccNUMA I/O model.

Figure 3.5.
ccNUMA provides for direct memory access.

ccNUMA is more an emerging technology than a fully developed product. By completely bypassing the I/O bus, it offers the greatest relief from today's processing bottlenecks. Unfortunately, it is also the least mature of the three I/O models, and will take quite some time to become generally available in low-end computing platforms.

3.2.4. I/O Model Implementation

Understanding these I/O models is important when you're developing a highly scalable cluster. Because it distributes a parallel processing environment across multiple computers, a cluster is intrinsically more I/O-intensive than a comparable amount of computing power contained in a single chassis. A cluster requires I/O to accept incoming requests, to access the requested data stored on disks, and to transmit the requested data.

What is more important, a cluster relies on I/O for its own management. Load balancing, fail-overs, and other intracluster messaging all rely on I/O. These characteristics require the highest level of performance possible. Failure to provide a robust network—a *Cluster Area Network* (CAN)—in this area will directly impede the capability of the cluster to manage itself.

Regardless of which I/O model is chosen, it should be hidden from the application by the operating system or the cluster management utilities. This will ensure identical application behavior, regardless of the physical platform.

Building in meaningful platform-independence will enable you to "future-proof" your cluster. As more sophisticated clustering hardware platforms become available (such as those that utilize NUMA or ccNUMA I/O models), you will be free to upgrade the physical platform without having to worry about re-engineering the application software.

As cluster-specific technologies and protocols emerge, these I/O models will become more familiar. They will be one of the keys to developing massively scalable clustering platforms by making the cluster area network a semi-internal function of each clustered node.

3.3. Scalable Coherent Interface (SCI)

One recent standard designed to overcome the performance limitations of I/O was defined in the IEEE/ANSI standards numbered 1596-1992. Cumulatively, they define a *Scalable Coherent Interface* (SCI). SCI is an interface that uses the NUMA I/O model. It is designed to provide scalability for clusters built from very high performance multiprocessor systems. Using SCI, these clusters theoretically can grow to a maximum of 65,536 nodes.

NOTE
SCI is intended as a replacement for traditional Local Area Network technologies in cluster interconnect networks. Improvements in network efficiency in this area directly affect the efficiency of cluster management.

SCI enables massively scalable clustering by focusing on performance scalability, which operates on the theory that capacity limitations are a function of performance limitations. Expanding the performance envelope is accomplished by providing a reliable, efficient, high-bandwidth intracluster message passing mechanism. This will enable hardware manufacturers to develop products with greater capacities so that more nodes can be networked together in a cluster without the performance limitations of traditional I/O.

SCI provides its efficiency and bandwidth via direct mapping of protected network memory across a highly specialized and efficient communications vehicle. This vehicle functionally extends the I/O bus of a computer to other external computers. Avoiding the high overhead conversion from I/O bus format to LAN frames enables the cluster's performance to be much more scalable. This scalability is possible because the disparity between the performance capacities of the CPU and network is substantially reduced.

Clustered nodes can be networked together directly, without traditional Local Area Networking, in one of two basic topologies: ring or switched.

Ring topologies, even an SCI ring, suffer from a basic flaw. Each connection in the ring constitutes a single point of failure. The failure of any one of them results in the failure of the entire ring. The risks inherent in this topology increase directly with the size of the cluster. It might be acceptable for small clusters of only a few nodes, but the risks become unacceptable as the number of nodes increases. For example, imagine a massive cluster of 8,000 nodes, each containing 8 CPUs that support a mission critical application. This cluster would contain 64,000 CPUs, the largest number that SCI can support. This cluster would contain 8,000 single points of failure. This would probably be considered an unacceptable level of risk by any rational person.

The SCI ring topology is illustrated in Figure 3.6.

Figure 3.6.
SCI ring topology.

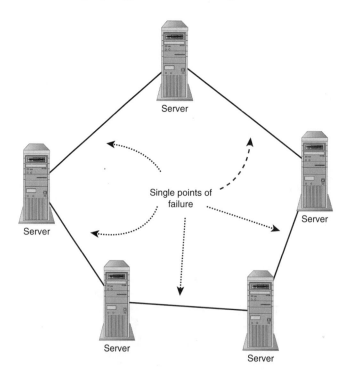

A better alternative is the switched topology. Switched topologies, in general, avoid many of the risks inherent in other network topologies. Each node enjoys its own dedicated connection to the switch. The switch also enables any-to-any connectivity through a hardware level mechanism. This ensures that switched connections occur at wire speed.

The SCI switched topology is illustrated in Figure 3.7.

Figure 3.7.
SCI switched topology.

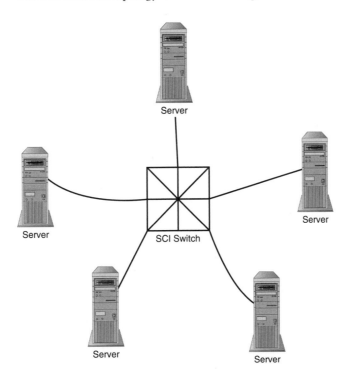

In theory, each of the cluster node connections to the SCI switch is also a single point of failure. The difference between the switched and ring implementations of this technology is that if a switched connection fails, the cluster "fails-over" to using the surviving nodes. In a ring topology failure, the entire cluster fails.

Early proponents of SCI include Novell, Sun Microsystems, and Data General. Each of these companies uses SCI as a component in its clustering products.

3.3.1. SCI Addressing

SCI uses a 64-bit address that is unique to SCI. Up to 16 bits of the address are used for node identification. Mathematically, this limits the number of potential nodes in the cluster to 65,536. This maximum is defined by the address architecture of SCI. It should not be misconstrued as a practical upper limit on the size of a cluster.

The remainder of the bits in the SCI address constitutes a single field that identifies a physical memory address in the remote node. This memory address field contains the actual page address in memory, as well as some attributes, that the remote node is requesting to access.

Figure 3.8 illustrates the SCI address structure.

Figure 3.8.
*SCI address
structure.*

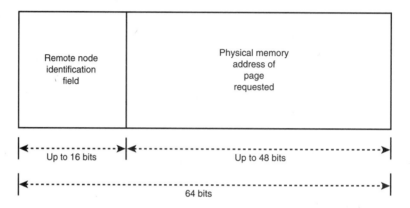

The memory address space can be segmented to contain both a physical memory address and a network control register address. Local memory addresses are mapped to remote memory addresses by SCI page descriptors. These descriptors are cached in the SCI adapter card and paged in on demand from PCI memory, allowing the PCI memory to be protected, yet remain accessible from the other nodes on the SCI network.

3.3.2. PCI-SCI Adapter

The SCI interface is available for the PCI bus. Support for other bus architectures might be developed in the future. However, the PCI-SCI adapter bridges the gap between many contemporary processing platforms that support NT, and the future. In theory, when the SCI adapter becomes available for different bus types, SCI will be able to integrate disparate processing platforms into one cluster. This assumes that the application, cluster management software, network operating system, and so on are similarly platform-independent.

The PCI-SCI adapter is a 32-bit card that operates at 33 MHz. It provides a translating interface between the PCI bus interface and the SCI interface. Figure 3.9 illustrates the functions of this adapter.

This adapter also features a 16-bit, 100 MHz path for linking to other cluster hosts. This path contains *Link In* and *Link Out* paths that can be used to build the SCI ring. A *scatter/gather* engine is used to access the processor's *Direct Memory Access* (DMA) channels and to move data between the PCI and SCI addresses.

Figure 3.9.
Functionality of the PCI-SCI adapter.

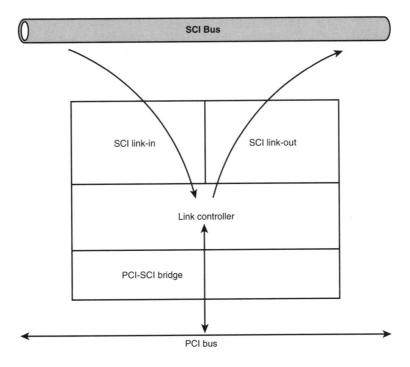

An address translation table, known as an SCI Page Table map, is used to map local SCI addresses to a remote one. This translation table resides in the SCI switch, and is updated by each of the SCI adapters' scatter/gather engines.

3.3.3. SCI Fault Tolerance

SCI was designed to be a cluster-enabling technology, so it should come as no surprise that it contains many native fault tolerance features.

Two basic diagnostic mechanisms are built in to SCI. First, the SCI adapter card can be detected via the loss of communications with other nodes on the SCI network. The second diagnostic tool is designed to detect software failures by monitoring a heartbeat signal in the remote node's memory. In combination, these tools enable the SCI network, and the cluster it interconnects, to detect and recover from failures.

For example, a failure in an SCI network undergoes the following diagnostic routine. If the SCI connection to a remote node is "up," but that node can't be communicated with, the heartbeat is checked. If the system itself had experienced a hardware failure, then, depending on the nature of the failure, either the communications link itself or the heartbeat would both cease. If the communications link remains up and the heartbeat continues to "beat," that node has suffered a software failure. The cluster can then take the appropriate remedial actions.

Other built-in fault tolerance mechanisms can be found in the topological choices supported by SCI. Small clusters might find that rings are the best approach. These are inexpensive, but contain single points of failure. Consequently, they are not very fault tolerant.

The switched topology offers more per-node fault tolerance by eliminating the multiple single points of failure that would exist in an SCI ring. The customer can select the configuration that provides whatever degree of fault tolerance they require or can afford.

3.4. ServerNet

Tandem Computers, Inc. has developed a semi-internal network specifically for use as a cluster area network. Because it is semi-internal, they regard it as a *System Area Network* (SAN). Tandem's trade name for this network technology is *ServerNet*.

ServerNet is designed to be the cluster area network for next generation, fault tolerant, parallel servers. It features the NUMA I/O model, and is designed to be the foundation for scalable clustering.

Like SCI, ServerNet provides the means for protected remote access of memory via DMA channels. It also provides for reliable, efficient, high-bandwidth message passing between clustered nodes without the overhead associated with network technologies that use the NORMA I/O model. An interesting twist is that ServerNet supports queuing of multiple interrupts with data. This minimizes the amount of overhead that would otherwise be required to get an interrupt and then pass data. This is known as *interrupt with data*, but is for use only with relatively small transfers.

To help ensure ServerNet becomes a de facto industry standard, Tandem has decided to license this technology to *Original Equipment Manufacturers* (OEMs).

3.4.1. ServerNet Addressing

ServerNet uses a 52-bit address. The first 20 bits identify the destination node. This provides a maximum of one million possible nodes in a ServerNet. As with SCI, this should be considered a mathematically possible maximum only and not a practical limit.

The remaining 32 bits are the *Address Validation and Translation Table* (AVTT) descriptor address. This address is used by the receiving, or destination, node to locate a descriptor in the AVTT.

The AVTT descriptor contains the following fields:

- PCI page number

- Upper and lower access bounds

- Source node ID

- Access rights

- Low-order, or last, 12 bits of AVTT address (This is an offset into the 4K page used by the ServerNet operation. It identifies whether the packet contains a READ or WRITE instruction.)

The ServerNet address structure is illustrated in Figure 3.10.

Figure 3.10.
ServerNet
address structure.

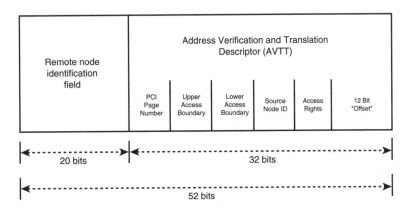

3.4.2. PCI ServerNet Adapter

The PCI-based version of the ServerNet adapter is a 32-bit card that operates at 33 MHz. It also contains two 8-bit ports, labeled "X" and "Y," that operate at 50 MHz. These ports provide the basis for redundant network topologies.

This adapter contains two *Block Transfer Engines* (BTEs) that move data between PCI and ServerNet addresses. The Address Validation and Translation Table (AVTT) is used to validate and translate the addressing between ServerNet and PCI memory.

Clustering for Scalability

Figure 3.11 shows a logical view of the ServerNet adapter's functionality.

Figure 3.11.
*Logical view of
the ServerNet
PCI adapter card
function.*

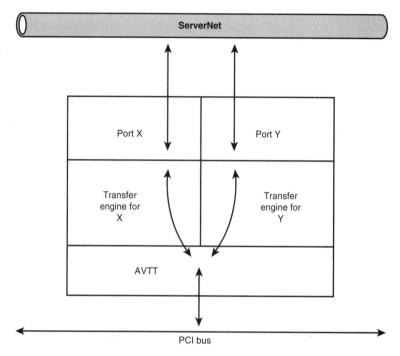

3.4.3. Fault Tolerance in ServerNet Networks

ServerNet provides several mechanisms for supporting fault tolerant operation of a cluster. A failure of the adapter card itself is detected by other ServerNet devices by a communications failure.

As happens with the SCI mechanism, software failures can be detected through the use of a heartbeat that is kept in remote memory and monitored.

ServerNet also supports development of redundant network topologies through the use of its X and Y ports. Figure 3.12 illustrates two separate ServerNet networks, the X and Y networks, that provide complete path redundancy for intracluster communications. These topological variations are at the customer's discretion.

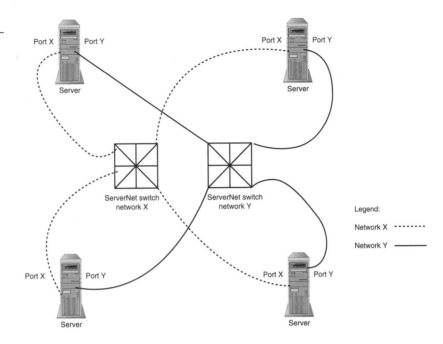

Figure 3.12.
Redundant X and Y System Area Networks in a single cluster.

3.5. Virtual Interface Architecture (VIA)

A relative newcomer to the field of low-end cluster scalability is *Virtual Interface Architecture* (VIA). VIA is still in draft stage, and is being reviewed by players in the low-end computing industry. Detailed information about VIA is not yet available, and even the information presented here is subject to change.

VIA was launched by Microsoft, COMPAQ, and Intel as a draft specification. The goal of this draft was to define a standard that would encompass all future clusters constructed of low-end computing components.

Although VIA includes provisions for supporting clusters of RISC-based computers, this initiative is distinctly aimed at x86-based servers. The goal is to make low-end clusters of x86 servers scalable enough to become competition for mid-range, and even mainframe, computers. Because of these provisions for RISC support, VIA, in theory, will enable the construction of mixed architecture

Clustering for Scalability

clusters. x86 and RISC machines will be able to interoperate in VIA-compatible clusters. This will facilitate the extension of low-end computers into the markets traditionally served by more expensive mid-range computers.

The breadth of its mission makes VIA an intentionally broad and generic proposal for a System Area Network. If it is successful, it will help speed the maturation of standardized clusters constructed from low-end commodity components. This, in turn, will expedite the development of cluster-aware commercial applications. In the absence of an industry standard, such applications would be slow to emerge.

3.5.1. An "Architecture," Not a "Product"

VIA, theoretically, will describe an interface architecture that allows for low-latency, high-bandwidth connections between clustered nodes. VIA is not a product, so eventually existing products might be modified for VIA compatibility. At least one manufacturer of SCI adapters is already gearing up to produce VIA-compatible PCI-SCI adapters.

Similarly, other manufacturers are investigating the potential to develop VIA-compatible ATM, Fast Ethernet, Gigabit Ethernet, and Fibre Channel adapters. These manufacturers are less interested in becoming VIA-compliant than in seeking other avenues for demonstrating the potential of their products.

Regardless of their motivations, VIA could help network technologies that were previously reserved for high-end systems into the affordable range of options for low-end computing systems and clusters.

3.5.2. Architecture by Committee?

Standardizing a far-flung collection of components can have its risks. These risks are magnified because the specification is being drafted by a large committee. Techno-politics are sure to be responsible for more than a little of the finished specification because the players are motivated to protect their own interests.

Even in this era of "open" computing, manufacturers have always tried to differentiate their product by adding bells and whistles. Sometimes, these features compromised the openness of the product. Thus customers could purchase open products but still find themselves tied to a single vendor, depending on how the products were implemented.

The nature of clusters, particularly VIA-compatible clusters, should preclude this behavior. The architecture must allow for disparate architectures to be so tightly coupled that they function as a logical, single computer. It seems logical, then, that the architecture be fairly loose so it can be as open as possible.

Loose architectures bring the risk of suboptimal performance levels. At least one participating manufacturer openly doubts the capability of VIA-compatible products to match the performance of its proprietary technology. This manufacturer isn't doubting that architecturally correct products will work; it's doubting that it will work as well as noncompliant products.

The draft VIA specification is currently being reviewed by more than 50 companies. These companies comprise the full spectrum of manufacturers in low-end computing. They include Hewlett-Packard, Novell, Oracle, Santa Cruz Operation, and many others. VIA appears to have momentum, but so did the ATM Forum in 1993. Only time, and the market, will tell whether VIA is ultimately successful and effective in satisfying its mission.

3.6. Clustering for Future Scalability

The goal of any future scalable cluster should be that it is easy to administer and use as a single, self-contained system. It should also be as easy to program as any multiprocessor system. These relatively simple goals can be deceptively difficult to achieve.

The following basic guidelines should help to future-proof the scalability of your cluster.

3.6.1. Networks

The network is probably the easiest component of a cluster to scale up. All the major Local Area Network(LAN) manufacturers presently make switching hubs that feature modular upgrades and multitopology support. In the short term, these hubs will make excellent platforms for supporting a cluster that is likely to experience significant increases in use.

Recognize, however, that conventional Local Area Networks contain a fair bit of latency and overhead relative to the demands of intracluster communications. The best way to proactively accommodate future scalability is to deploy the highest bandwidth, lowest latency networks possible for intracluster communications.

Another way to extend the life of conventional LAN technologies in a cluster is to deploy one for each of the cluster's network functional areas. By using one LAN for client access, and another for intracluster communications, both networks will be able to better serve their intended purpose. Thus, they will both be able to serve longer as the cluster scales upwards.

Clustering for Scalability

In the long term, as the semi-internal bus extension networks of NUMA and ccNUMA become stable and well supported, consideration should be given to using them instead of a formal Local Area Network technology for intracluster communications. Given this as a likely future migration path, it is logical to establish whether or not the products you use in assembling your cluster will support this change in I/O models.

3.6.2. Platforms

Processing platforms can be easily built for future scalability, up to a point. Developing a cluster with lightly loaded symmetrical multiprocessors creates the opportunity to provide future scalability by adding memory, CPUs, and disks as they are needed. This is the easy way to provide scalability and is directly analogous to using modularly upgradable switching hubs. Both provide the capability to add capacity incrementally—without a forklift.

Depending on your choice of cluster management software, an SMP cluster can be scaled beyond the internal limitations of its nodes by adding additional nodes. Again, the degree to which this form of scalability can be utilized will depend directly on your choice of cluster management software. Most of the products available for low-end computing are focused on reliability. Scalability has distinct and finite upper limits because of the performance issues described throughout this chapter. These limits will be eased somewhat over time as the cluster management software matures.

In the long term, the only way to provide high levels of scalability is to eliminate bottlenecks. This must begin with a thorough understanding of the clustered applications resource needs and end with implementation of technologies that are well suited to those needs. Given the intrinsic relationship between the performance of cluster management and I/O, eliminating I/O bottlenecks will be a priority for any cluster, regardless of the application.

Improving the throughput of I/O functions can be done by building your cluster with the most robust bus architecture possible. Then, further improvements can be gained by streamlining external I/O functions using either a NUMA or ccNUMA technology to extend that I/O bus to other clustered nodes.

3.6.3. Cluster Topologies

Cluster topologies, too, can directly affect the future scalability of your cluster. Shared disk topologies, although relatively inexpensive to build and maintain, are not very scalable. The complexities of trying to share disks across more than two or three clustered nodes become obvious quickly. The increased competition for disk access will also adversely affect the performance of a clustered application.

The bottom line is avoid shared disk clusters, if your future goal is scalability. Shared nothing clusters are much more versatile and scalable, though they are a bit more expensive to purchase and operate.

Some additional topological customization can also make any cluster slightly more scalable. Chapter 4, "Complex Clusters," presents several ways that the functions of a clustered application can be split among two or more nested or layered clusters. This functional segregation permits each cluster's hardware to be optimized for its particular function. This increases the effectiveness with which it can perform, and might well forestall the need for reinvestment as the cluster's workload increases.

3.6.4. System-Level Software

The system-level software in a cluster includes operating systems and cluster management software. Both are equally important to the future scalability of a clustered application. They should work together to hide component failures from the users and applications. They should also be well matched to each other's performance levels. Otherwise, it is possible that one or the other will become a new bottleneck. Unfortunately, this type of bottleneck will become apparent only after the cluster has been implemented and actually starts to experience increased usage.

Make sure that both the operating system and the cluster management software are capable of handling the projected work load. More importantly, verify that both are capable of handling the specific types of processing that the cluster will support. Different application types can have very different processing and resource requirements.

3.6.5. Application Software

Finally, consider the application software itself. Building the most technically elegant cluster will do your users no good if the application software is not cluster-aware! Whether you install shrink-wrapped software or have an in-house custom development group, the application software must be aware of the features and services of the cluster. This software must be able to interact with either the operating system or the cluster management software. Thus, it is critical that they use industry standard Application Programming Interfaces (APIs).

More importantly, the application should be engineered with future scalability in mind. Each application can have its own performance bottlenecks that must be minimized. The application must be designed not only to process in parallel, but to process in distributed parallel.

3.7. Summary

There is no one thing that can be done to ensure the future scalability of your cluster. Rather, scalability is the aggregate benefit of many underlying factors. Each one must be identified, understood, and either eliminated or worked around in such a way that the resource intensity of the application and cluster is reduced. Minimizing resource intensity is the surest way to build future scalability into any application, clustered or otherwise.

Chapter

4

Complex Clusters

The basic clustering concepts and topologies presented in Chapters 2, "Clustering for Availability," and 3, "Clustering for Scalability," can be mixed, matched, stacked, and applied in almost infinite variety. This flexibility can be used to customize the performance of a cluster, so that it will better satisfy the requirements of its applications.

This chapter presents some of the ways that complex clusters can be developed, along with tips for customizing clusters to maximize their performance.

4.1. What Is a Complex Cluster?

By now, the amorphous nature clusters should be well understood. This attribute is simultaneously a weakness and a strength. It is problematic because clusters defy easy definition, which makes the learning curve for clusters a bit steeper.

Their chameleon-like topologies, however, can also be a source of considerable strength and advantage. For example, if the only measure of a cluster's success is how well it serves its intended business purpose, then topological correctness is moot. Therein lies the potential for customization. Clusters are flexible enough to be mixed and matched, stacked, or nested in a nearly endless variety of combinations. These varieties can be used to fine-tune a cluster's fit to specific business requirements and infrastructures.

There are two primary means for creating additional topological, and therefore functional, complexity. The first method is through the layering of somewhat conventional cluster topologies. Each layer would be applied to a specific purpose.

The second method is through actual hybridization. Two or more different conventional cluster topologies are interconnected to form a unique, compound cluster.

Both of these methods can be used to create complex, multitier clusters of clusters. Each tier, or cluster, can be optimized for a specific function, like transaction processing, database mining, and so on. Thus, performance tuning can be added to scalability and reliability as cluster's main virtues.

4.1.1. Layers

Layering is a clustering technique that serves two purposes. First, it further spreads responsibility for the work. This improves reliability by further reducing the impact of any failure in the cluster. Second, it can be used to uncouple functions within the clustered application. Uncoupling across layers enables each layer to be configured for optimal performance.

Layers can be designed to satisfy many other objectives. Developing a layered, or tiered, cluster architecture must begin with an understanding of the clustered application's functionality. For example, a particular application might have a client front-end, on-demand processing, and database management functions. Each function lends itself to optimization via layering.

These functions can be layered logically with commercially available software without altering the physical cluster topology. Relational database management software, transaction processing management software, and queuing management software usually contain some provisions for either fail-over or load balancing. With the right platform, there is no reason why these functions would require their own dedicated processing platform. Therefore, logical layering can occur within the confines of basic cluster topologies.

Alternatively, the functions can be physically uncoupled and run on separate platforms. One such physical uncoupling of functions results in a multitiered cluster that can best be described as a *client/server/server* model.

Using a two-tiered server model and physically uncoupling the application from the data achieves tandem goals: performance optimization and increased reliability.

Each type of work imposes different requirements on the host, and this arrangement offers system architects the ability to customize each server's configuration according to its specialized function. For example, the application servers can be optimized for either transaction processing or computation, depending on the nature of the application. Similarly, the data server can be equipped with high speed I/O capabilities and large disks.

Physical layering distributes a fixed amount of work across an increased number of physical resources, which automatically increases the reliability of the overall cluster. Quite simply, there is more redundancy.

As Figure 4.1 demonstrates, a cluster of application servers can process incoming user requests. This cluster then shares access to another server that "owns" the data and database subsystem. This configuration enables one class of machines to focus on database management and another to be dedicated to performing application work.

The small, private FDDI ring that interconnects the three servers in Figure 4.1 is used to segregate inbound traffic from I/O requests. This network can also be used for interhost communications if either load-balancing or fail-over mechanisms are used.

For applications that cannot afford a single point of failure, the cluster's data server can be clustered, too. Thus, two or more fully redundant servers could function interchangeably as the cluster's server for database management.

Complex Clusters

Figure 4.1.

*Client/server/
server clustering.*

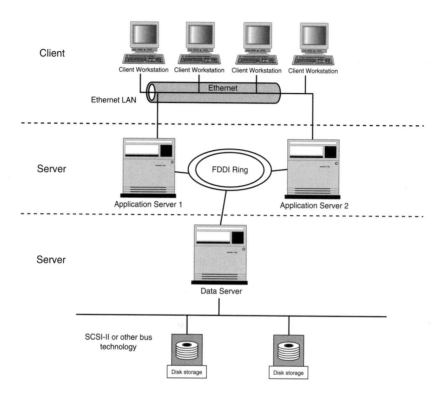

In Figure 4.2, the single point of failure evident in Figure 4.1 is eliminated by introducing a fail-over cluster in the role of the primary cluster's data server. Depending on the amount of use anticipated, either a more robust LAN or a separate LAN (or both) might be required to further segregate "keep alive" communications from I/O requests between the two clusters. This example, however, shows the two clusters sharing a common *Cluster Area Network* (CAN).

Layers do not necessarily have to be vertical. They can be horizontally nested. Figure 4.3 shows a cluster of clusters in which the two clusters are peers.

In theory, a horizontal layering of functions can be used to introduce application-level diversity. The peer-to-peer complex cluster in Figure 4.3 provides the two separate load-balancing shared disk clusters with a completely redundant fail-over cluster. The fact that the applications already execute in a fairly redundant environment makes it highly unlikely that any single hardware failure would render an entire cluster unavailable; however, application-layer errors might.

Horizontal layering requires you to have cluster management software that supports two distinct levels of clustering. The first and most obvious is the application load-balancing level. Fail-overs at this level would enable the cluster to recover from the loss of any node in that primary cluster.

Figure 4.2.
Client/server/ server double cluster.

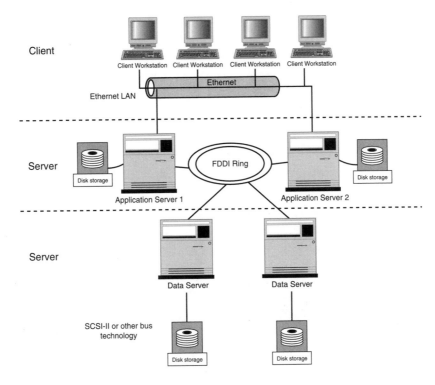

Figure 4.3.
Peer-to-peer, or nested, clustering.

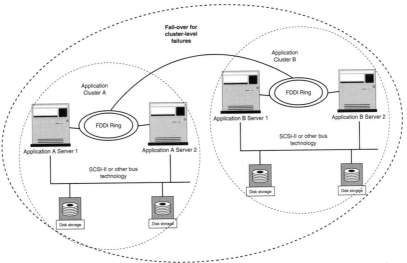

The second level of clustering in this example is more of a disaster recovery scenario. If the entire primary cluster fails, the backup cluster assumes its processing load. Again, this is a fairly complex and highly specialized scenario. It is presented to demonstrate only the potential flexibility of clusters. Whether support for this sort of nested clustering will become widely available remains to be seen.

4.1.2. Hybridization

Hybridization is a technique for building complex clusters by stacking clusters of different topologies.

The client/server/server cluster presented in Figure 4.2 can be further modified to demonstrate layering clusters of different topologies. Figure 4.4 illustrates the same clustered application as was shown in Figure 4.2. The primary difference is that the cluster tasked with data management uses a shared disk topology. The cluster that provides the on-demand processing for user requests remains a shared nothing topology.

Figure 4.4.
Client/server/ server clustering, with mixed topologies.

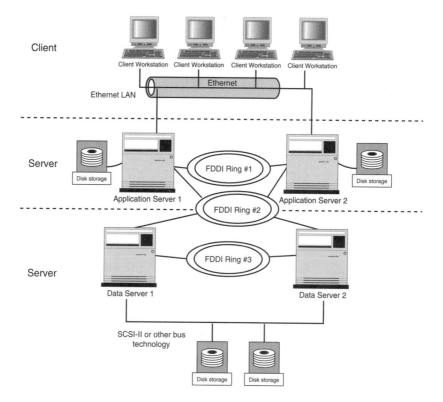

Figure 4.4 also shows how cluster performance can be improved by keeping the cluster area network to an absolute minimum. In this illustration, there are three separate FDDI cluster area networks. The first of the FDDI rings provides connectivity between the clustered application servers for cluster management. The second FDDI ring connects the application servers with the data servers. The traffic on this CAN will be I/O and other application functions. The third FDDI ring provides intracluster connectivity for the cluster management activities of the shared disk data cluster.

4.2. Disaster Recovery Clusters

Disaster recovery clusters, though not necessarily either a hybridized or a layered cluster, are an important complex variant that warrants further attention. This last variation is built around the remotely distributed, shared nothing cluster. Properly planned and implemented, this topology can provide application-level disaster recovery. This requires that clustered servers, and their storage facilities, meet certain criteria. These criteria are as follows:

- They must have sufficient spare capacity to instantly absorb the processing and I/O demands of the application that they are backing up.

- The Local and Wide Area Networks interconnecting the user base and the clustered hosts should have adequate spare capacity to automatically accommodate the shift in traffic patterns that will result from implementing the disaster recovery contingency plans.

- The servers should be geographically separated from each other to ensure that regional disasters do not simultaneously impact both an application's primary and backup hosts.

- If the users are located with their cluster, they must be provided with back-up facilities, too. This includes work surfaces, client machines, and appropriate networking.

- Provisions must be made for maintaining current copies of the application software and data at the emergency host.

Using a variation of the remotely distributed, shared nothing cluster enables system architects to accommodate disaster recovery requirements without incurring the costs normally associated with fully redundant, emergency backup systems.

Figure 4.5 depicts a typical disaster recovery cluster.

Complex Clusters

Figure 4.5.

Clustering for disaster recovery.

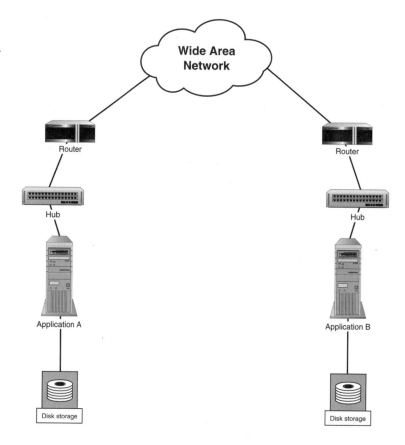

This basic disaster recovery topology features a shared nothing topology that supports two different applications in a dedicated fashion. Application A is solely supported by Node A. Its workload is not distributed. Application B is similarly supported by Node B. Node A provides disaster recovery backup to Node B and vice versa.

Disaster recovery clusters can be developed with clusters of clusters as well, as presented in Figure 4.6.

In Figure 4.6, applications A and B are supported by different shared disk clusters. Depending on the cluster's performance requirements, a shared nothing cluster could just as easily have been used. In the event of a disaster that cripples either location, the stricken cluster's workload would fail-over to the backup location. Looking at Figure 4.6 from a disaster recovery perspective, the clusters at each location are unrelated to each other, except for their mutual fail-over protection. Even though both clusters are shared disk clusters, they form a shared nothing, disaster recovery cluster.

Figure 4.6.
*Clustering
clusters for
disaster recovery.*

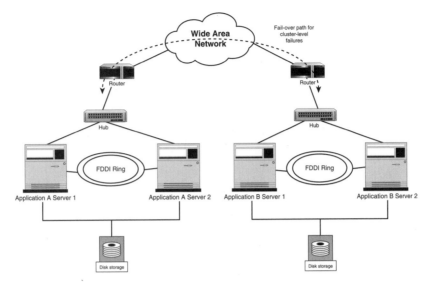

4.3. Tips for Developing Complex Clusters

As explained in section 4.1, the only valid measure of a cluster's success is how well it satisfies the business requirements of the applications that it supports. Consequently, topology is fair game. Some limits on topological variety will be imposed by the cluster management product that you purchase, so it is imperative that any cluster design exercise begins with a clear understanding of its operational performance goals. These goals can be used to help evaluate potential clustering products.

Before you can select a clustering product, it is important to have developed the solution set of potential cluster topologies. This set should contain all the possible cluster designs that are, at least in theory, capable of delivering the level of performance that is required.

The remainder of this section identifies some of the basic architectural concepts that you shouldn't lose sight of when you're developing complex clusters.

4.3.1. How Much Is Enough?

First, too much of anything, even a good thing, can be bad. Adding complexity can be beneficial, but only up to a point. After that, you begin to experience what economists call "diminishing returns." That is, the benefits begin to decrease. Taken to the extreme, a cluster's performance actually suffers with any additional complexity. At this stage, the cluster's performance will improve by removing layers of complexity.

Complex Clusters

Complexity, regardless of whether it is stacked, nested, or otherwise achieved, comes at a price. Additional hardware translates directly into increased hardware and software intensity. This leads to increased response times. The key is to develop an appropriate level of complexity that, in the aggregate, delivers acceptable levels of performance for all of the cluster's performance metrics.

4.3.2. Does It Have to Be Symmetric?

Although it is quite possible to improve performance at minimal cost by modifying only one of the clustered nodes, this is a dangerous game. Such asymmetric clusters, by their very nature, are not perfectly interchangeable because the modified node is different from its peers. Ostensibly, this makes it capable of performing different tasks or of performing at a higher level. In either case, this might compromise the cluster's capability to balance workloads. Worse, asymmetry in a cluster might result in less than complete fail-over protection. Figure 4.7 illustrates an asymmetric cluster.

Figure 4.7.
Asymmetric clustering.

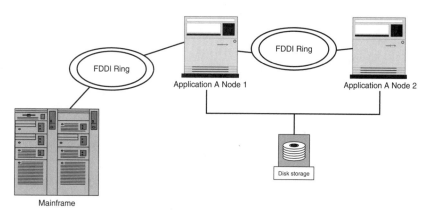

This asymmetric cluster supports an application's on-demand processing. Node 1 is solely responsible for queuing messages to the mainframe. Node 1 also supports the on-demand processing. If it fails, the surviving nodes can assume its processing load, but are not equipped to take over its queuing.

A better approach is to have all the clustered nodes provide their own queuing. This is illustrated in Figure 4.8.

If you find yourself developing an asymmetric cluster, stop! You need to think of a symmetric approach that satisfies your requirements. Asymmetric clustering is a bad practice, and a risk not worth taking. Although you can probably get away with building and using an asymmetric cluster, you don't want to be around when you are finally proven wrong.

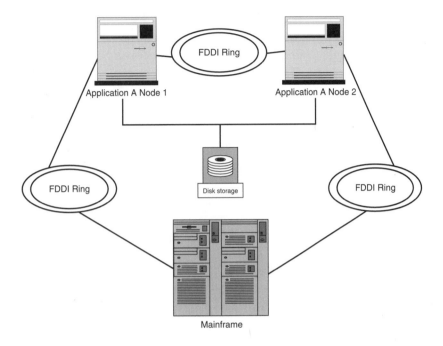

Figure 4.8.
Distributed processing and queuing.

Application A Node 1

FDDI Ring

Application A Node 2

FDDI Ring

Disk storage

FDDI Ring

Mainframe

4.3.3. Keep It Simple!

The last thing to remember as you begin to develop cluster architectures is that complex is not necessarily better. The old "keep it simple, stupid" (KISS) principle might be an old saw, but it still cuts true. Any complexity must be validated in terms of improved cluster performance.

Cluster performance is a nebulous term that can mean many different things. The characteristics of performance that you need to worry about should be embodied in the customers' requirements. If any sort of complexity compromises a requirement or does not contribute to the satisfaction of a requirement, it does not belong in the cluster.

4.4. Summary

This chapter's sampling of complex clustering configurations, though by no means complete, should adequately convey the degree of flexibility that clustering affords. Topologies and their variations can be mixed and matched and even nested together to accommodate business requirements. Individual computers within a cluster can also be tailored to meet specific performance and functional requirements, though this incurs some risk by compromising the interchangeability of clustered nodes.

Complex Clusters

Which one is right for you? Although it is likely that any one of the cluster variants presented in this book can be used satisfactorily, the success of a cluster must be measured in terms of how well it satisfies the users' requirements.

Given this, it is possible that none of the cluster variants presented in this book are right for you. It is also possible that your application can be adequately supported with one of the basic topologies. It is also possible that any one of the cluster variants in this book can be further adapted and customized to better fit your particular situation and requirements.

The right answer might well be determined by your choices of cluster products. The variations presented throughout the first section of this book are intentionally generic. Not every cluster management product will be able to support every possible topological variation. Thus, it is in your best interest to have well-defined cluster performance requirements before you start shopping for cluster management products and cluster-aware operating systems.

Chapter

5

The Anatomy of a Fail-over

So far this book has focused on describing the various macro-mechanics of clusters, their architectures, and the strengths and weaknesses of each. Although this approach provides you with a general understanding of clustering, it stops short of describing the internal mechanics of an NT Server–based fail-over.

This chapter examines the anatomy of a fail-over. However, although it focuses on fail-overs in NT Server–based clusters, it does not describe the fail-over process of any particular cluster management product. Rather, it describes the typical fail-over in an NT Server cluster. The steps described here are somewhat abstracted, and might differ slightly from the processes used by a particular cluster management product.

5.1. Fail-over Activities

The typical fail-over scenario requires several important steps to successfully transition processing to an alternative platform. These steps are as follows:

- Detecting the failure

- Identifying stricken resources or groups of resources

- Notifying the other cluster nodes about the failure

- Removing the stricken resources from active service

- Identifying alternative resources or groups of resources

- Activating the alternative resources

- Notifying impacted applications of the resource status change

- Replicating any in-use data to an alternative node's memory

- Replicating current application states to an alternative node

- Resumption of application activity

Although this might seem a lengthy and time-consuming sequence of events, the times to fail-over completion can be as quick as a few seconds. On the other hand, replicating application and data states for some applications can force the fail-over to take 90 or more seconds.

Each of these activities plays a vital role in the proper functioning of a fail-over. Unfortunately, what constitutes a failure (and therefore triggers a fail-over) can be as diverse as clusters themselves. Before inspecting these activities, it is necessary to acknowledge that fail-overs are not homogeneous. Consequently, what follows is only an approximation of the necessary activities (and their sequence) that will occur during a fail-over.

The time required to complete this sequence can vary considerably as well. Factors like the degree to which the entire cluster was aware of and able to use the cluster's features, the application type, and even the workload, can all affect the amount of time required to successfully complete a fail-over. Times can range from a few seconds for simple, well-integrated solutions, to 90 seconds or more!

5.1.1. Fail-over Scenarios

There are four basic fail-over scenarios that you can encounter in an NT Server–based cluster. These four scenarios are based on two variables: Fail-overs can be manual or automatic, and complete or partial. Together, these variables yield the following potential fail-over scenarios:

- Automatic complete fail-over

- Automatic, partial fail-over

- Manual, partial fail-over

- Manual, complete fail-over

The mechanics, and even the functional significance, of these four scenarios can be very different. After more thoroughly examining each of the fail-over activities, these scenarios will be reviewed. For the sake of brevity, this chapter assumes that the cluster was well designed and well constructed, and that details like data and application redundancy have already been taken care of.

5.2. Detecting the Failure

Detecting the failure is the first step in a fail-over. On the surface, this appears to be a fairly simple task: something ceased working, so let's tell the rest of the cluster. Unfortunately, it's not that easy. There are some significant logistics that exacerbate failure detection.

Ideally, the node experiencing the failure will realize it, and have enough time to identify the stricken resources and initiate the appropriate fail-over and recovery procedures. This might well be the case for minor failures of individual resources and groups.

Unfortunately, sometimes failures are catastrophic and can disable a node before it can take any remedial actions. In such cases, it is virtually impossible to save any work that was in progress. Regardless of what the vendors advertise, the fail-over will be noticed by the users. The best you can hope for is that the surviving nodes will recognize the loss of a peer and assume its workload.

Another challenge in detecting failures is that the subsystems that aren't cluster-aware might be the first to detect a failure. For example, if the cluster uses a Small Computer Systems Interface II (SCSI-II) bus to chain disk drives, the SCSI driver set might be the first component to recognize a drive failing to respond. The SCSI adapter would attempt to write to the failed device, according to its preset parameters, and eventually declare the drive out of service.

Unfortunately, this subsystem isn't cluster-aware, so its identification of a stricken resource would not be communicated. It is up to the operating system to recognize the accumulated I/O errors, or even the change in the resource's operational status. This takes time. Depending on what caused the failure, the time required for the operating system and/or cluster management software to recognize the failure might make the difference between an invisible fail-over and a painfully obvious one. Although this example picked on SCSI-II bus technology, the implications of using non-cluster-aware components apply universally to all subsystems, application software, and even to the operating system.

As a result of the challenges described in this section, many mechanisms must exist for detecting the myriad types of failures that can occur and warrant some type of fail-over.

5.2.1. Detecting Severe Failures

Clustered nodes are given mechanisms for continuously monitoring the status of other nodes in the cluster. These mechanisms are cumulatively regarded as a *heartbeat*. The heartbeat is a signal that is almost continuously broadcast and asserts the originating node's availability.

> **NOTE** Transmitting heartbeats is a critical function that cannot be trifled with. Although it is technically feasible to ship heartbeats and other cluster management activities across LANs that also provide client-to-cluster connectivity, to do so would be foolish. This function absolutely should be handled by its own private network, the cluster area network (CAN). The CAN is a private local area network that serves only to interconnect clustered nodes and support cluster management functions, including disk mirroring, heartbeats, load balancing, and fail-overs. In time, technologies will emerge that will enable extending and switching each node's I/O buses, and direct memory access. Such technologies (known as System Area Networks) will make the cluster area network obsolete.

In the event that clustered nodes cease receiving responses or status messages from one of their peers, they automatically assume that the peer has ceased functioning and implement their fail-over procedures. This form of failure detection has deep implications for the fail-over.

That a node was unable to detect its own severe failure implies that there is very little that can be done to salvage any work that was in progress. The node likely experienced a sudden and catastrophic error. Such errors can be impossible to gracefully recover from and, usually, the node goes down hard and fast.

Windows NT usually manifests sudden and catastrophic failure via the *Blue Screen of Death*. This screen, featuring white text on a blue background, is a debug screen that indicates an unrecoverable failure has occurred. Your only recourse is to reboot the machine and hope you didn't lose too much work. A blue screen failure on an NT Server will drop all user connections. Any data that existed solely in memory will be lost. The application, too, has little chance of replicating its state to the alternate node.

5.2.2. Detecting Minor Failures

Successfully identifying the less severe failures requires the cooperation of multiple cluster components. Less severe failures can include the loss of a single resource. In turn, this singular loss can impair the functionality of any resource groups that it might belong to. Such a loss might be identified by any one of three different cluster components.

The first component that might recognize a low magnitude failure would be the application that needs the stricken resource. Applications that are cluster-aware or cluster-enabled will likely be able to notify the operating system of the failure. The operating system, working in conjunction with the cluster management software, would then initiate the fail-over sequence.

There are several drawbacks to relying on applications as a detection mechanism. First, failures are usually only detected when the application attempts to use a stricken resource. This is too late! The user will notice the failure immediately. If the application wasn't cluster-aware, things would deteriorate quickly because the application wouldn't be able to communicate the failure to the operating system. Even worse, when the operating system did figure out what was happening, the application would not be able to understand the operating system's attempts to replicate its state to the fail-over node.

Another component that could recognize the loss of a service or resource is the operating system. Given that Windows NT 5.0 will be cluster-aware, it is quite possible that NT would recognize the failure independent of any other detection mechanism.

Ideally, your cluster will feature many cluster-aware mechanisms. Each one should be capable of detecting failures, notifying other node-level resources, and initiating the sequence of fail-over events. It is in your best interest to use only cluster-aware technologies. If this is not practical (as illustrated with the example on SCSI-II bus technology), understand the implications of the lack of cluster-awareness on failure detection and try to compensate accordingly.

5.3. Identifying Stricken Resources

Compounding the problems inherent in fault detection are the problems inherent in fault identification. It is one thing to figure out that a problem exists. It is vastly more difficult to figure out exactly what the problem is. Unfortunately, until the stricken resources are identified, it might be impossible to take appropriate remedial action.

NT Server is resource-oriented. A resource is any single system-level service, function, or asset. These provide a service to either client applications or other cluster resources. NT Server typically supports resources with dedicated DLLs. Examples of resources include the following:

- Disk drives

- Databases

- File shares

- Print queues

- IP addresses

- DNS or NetBEUI network names

- System services

Some resources can be deceptively difficult to diagnose. For example, if a DNS name ceases responding, there can be multiple potential causes: The DNS could have failed, the named resource might have failed, or the name could have changed. In any of these events, the source of the failure is external to the cluster and, consequently, immaterial.

Internal cluster resource failures can prove equally difficult to diagnose. For example, if a two-node, shared nothing cluster experiences a network failure in its cluster area network, each node will assume that the other has failed because it has lost contact. Consequently, each will try to assume responsibility for the other's workload. Such a response is predictable, but inappropriate.

The key difference between these two examples is that the external failure does not alter the fail-over sequence and might not be remedied via fail-over. Failures that are internal to the cluster, if misdiagnosed, can generate inappropriate activities that will further detract from the cluster's ability to process its workload. Typically, cluster management software won't have strong diagnostics. It will limit its trouble analysis efforts to merely identifying the failed resources and taking steps to logically migrate those resources to another node.

> **NOTE** Diagnostics can be time-and resource-intensive endeavors that are contrary to the mission of a cluster. Though this might seem counter-intuitive, the purpose of a cluster is either high scalability or high availability. High availability does not require strong diagnostics, just the tandem capabilities to identify the resources impacted by a failure and to automatically recover from that failure.

5.3.1. Resource Groups

Once a stricken resource is identified, the next step is to identify its interdependent resources. Resources are often grouped logically because of such functional interdependencies. These structures, known as *resource groups,* must always reside together on the same node. In the event of a failure of a resource, all resources that are grouped with the stricken resource must fail-over in unison. If you failed to identify all resource interdependencies when you designed your cluster, you will experience erratic cluster and application behaviors during fail-overs.

It is important to note that an application is a cluster resource. As such, the cluster must be aware of any hierarchical dependencies that an application might have. For example, assume a two-node, shared disk cluster with two applications. The first is an inventory application. This application and its database reside on a SCSI disk drive. All three—the application, database, and disk drive—are cluster resources.

An unrelated employee time reporting application also resides on this disk drive, but it has its own database. This application and database are two more resources. The result is a pair of logical, interrelated hierarchies (or groups) of dependency with a common element. This hierarchy of dependencies is illustrated in Figure 5.1.

Figure 5.1.
Hierarchical resource dependencies.

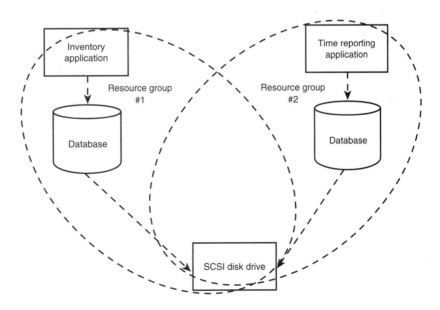

If the disk drive skips ahead off the platter's surface, it makes an interesting noise, but permanently compromises the functionality of the entire drive and its contents. This includes the database. The database failure, in turn, renders the application at least partially unusable. This is the essence of hierarchical dependencies in a cluster. The impact of this failure on the hierarchy shown in Figure 5.1 is presented in Figure 5.2.

Figure 5.2.

Effects of disk drive failure on hierarchically dependent resources.

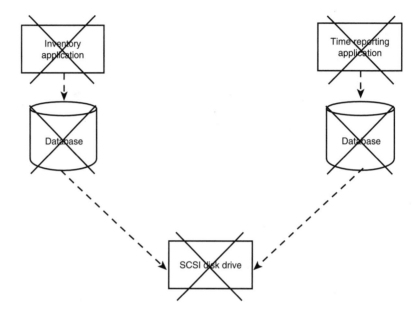

A different failure scenario (with the same basic set of resources, however) yields a different set of downstream impacts. If the inventory database indices become corrupted, the database becomes unstable and unusable. Consequently, the inventory application and its database would both be flagged as unavailable resources. The disk drive would remain viable. The time reporting application, tragically, would remain unaffected by the database failure. The impact of this failure on the hierarchical resource dependencies is illustrated in Figure 5.3.

The moral of this story is this: Pay excruciatingly close attention to the detailed policies that will guide your cluster's behavior. Your fail-over will depend on it. For more information on setting cluster policies, please refer to Chapter 7, "Microsoft's Cluster Server."

Figure 5.3.

Effects of database failure on hierarchically dependent resources.

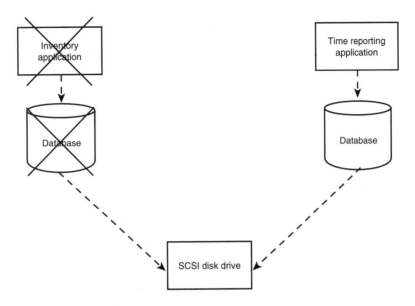

5.4. Notifying the Other Nodes

After the node's cluster management software or operating system has identified the stricken resources, it must notify the other nodes of their failure. Much like failure detection, there is more to notification than is readily apparent. Failure notification can happen in one of two ways: proactively or by inference.

A proactive fail-over notification occurs when a node detects the failure of one or more of its own resources, and proactively initiates their fail-over to the alternative node. The usefulness of this type of notification is limited to failures at the resource or group level, or for voluntary fail-overs. Unanticipated failures at the node level seldom provide enough lead time for the soon-to-be-stricken node to do anything about it.

For nodal failures, a more plausible scenario is notification by inference. It is not inconceivable that the primary node will experience a massive failure that almost instantaneously renders it inoperable. The node itself would be helpless to initiate the fail-over sequence. The first sign of trouble that the other cluster nodes would receive is the loss of the stricken node's heartbeat across the cluster area network. Under these circumstances, there can be no opportunity to replicate data that is resident in RAM, or the application's state at the time of failure. Any work in progress is lost. Any connections to the stricken node are dropped and the users must re-initiate the connection by addressing the logical cluster name. Ideally, when they try to reconnect to their application server, the cluster will have recognized the failure and completed the fail-over to a healthy node.

5.4.1. Mechanics of Inferential Notification

Notification by inference is an imprecise solution to a nearly impossible dilemma. Depending on the nature and severity of the failure, a stricken node might be incapable of notifying the other clustered nodes about that failure for more than one reason. As explained in the previous paragraph, cluster nodes might have to infer awareness of a node-level failure from the loss of a heartbeat. Figure 5.4 illustrates this situation.

Figure 5.4.

Node 1's "heartbeat" fails.

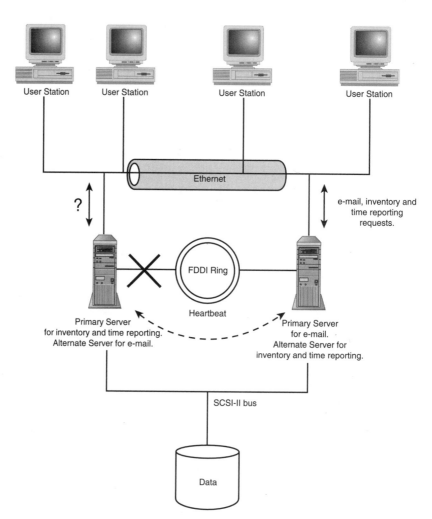

Even though Figure 5.1 demonstrates a viable approach to detecting node-level failures, this type of inference is not foolproof. In Figure 5.4, it is not entirely clear why the heartbeat ceased. The primary application server for inventory and employee time reporting may or may not still be functional. Its alternative node, the primary server for e-mail, must assume that because its connectivity with the cluster area network appears fine, the other node has failed. Thus, it will initiate its fail-over sequence and begin accepting requests for the inventory and time reporting applications.

The cluster area network, too, can fail in ways that appear as a node-level failure to other cluster nodes. All clustered nodes might be functioning perfectly, but be unable to communicate with the other nodes because the interconnection between them has failed.

> **NOTE** This hypothetical situation is presented solely to illustrate the complexity introduced through externally distributed parallelism. Depending on the network technology used and the exact manner in which it fails, at least one of the nodes should be able to detect a problem with the network. This node would flag that resource as unavailable and rely on established policies to determine appropriate actions.

In such cases, each cluster node will detect the loss of a heartbeat. Depending on the exact nature of the network failure, the individual nodes in the cluster might not be able to determine that the network is the culprit. Consequently, they might each assume the other node failed and reactively initiate their fail-over sequence. This situation is illustrated in Figure 5.5. Both nodes, in this hypothetical situation, would try to execute their fail-over plan and assume the workload for the other node.

This situation can be a particular nuisance in clusters that do not share applications. Shared application clusters, whether they feature dynamic or static load balancing, would not be as greatly impacted. Figure 5.6 illustrates that inbound client requests could still be accepted by both nodes. The cluster would be functioning as two independent nodes in fail-over mode. Any functions that would be compromised in fail-over mode would be compromised in this scenario. Depending on the nature of the application and the degree to which shared data is required by both instances of the application software, this situation could precipitate data integrity problems.

Figure 5.5.
*Cluster area
network failure.*

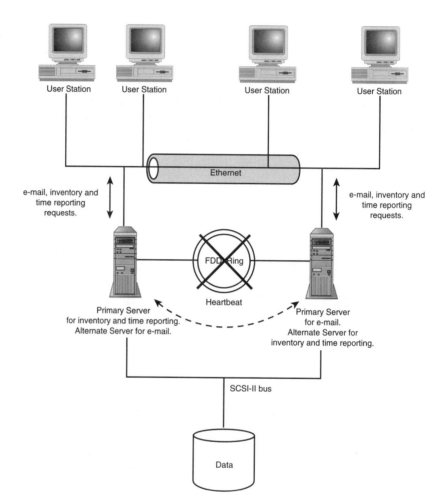

User Station   User Station   User Station   User Station

Ethernet

e-mail, inventory and
time reporting
requests.

e-mail, inventory and
time reporting
requests.

FDDI Ring

Heartbeat

Primary Server
for inventory and time reporting.
Alternate Server for e-mail.

Primary Server
for e-mail.
Alternate Server for
inventory and time reporting.

SCSI-II bus

Data

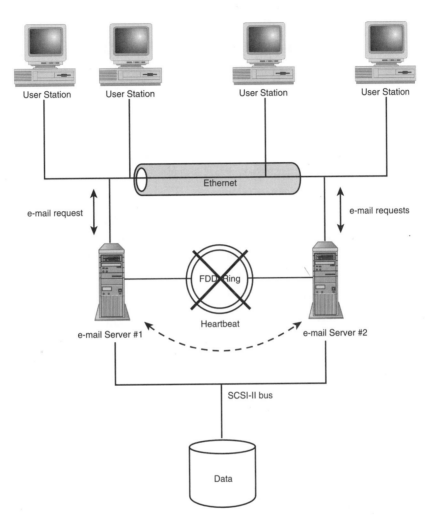

Figure 5.6.
Cluster area network failure in a dynamic load balancing cluster.

One potential means of preventing this particular situation would be to implement redundant networking for intracluster communications. This provides a robust and dedicated backup to the primary cluster area network, and can prevent network failures from causing unwanted fail-overs. This alternative is illustrated in Figure 5.7.

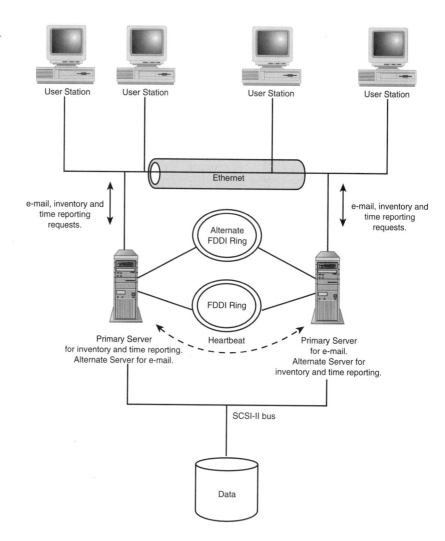

Figure 5.7.
*Redundant
cluster area
networks.*

This hypothetical situation was intended solely to demonstrate the less than perfect ability of a remote node to make inferences about the status of another node. Fail-over policies must be extremely carefully thought out before they are implemented.

5.5. Resource Deactivation

Resource deactivation is significantly less complicated than many of the other fail-over processes. Deactivation simply means that a resource has been removed from the cluster's pool of active and available resources. There are only two variations: automatic deactivation or voluntary deactivation.

Automatic deactivation is the functional goal of any clustering product. Any resources that fail to respond to requests are, de facto, out of service. Consequently, it is simply a matter of detecting the problem, identifying all impacted resources, and flagging them as out of service. Once they are identified to the cluster and the clients as being out of service, they can no longer be used. All requests for those resources are automatically channeled to the alternative resources instead.

Voluntary resource deactivations occur when a resource is manually and voluntarily taken out of service by the host administrator. This results in the logical "migration" of that resource to its alternative cluster node, even though the primary resource did not experience a failure of any kind.

The important distinction between a voluntary and an automatic resource migration is the nature of its fail-back. Generally speaking, once a resource or group of resources becomes deactivated, the cluster management software can and should automatically begin to recover by making the alternative resources available and active. However, if the resource migration is voluntary, the cluster management software should *not* attempt an automatic fail-back; it should wait for the cluster administrator to manually restore the deactivated resources to service.

5.6. Identification of Alternative Resources

The next step in the fail-over process is the identification of appropriate alternative resources. This is done using the cluster management policies that must be developed during the cluster's logical construction. Primary and secondary resources and resource groups must be identified in these policies.

Extending the example presented in section 5.3.1, it is easy to see how a cluster can identify alternative resources. That example presents a two-node, shared disk cluster that supports two applications (inventory and employee time reporting), two databases, and one disk drive.

The cluster depicted in Figure 5.8 shows that the primary copies of both the inventory and the time reporting applications reside on Node 1. Node 2 runs a completely unrelated e-mail post office, but each has sufficient spare capacity to accept fail-over work from the other. The copies of the inventory and the time reporting applications residing on Node 2 are the alternative resources. In the event of a failure of any related resource on Node 1, these would become active.

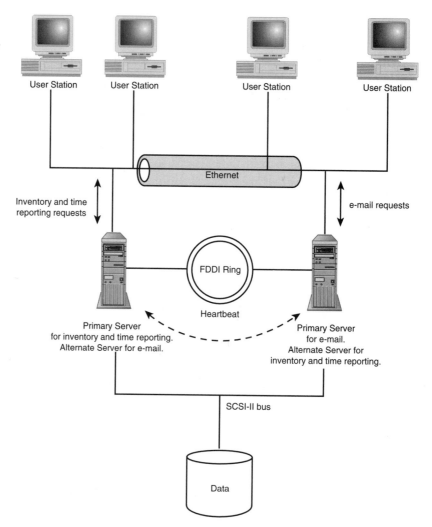

Figure 5.8.
*Primary and
alternative cluster
resources.*

As powerful as clustering can be, it cannot be taken for granted. It's up to the administrator of the clustered nodes to ensure that the distributed, redundant copies of application software and, more importantly, data, stay current and synchronized with each other. This absolutely requires that good *operations, administration, and maintenance* (OA&M) procedures be established and adhered to. That isn't to say that clusters aren't capable of automatic replication. In fact, there are many tools, including RAID striping, distributed lock management, and so on, that can help maintain consistency and integrity. The point is that a cluster is only as good as its design, and its design can suffer from the entropic effects of poor OA&M practices. Over time, the cluster's policies can become outdated if they aren't diligently maintained.

5.7. Alternative Resource Activation

Only one instance of any given cluster resource or group of resources can be active at a time. These resources can and should be duplicated across all nodes in a cluster, but only one can be "active." The others must remain in one of two possible states: inactive or ready.

Each manufacturer has different terms for these states. The actual phrasing does not alter their meanings. An active resource is the one that is up and running. Calls for that resource are directed to the active resource only.

Redundant copies of that resource existing on other cluster nodes can be inactive. Inactive means that they are present, but not online or usable. Typically, some effort will be required to make them usable beyond changing their status to active. Depending on the type of resource, this could require

- Loading them into memory

- Initializing hardware

- Spinning up a disk

- Mounting a file system

- Using some combination of the above or any other physical processes needed to ready the resource for use

Ready resources means that they are present and ready for use. No additional effort is required to prepare them for use as primary cluster resources. All of the possible preparations just mentioned have already been performed; disk drives are already spinning, file systems already mounted, and so on. All that remains is to change their status to active. This process is automated sufficiently to make it appear that a single resource has migrated to an alternative platform within a cluster.

5.8. Notification of Impacted Applications

Applications, it would seem, would be the first to know if a resource failed. In reality, many applications lack the logic necessary to detect a resource failure. They will be the first to know that a resource is inaccessible, but they might not be able to do anything about it. The application's usual behavior for accessing failed resources is repeatedly trying to access that resource until some threshold is reached. At that point, the application would offer the client a choice of either continuing to try, or aborting the request.

Implicit in this behavior is that applications can't recognize a resource failure until they've failed to access that resource. This is too late. In any structure that strives for high availability, like a cluster, this approach is unacceptable. Too much time can elapse before the failure is detected. This wasted time could have been used to enact contingency plans to minimize the effects of the failure. Cluster management services are designed to identify failures early and take advantage of the highly redundant, distributed nature of clusters to remediate failures before they are required by an application or requested by a user.

5.8.1. Chain of Notification

The examples presented in section 5.3.1, and expanded in section 5.6, demonstrated that applications might not be the first to recognize a resource failure. The typical chain of notification for this example would be as follows:

- The SCSI device controller will likely be the first component to notice the failure.

- The operating system will be informed by the device controller.

- The operating system can then inform the cluster management service that the resource is, suddenly, unavailable.

If the application wasn't trying to access data when the failure occurred, it would have no way of knowing about that failure.

In a cluster, the partnership of the operating system and cluster management product will be responsible for interfacing with applications and any applicable subsystems to identify a resource failure. The cluster's policies, which include definition of resource dependencies, are used to identify all impacted applications. These applications may or may not have experienced the failure. Regardless, they must be notified of the change in that resource's status so that their fail-over can begin.

5.9. Data Replication

After the cluster management service has successfully activated the requisite alternative resources, it can attempt to minimize the damage of the resource failure on any work that was in progress. An important part of this is to save any data that was in use at the time of the failure. In-use data would reside in memory only. Thus, it is volatile and subject to loss if it's not saved to a less volatile medium like a disk. Replicating this data permits the application to logically "move" to its alternative platform without disrupting processing; even work in progress is preserved and moved.

Applications that are cluster-aware will be able to respond to function calls through their application programming interface (API) and work with the cluster management service to replicate volatile data to the alternative node.

Applications that aren't cluster-aware won't respond to attempts to replicate volatile data. Consequently, any volatile data will be lost.

5.10. Replication of Application States

In addition to replicating volatile data to the alternative node, clusters permit even the state of an application to be replicated to the alternative node. In combination with the replication of volatile data, state replication ensures that the application can resume processing on its new host, starting from exactly where it left off on its original host when the resource failure occurred.

Every facet of the application's state, from the contents of registers, to the exact point in the application's logic that was executing, to the connection from the user station, is replicated to the backup node. Once everything has been replicated, the application resumes processing automatically.

As with data replication, this functionality is only available to cluster-aware applications. Legacy applications that aren't aware of their clustered platform are not equipped to respond to cluster function calls. Consequently, in the event of a failure, any applications that aren't cluster-aware will go down hard, lose data, and will not be failed-over gracefully.

5.11. Resumption of Application Activity

In a normal fail-over sequence, one of the last steps is to actually resume application processing on the alternative node. As with any clustered function that involves the application, the degree of automation with which processing is restored depends directly on the application. Applications written to a recognized clustering API will be able to respond to function calls, replicate volatile data and application states, and even automatically restart on the alternative cluster node. Even the network connections from users to the cluster node will be "moved" to the alternative node. In short, the users will experience a slight delay, but no disruption, in processing as the application fails-over to the alternative node and resumes.

Applications that aren't cluster-aware will have a much more difficult time. Volatile data will be lost. The application's state at the time of the resource failure, too, will be lost. It is possible that the application will have to be manually failed-over and restarted. User connections will have no hope of "moving" to the new node. Users of clustered legacy applications, that is, non-cluster–aware applications, will notice the resource failure.

5.12. Fail-back

The last activity in any fail-over is the restoration of service to the primary node. Known as a *fail-back*, this is the final process that completes a fail-over. It restores service in the cluster back to its original form before the fail-over occurred.

After the original node and all its resources are fully operational, its workload can be restored in one of two ways. If the cluster is configured to automatically restore service to the designated primary node, it should recognize the return of that node to operational status. At that point, it will use its policies to determine which resources and resource groups can be returned to that original node. Rendering them inoperative should allow them to revert back to their original platform. Any data or application state replications should also be handled automatically by the cluster management software.

The second option for service restoration is another manual effort. This might be required if your cluster management software doesn't support automatic service restoration, or isn't configured for it.

These two fail-back options should be considered the final step, the recovery step, that completes any fail-over. Section 5.13 describes the four fail-over scenarios in more detail. For the sake of brevity, these process descriptions end with the restoration of service on the alternative node, but they do not describe fail-backs.

5.13. Fail-over Scenarios

After reviewing the mechanics of fail-overs, the next logical step is to look at the fail-over sequences that occur during the four distinct fail-over scenarios described in section 5.1.1. These four scenarios are *manual, partial; manual complete; automatic, partial;* and *automatic, complete* fail-overs.

5.13.1. Manual, Partial Fail-over

The ability to manually trigger a partial fail-over affords you the ability to conduct resource-level static load balancing within a cluster. Additionally, it can be beneficial to take a node partially out of service to conduct upgrades to some of its resources. Under such circumstances, it might be possible to identify the impacted resources and manually initiate their fail-over to their alternative node. In either event, the ability to manually trigger a partial fail-over affords the administrator the ability to optimize the cluster's overall performance and "health" without incurring any downtime.

One other possible application of this scenario is to manually initiate the fail-over of any resources that failed, but did not automatically fail-over. This cluster behavior is contrary to what a cluster is supposed to do. However, the possibility exists that a bug in the cluster management software, or even improperly defined cluster management policies, can cause unexpected cluster behavior. Thus, a manual, partial fail-over can be the last resort for providing high application availability in a cluster that is experiencing operational difficulties.

The typical manual, partial fail-over begins with the manual identification of resources to be failed over. The cluster management software identifies any interdependent, grouped resources that must fail-over in unison with the identified resources. Its management policies are then used to identify the appropriate backup node. These resources are deactivated and the backup node is notified of the change in operational status.

The backup node readies and activates the necessary resources, and begins accepting requests from the failed node's groups. Once these alternative resources are ready and active, it is possible to begin replicating the data and application states of the impacted applications (from the original node to the backup node). This can only happen if the applications are cluster-aware. Clustered applications that aren't cluster-aware cannot perform these replications and might lose any data or work that is in process at the time of the fail-over.

5.13.2. Manual, Complete Fail-over

Manually triggering a complete fail-over can be used to take a node down for proactive maintenance, upgrades, or even physical replacement, without impacting the availability of the clustered application. As happens with a manual, partial fail-over, a complete manual fail-over can also serve as a last resort if a failure occurs and the cluster cannot, or does not, automatically fail-over.

In this fail-over scenario, there is no resource failure to detect. Thus, the cluster management software is spared the effort of isolating stricken resources and any interdependent, grouped resources. The fail-over begins by identifying the node itself as "stricken." Consequently, all the resources, resource groups, and hierarchies of resource interdependence are identified for fail-over.

The stricken node uses its management policies to correlate these resources and groups with their backup node. It notifies the other nodes of the impending change in resource status, requests that they activate their counterpart resources, and then removes the primary resources from active service. Once the alternative resources are activated, that node begins accepting requests for them.

Once the peer nodes have been notified and their resources activated, off-loading any work in progress from the stricken node can be coordinated. If the applications are cluster-aware and enabled, the cluster management software will work with them to replicate their current states and memory-resident data to their alternative nodes.

5.13.3. Automatic, Partial Fail-over

In a clustered operation, the automatic, partial fail-over will likely be the most common fail-over encountered. In fact, this scenario provides the type of high availability and fault resilience that would prompt the development of a cluster! NT, a cluster-aware operating system, excels at identifying failed resources. The operating system works with the cluster management software to identify the failed resources as well as any interdependent, grouped resources. The fail-over begins by identifying these resources as unavailable.

The stricken node uses its management policies to identify the appropriate alternative resources and their hosts. The alternative hosts are informed of the need to ready and activate the impacted resources and groups. Once they are made available, they can be used to satisfy requests. After they are available, the clustered nodes can begin coordinating the replication of any impacted data and application states. As usual, if the impacted applications are not cluster-aware, there can be little hope of successfully replicating their memory-resident data or application states.

5.13.4. Automatic, Complete Fail-over

Automatically performing a complete fail-over is the basic level of fault recovery in a cluster. In this fail-over scenario, the failure renders the entire node unserviceable. Unlike the failure of individual resources, or even groups of resources, there is no need to isolate specific, component-level failures or recover from them. The entire node and all of its resources are out of service. In this event, a fail-over can happen in one of two ways: proactively or reactively.

A proactive fail-over occurs when the stricken node detects deteriorating system conditions and proactively initiates the fail-over of operations to the alternative node before the condition becomes fatal. The failing node initiates the fail-over sequence by declaring all resources out of service. Its management policies are used to correlate these resources and groups with their alternatives. These alternative nodes are notified of the change in availability of the primary resources. They activate their resources and begin accepting requests for those groups.

Once the peer nodes have been notified, it is possible to coordinate the off-loading of work in progress from the stricken node. This is done by notifying the clustered applications of the change in the status of their resources. If the applications are cluster-aware and enabled, the cluster management software will work with them to replicate their current states and memory-resident data to their alternative nodes.

As explained in section 5.1.2, the Blue Screen of Death that typifies a sudden and massive failure in an NT operating system makes proactive automatic fail-over a fairly improbable scenario. A more plausible scenario is the reactive fail-over. The primary node experiences a massive failure that almost instantaneously renders it inoperable. The node itself would be helpless to initiate the fail-over sequence. Instead, the other cluster nodes would detect the loss of that node's heartbeat across the cluster area network. Under these circumstances, there can be no opportunity to replicate data that is resident in RAM, or the application's state at the time of failure. This work in progress is lost. Any connections to the stricken node are dropped and the users must re-initiate the connection by addressing the logical cluster name. Ideally, when they try to reconnect to their application server, the cluster will have automatically completed the fail-over and a healthy node will accept their inbound request.

5.14. What Causes Sequence Differences?

The sequences described in section 5.13 are not chiseled into stone. Rather, they are only an approximation of the activities and their sequence that will occur during a fail-over in an NT cluster. The actual sequence in which your cluster fails-over will depend on several variables. Differences in cluster management products, the degree to which your application software is cluster-aware and enabled, and even the nature of the failure that triggers the fail-over, all directly affect fail-over sequencing.

The primary factor that determines the sequencing is the cluster's functionality. Load-balancing clusters can much more readily absorb the incremental workload of another node. Clusters that do not share a common application have more work to do in activating resources. Consequently, they require more time to complete the fail-over process.

Some of the key functional areas that differ by implementation include the following:

- The granularity of resource fail-overs

- The degree to which fail-overs can be controlled

- The manner in which data and application state replication is coordinated and performed

- The manner in which data access and modification ("locking") is coordinated and performed

These are some of the primary functional areas in which the various NT Server-based clustering products vary. Each of these, in turn, can directly impact a fail-over's activities. For example, whether or not a cluster management product supports the fail-over of individual resources, or groups of resources, has a great impact on the fail-over process. As illustrated in the preceding sections on fail-over scenarios, clusters that are limited to an "all-or-nothing" fail-over are spared the burden of identifying the impacted resources. They function until a failure of sufficient magnitude occurs to initiate the fail-over sequence.

Cluster management products—like Microsoft's Cluster Server—that can detect and fail-over individual resources or small groups of resources are much more adept at maintaining the availability of the clustered application. When it's combined with the ability to voluntarily migrate resources, the added flexibility provides cluster administrators with powerful management capabilities. This is particularly useful in statically balancing workloads, preparing for scheduled downtime, or any number of other uses.

Another key area of cluster functionality that could affect the sequence, and even the processes, involved in a fail-over is the manner in which data and application state replication is coordinated and performed. Successful data and state replication is predicated on having cluster-enabled application software. If the application is not cluster-enabled, any attempt by either the operating system or the cluster management software to initiate replication en route to a fail-over is ignored or misinterpreted by the application.

The last area of cluster functionality that impacts sequencing is the manner in which data is accessed and modified. Different implementations rely on different mechanisms to conduct this access arbitration. For example, a cluster-aware subsystem like Oracle could be used to lock records and arbitrate access to shared data. Alternatively, a proprietary mechanism could be embedded into either the operating system, the cluster management software, or even some other non-cluster-aware subsystem, to provide this function.

5.15. Summary

As emphasized throughout this book, there is no single, right way to design and build a cluster. Consequently, there can be no single explanation of how a fail-over occurs in a cluster. The typical anatomy presented in this chapter should serve only to increase your appreciation for some of the mechanics of your cluster's fail-over capabilities and reinforce the need for careful maintenance of the cluster's fail-over policies.

The Anatomy of
a Fail-over

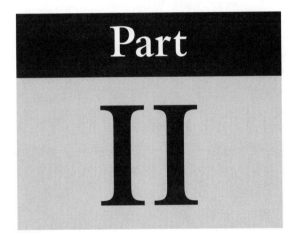

Part

II

Microsoft's Cluster Server

Chapter

6

Windows
NT Server

Since its inception, Microsoft Windows NT Server has been steadily upgraded and enhanced with an eye on the future. The next release, NT Server 5.0, continues this tradition. This chapter describes the forward-looking, enabling attributes of NT Server, and explains their benefits in a clustered environment.

6.1. Developing a Cluster-Aware Operating System

Traditionally, software development lags behind hardware development. Hardware is developed with new and enabling features, and is almost always made generally available before any software manufacturer can deliver software to take advantage of those features. Co-development agreements and strategic partnerships have mitigated the effects of this practice, but they have not eliminated it.

Microsoft is attempting to reverse this paradigm in many important ways with Windows NT Server. Microsoft steadfastly maintains that NT is its strategic product, and has positioned it for the future. While many other interim products were produced with great fanfare (one of them even lent NT 4.0 its user interface), NT's strategic positioning remained constant.

Consequently, NT has been treated to a steady diet of upgrades and enhancements that were not extended to its siblings. Many of these are years ahead of the hardware required to exploit their potential. This incremental, forward-looking approach to updating NT Server is about to pay off. It is now well positioned for its future as a highly scalable, highly reliable, cluster-aware operating system for low-end computing architectures. Some of its native attributes include support for 64-bit computing (which directly translates into massive scalability), interoperability, and portability.

6.2. Scalability

Scalability is a measure of the efficiency with which linear expansion can occur on any given platform. In other words, if we add a CPU to a symmetrical multiprocessor that only has one CPU already installed, the theoretical processing power has doubled. In reality, actual performance improvement will be less than 100%. This ratio of performance improvement to linear expansion is known commonly as scalability. Figure 6.1 illustrates the relationship between scalability and the linear expansion of a computing platform.

The problem with determining platform scalability is that it is extremely application dependent. Adding CPUs will only improve performance if the application is CPU-intensive and if that was the resource constraining its performance. Consequently, scalable platforms can be remarkably difficult to design and implement.

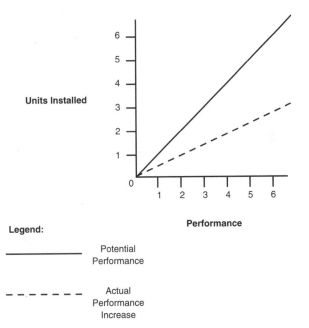

Figure 6.1.
Scalability versus linear expansion.

Units Installed

Legend:

—————— Potential Performance

— — — — — Actual Performance Increase

The hallmarks of highly scalable platforms are consistently scalable hardware and software. In a cluster, scalability can be achieved either via an internal or an external linear expansion of resources. Chapter 3, "Clustering for Scalability," described many features of scalability in clusters. Having a physical platform that is capable of massive expansion is only part of the solution. An equally critical component is an operating system that is capable of recognizing and addressing massive quantities of system resources.

Windows NT, as a *network operating system* (NOS), supports massive scalability in several important ways. These features have been folded into NT slowly, but steadily, in maintenance releases and major new releases since release 3.1 back in 1993. These features are described below.

6.2.1. File System

One of the more significant scalability-enhancing developments was the NT File System, known more commonly as NTFS. NTFS was introduced in NT 3.1, and featured support for a true 64-bit file system. The scalability of a 64-bit file system is a little hard to comprehend. The maximum size of a file is 17 million terabytes. Two mnemonics are required, because of the lack of readily comprehended mnemonic names for such a very large number. Seventeen million terabytes is also the maximum size of a volume in an NTFS File System. All totaled, Windows NT can support a maximum of 408 million terabytes of disk storage.

Windows NT Server

One look at these figures makes it quite clear that NT's potential scalability, at least from a storage addressing perspective, has quite a long life ahead of it. It will be quite some time before hardware becomes available (and affordable) that can actually use the massive scalability of a 64-bit file system. However, a 64-bit file system should be prerequisite to any cluster that has scalability as its long-term goal.

> **NOTE** It is important to remember that these values are mathematical and theoretical maximums. Your mileage may vary.

6.2.2. Memory

Another crucial system resource that can easily constrain application performance and, consequently, directly impact scalability is memory. Today, memory is usually limited by physical hardware constraints. There are only so many physical slots on the motherboard for memory modules, and there is also a finite amount of memory that can be put on a single memory modules. The maximum amount of memory capacity varies by manufacturer, and can be quite a substantial amount, but it is still finite.

NT Server is already capable of addressing far more memory than any low-end computing architecture can physically contain. The Enterprise Edition of Windows NT Server can address up to a maximum of 4 gigabytes (GB) of *random access memory* (RAM). Included with this operating system is a tool known as *4 Gigabyte RAM Tuning* (4GT). 4GT allows the operating system to dynamically reallocate up to 3 gigabytes of memory to RAM-intensive applications.

The NT 5.0 Server Enterprise Edition will expand this capability even further. This next release will support 64-bit memory addressing. This concept, known as *Very Large Memory* (VLM), will permit the direct addressing of up to 32 gigabytes of memory. This feature will require a 64-bit processing platform like the DEC Alpha or Intel's planned product, code-named "Merced."

For more information on VLM, and NT Server 5.0, see section 6.5, "Windows NT Server 5.0."

6.2.3. CPU

Scalability also applies to the internal CPUs of a symmetric multiprocessor (SMP). Many x86 and RISC-based systems are capable of symmetrical multiprocessing. NT Server is capable of recognizing the presence of multiple CPUs, and of supporting multiprocessing as a native feature.

As it becomes cluster-aware, NT Server will be able to support the internal and external scalability of a cluster. That is, it will recognize and support additional microprocessors added to vacant CPU slots in the clustered nodes as easily as it will support the addition of nodes to the cluster.

6.2.4. NT Scalability, Revisited

NT Server had been incrementally developing a migration path to true 64-bit computing long before most hardware manufacturers began developing a 64-bit platform. This pre-existing support for 64-bit computing will make NT Servers (and clusters) much more scalable.

6.3. Portability

Windows NT Server can be run on a wide variety of architectures, although it is most commonly paired with the Intel x86 microprocessor family of products. It can also run on RISC processors like the 64-bit DEC Alpha. This native flexibility is rooted in the hardware-independent architecture of NT Server's microkernel.

Hardware independence means not only that it can run on many of today's more popular processing platforms; it also means that it will continue to be a viable network operating system for future processing platforms. Thus, as 64-bit computing platforms become the norm, NT Server will already be positioned as a viable network operating system that can immediately benefit from their increased scalability.

6.4. Interoperability

NT 4.0 defines interoperability in the low-end server network operating system market. It can interoperate with Novell's NetWare, UNIX, Apple's Macintosh, and the other forms of Windows operating systems.

Open communications is assured by the native residence of a TCP/IP protocol stack. TCP/IP, known more formally as the Transmission Control Protocol/ Internet Protocol suite, has become the de facto standard for open communications in client, server, and even some mainframe environments. Its inclusion with NT Server guarantees the capability to communicate across IP networks with other computers, regardless of their physical architecture or operating system.

Software products exist, too, that enable X-terminal users to use a Windows presentation layer, as well as Microsoft's office automation applications like Word, Excel, Exchange, and so on. In short, Microsoft has quickly supported all the standards required to maintain broad interoperability with other leading platforms.

6.5. Windows NT Server 5.0

Microsoft's Windows NT Server Release 5.0 will be a dramatic and significant change from its predecessor, NT Server Release 4.0. Entire books can, and will, be written describing this network operating system. Obviously, it is impossible to adequately describe the entire operating system in just a few paragraphs, so this section will be limited to just those features of NT Server 5.0 that are directly pertinent to clustering.

Topics covered in this section are

- Active Directory Services (ADS)

- Replication services

- 64-bit memory access

Each of these technologies, or sets of technologies, contributes to the positioning of NT Server Release 5.0 as the server operating system of choice for clustering applications on low-end computing platforms.

6.5.1. Active Directory Service (ADS)

One of the more powerful new features introduced in NT Server 5.0 is the *Active Directory Service* (ADS). ADS is an advanced directory service designed to facilitate intranet scaling. It is both open and extensible, yet tightly integrated with NT Server. The best way to describe ADS is as a combination of DNS (Domain Name Service) and X.500.

> **NOTE**   *Domain Name Service*, better known as DNS, is a network service that provides translation between numeric IP addresses and their mnemonic counterparts.
>
> X.500 was originally an OSI protocol developed by the *International Telecommunications Union* (ITU-T) to manage online directories of users and resources. Although X.500 recognizes X.400 and can support other messaging systems, it is not just an e-mail directory. X.500 provides a hierarchy based on a geographical classification system: countries, states, cities, streets, houses, families, individuals, and so on. The result is a directory service that can be used anywhere in the world, from any computing platform that complies with the ITU-T standards.

Combining DNS and X.500 into a single mechanism enables NT Server to logically centralize all resources, regardless of how they are referenced. This centralization results in all networked resources, known as "objects," to be much easier to manage and access. The user is relieved of the burden of finding resources: they are all in the active directory of ADS.

ADS is open because it is based on a rich palette of open, industry, and Internet standards, including DNS, X.500, X.509, Kerberos, LDAP, and HTTP. Consequently, ADS can be used to provide a homogeneous suite of network services for network users. Alternatively, it can be highly customized to meet the unique requirements of user groups or of individual users.

The following are benefits of this NT Server feature:

- High scalability of the network infrastructure without compromising usability

- Enhanced accessibility of networked resources

- Reduced network management cost through centralization of the directory function

> **NOTE** Centralization of the directory function refers only to its consolidation into a single mechanism. Multiple ADS "stores" can be distributed throughout the network's infrastructure.

- increased potential for developing reliable networked applications

- increased capability to provide customized network services to selected communities of users

- support for a single client network logon from anywhere in the network and from any networked computer

ADS can support more than 10 million objects per store. This enables it to gracefully accommodate the exponential growth of an intranet without necessitating rebuilding the its directory. This growth rate can be experienced by young and rapidly growing companies. Large, established companies can experience a similar intranet growth rate if they are aggregating departmental resources into an enterprise infrastructure. In either event, a highly scalable directory is critical to the scalability of the intranet.

Although ADS is intended to facilitate an intranet's scalability, it also contributes to establishing NT Server as an operating system for supporting and accessing scalable NT Server-based clusters.

6.5.2. Microsoft Replication Services

Another important feature of NT Server's functionality is its replication services. These services allow you to automatically replicate data between servers, even across domain boundaries. In Release 4.0, these services were optionally available by purchasing Microsoft's Site Server. In Release 5.0, these replication services are integrated into the operating system.

Microsoft's replication services are designed to be easy to use, and can be used on data ranging from Web-based hypertext to the more conventional Office application data types. Typically, a source/destination relationship is established between two servers. Files are replicated automatically, according to predetermined operating parameters, between these source and destination servers.

Some of the replication services supported include the following:

- File synchronization, or standard replication, allows files that have been added or modified to be synchronized on demand between the source and destination servers. Deleted files, too, can be automatically synchronized in this manner.

- Incremental synchronization enables replication to be much more efficient by only replicating those files that have been added, changed, or deleted since the last replication.

- Transaction-based replication automatically replicates any changed content into a temporary directory. Once the transaction is completed, the entire transaction is replicated to the destination server. This reduces the opportunity for data inconsistency that would otherwise occur if a server or network failure disrupted the replication in transit.

- Automatic replication (similar to the transaction-based replication service) replicates a file as soon as it is added, modified, or deleted.

- Replication can also be scheduled to run automatically at pre-determined times.

- Content can also be "pulled" from Web or FTP sites by the destination server. Such sites, passive by nature, would otherwise not benefit from content replication.

Microsoft's Replication Services also feature replication roll-back. This enables the replicated data to be restored to a previous state in the event that the current state becomes unusable or unreliable. Additional data protection can be achieved by using the replication services in parallel with multiple destination servers.

One other feature of this suite of replication services that warrants mention is support for host authentication. Transmissions from source servers can be digitally "signed" using the MD5 standard for digital signatures. This protects data streams from being intercepted or falsified.

NOTE	MD5 is a fairly popular one-way hashing function that is frequently used to create digital signatures.

WARNING	Digitally signing replication transmissions is a CPU-intensive operation that will slow down replication and everything else on the source machine. Use this feature only if you are replicating across unsecured transmission facilities, or if the data is extremely sensitive.

These replication services will be an integral part of the Windows NT Server 5.0 operating system, and will be completely integrated with ADS. This solidly positions NT Server 5.0 as the operating system to use for ensuring data integrity when replicating it across an intranet, or between nodes in a fail-over cluster.

6.5.3. Very Large Memory (VLM)

The NT 5.0 Server Enterprise Edition builds upon Microsoft's long-standing tradition of supporting addressing for more RAM than can be installed in most computing platforms: NT 5.0 will integrate support for 64-bit memory addressing. This concept, known as *Very Large Memory* (VLM), will allow direct addressing for up to 32 gigabytes (GB) of memory. Operating systems that use only a 32-bit memory addressing scheme are limited to a maximum of 4 GB of RAM.

Using a 64-bit processing platform like DEC's AlphaServer as an example, it is easy to see the advantages of VLM. The AlphaServer supports a maximum of 14 GB RAM. Using NT 4.0, or any other server operating system with a 32-bit memory addressing scheme, a maximum of 4 GB is accessible to both the operating system and the application(s). With NT Server 5.0, all 14 GB of this memory is directly addressable.

The benefit of being able to directly address a very large amount of memory is the reduction in the need for *Input/Output* (I/O) operations.

> **NOTE** I/O is the most expensive operation a computer can perform. This is because of the speed mismatch between the CPU, the I/O bus, and the various I/O devices. Even a very fast I/O bus and device are substantially slower than the CPU, which creates the potential for inefficiency, as the CPU might have to execute many *nops*, or "no operations," waiting for its I/O request to be fulfilled.

Used wisely, VLM can improve the performance of memory-intensive applications by reducing or eliminating the need for unnecessary I/O operations like *paging*. Paging is a technique that was developed for memory sharing. Blocks of data stored in memory awaiting processing are temporarily swapped out to a disk drive so that another, higher priority task can use the memory they were occupying. Applications that are severely constrained by memory limitations might find themselves spending more time paging than actually processing. VLM, when paired with the right physical platform, can mitigate this problem significantly. In fact, depending on the size of the database being used, it might be possible to read the entire database into memory and avoid I/O during the application's processing entirely!

This is an extreme example, but the point is clear: VLM will make NT Server 5.0 a much more viable platform for memory-intensive applications like decision support systems. As the appropriate application software becomes available, VLM will prove to be an invaluable contribution to NT Server–based clustered applications.

6.6. Summary

Windows NT Server has been constantly proactively upgraded, often beyond the capacity of most of the existing platforms that hosted it. This forward-looking commitment has resulted in a network operating system that is almost completely ready for 64-bit computing, long before most hardware manufacturers are!

Microsoft's strategy for NT Server is paying off. International Data Corporation (IDC) recently released the results of a survey that showed Microsoft clearly taking market share from Novell in the server operating system market. New NT Server licenses purchased last year outnumbered new NetWare 4.x license purchases by more than 2 to 1.

NetWare, however, still has a greater installed base and enjoys greater total sales— if one includes upgrades to existing systems. During 1996, Novell accounted for 37% of all server operating system license sales, while Microsoft logged only 27%. Still, the trend is undeniable: Novell's share of the market was down 4% from 1995, while Microsoft's NT market share was up 10% over the same time period. This survey was based on reports from vendors, although IDC cross-referenced this information against user surveys.

Given this validation of its strategy, Microsoft is likely to continue with its proactive development of 64-bit technology support for NT Server. Clusters of 64-bit multiprocessors and NT Server will be extremely powerful, highly scalable, and very reliable structures capable of supporting true enterprise-level, mission critical applications.

Future developments will continue to reinforce NT Server's position in enterprise-level computing. Future enhancements will likely be more and better cluster management utilities, tightly integrated support for cluster-aware application software, and increased support for scalability.

Perhaps the most important addition to NT Server 5.0 is its native support for clustering, courtesy of an *Application Programming Interface* (API). Chapter 7, "Microsoft's Cluster Server," focuses on this API and the Microsoft Cluster Server product (formerly known as Wolfpack).

Chapter

7

Microsoft's Cluster Server

Microsoft's Cluster Server, formerly known as "Wolfpack," is cluster management software designed specifically for the Microsoft Windows NT Server network operating system. Cluster Server is designed to run as an adjunct to Microsoft's Windows NT Server versions 4.0 and higher. Thus, it can be expected to run on any processing platform supported by that operating system. It enables applications to remain available by providing clustered fail-over support.

This chapter explains Cluster Server's components and their features and functions and describes the overall architecture of Microsoft's initial release of Cluster Server.

7.1. Introduction

Microsoft's much publicized clustering technology, code named Wolfpack, has matured into a commercially available product called Cluster Server. Cluster Server is designed to provide high availability for NT Server-based applications.

Cluster Server is composed of three categories of resources:

- Nodes

- Individual resources

- Resource groups

Figure 7.1 provides an overview of this component architecture. This component perspective is only intended to show the relationship among Cluster Server's main components. The technical architecture of Cluster Server will be discussed in more detail throughout this chapter.

Microsoft's plans call for a phased implementation. The initial Cluster Server is a modest offering that supports only fail-over capability in a two-node, shared disk cluster. Each node in the cluster can contain up to four CPUs. Figure 7.2 illustrates the typical Phase One Microsoft NT Cluster Server implementation. This cluster is a two-node, shared disk cluster that enables two separate applications, each residing on its own dedicated processor, to fail-over to the other node in its cluster.

Phase Two will bring with it support for up to sixteen multiprocessing nodes in a shared nothing cluster. Additionally, this version of Cluster Server will support parallel applications that can actually use the distributed parallelism of a cluster. The last planned improvement for Phase Two will be the elimination of traditional local area networking in the cluster interconnect role.

Figure 7.1.
Cluster Server
component
architecture.

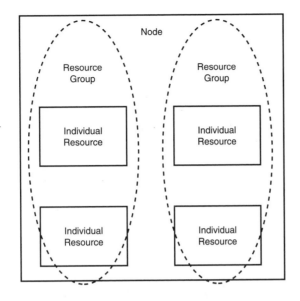

Figure 7.2.
Typical Phase
One Microsoft
NT Cluster
Server implemen-
tation.

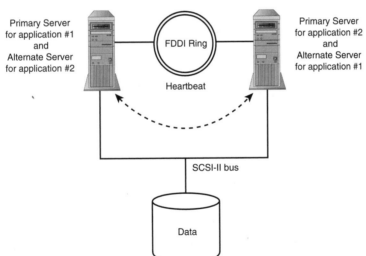

Microsoft's Cluster Server

NOTE   Emerging technologies will enable the clustered server's I/O buses to be extended and interconnected via robust I/O switches. For more detailed information on the extension of I/O buses in lieu of conventional LANs to interconnect cluster nodes, please refer back to Chapter 3, "Clustering for Scalability."

Figure 7.3 illustrates what is expected to be the typical Phase Two NT Cluster Server implementation. This cluster supports a company's *World Wide Web* (WWW) site, and the demand for service is dynamically balanced across the four nodes in the cluster. Although Phase Two of Cluster Server will be able to support up to sixteen nodes in a cluster, this illustration presents only four in a shared nothing topology. Each node is a symmetrical multiprocessor. More importantly, there is only a single application. This application's processing load is dynamically balanced across all CPUs in a node, or system, and across all nodes in the cluster.

In this configuration, all nodes have access to all data, regardless of where it is stored. Given that this cluster supports a single application in a shared nothing topology, the need exists for some mechanism to provide distributed lock management of the shared, but distributed, data.

Figure 7.3.

Typical Phase Two Microsoft NT Cluster Server implementation.

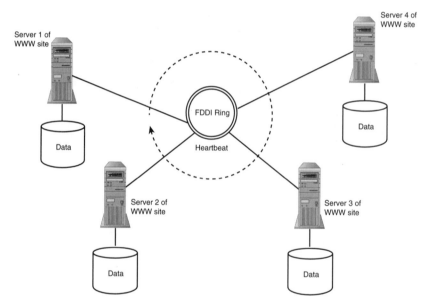

The Phase Two Cluster Server will be a very flexible product. It can, and will, be used to support many different types of clusters. The example presented in Figure 7.3 is just one of these potential clusters. It was selected as an example to highlight the functional differences between Phases One and Two.

7.1.1. Nodes

Cluster nodes are the individual, stand-alone computers that are logically bound into a cluster. Although these machines maintain an individual identity, they should be completely fungible. Further, their individual identities should be superseded, from the client's perspective, by their membership in the cluster.

The cluster has its own identity, separate and distinct from the clustered nodes that it encompasses. This is the logical identity that is viewed by the clients. This perspective enables the cluster to "heal" itself of failures in an almost completely invisible manner.

Invisible recoveries require each node in the cluster to be:

- fully interconnected, via a cluster or system area network, to every other clustered node

- able to monitor the availability of every other node

- functionally equivalent to every other node

- able to offer clients undisturbed access to data, services, and any other needed resources

These basic criteria apply to all clusters, regardless of their topology or functionality.

The concept of current status, known more commonly as *state*, is an important one throughout the architecture of Cluster Server. A node may experience any one of three different states, each of which has direct implications for its cluster peers.

The first state is *online*. A node that is online is an active member of the cluster that supports both cluster management activities and resource ownership.

An *offline* node is defined to be a member of a cluster, but it is not active. This state is the initial state assigned to a cluster node. It is not necessarily indicative of whether or not that node is up and running. It simply means that it hasn't joined the cluster yet or has temporarily suspended participation.

The last node state is *paused*. A node that has paused is an active member of the cluster in that it participates in cluster management activities, but it does not currently own any cluster resources. Consequently, it is not actively supporting the cluster's workload. Should a fail-over occur, it is fully ready and capable of immediately assuming ownership of resources.

7.1.2. Cluster Server Fundamentals

Cluster Server adheres to a fairly basic set of fundamental principles. These guide the interaction of Cluster Server with other Microsoft Windows NT Server system resources by establishing their hierarchy.

Figure 7.4 demonstrates that each node, a computer capable of stand-alone processing, is also called a "system." A cluster is two or more systems loosely coupled under a common logical identity. Each system, or node, runs its own copy of Cluster Server. This package contains a Communications Manager that is responsible for all intracluster communications. The presence of an active Cluster Server is what makes a system a cluster.

> **NOTE** Using Cluster Server, it is possible to have a cluster of just one node or system. Though this appears contrary to the definition of a cluster presented in Chapter 1, "Introduction to Clustering," it is essential to the normal start up and operation of a cluster using Cluster Server.

Figure 7.4.

Logical view of a cluster using Cluster Server.

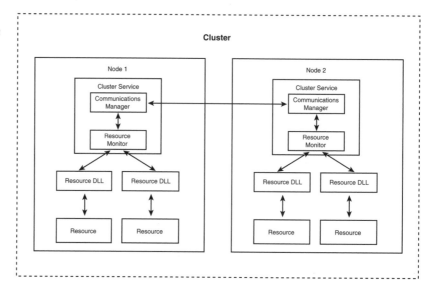

Each system also has one or more Resource Monitors that interact with the Cluster Service. These monitors keep the Cluster Service "informed" as to the status of individual resources. If necessary, the Resource Monitor can manipulate individual resources through the use of Resource DLLs.

> **NOTE** DLL is the acronym for Dynamic Link Library. This is a feature of both IBM's OS/2 and Microsoft's Windows operating systems that lets small, system-level modules be loaded on demand and linked at runtime instead of at compile time. This greatly facilitates the ability to upgrade software.

Resource DLLs are narrowly focused. Each type of resource requires its own specific Resource DLL. These DLLs actually perform the resource monitoring and management for the Resource Monitor.

This basic outline of cluster concepts and fundamentals should serve as the context for a more rigorous exploration of Cluster Server's innards.

7.2. Resources

Microsoft's Cluster Server establishes resources as the basic unit of system assets that can be failed-over. Resources are basic, system-level components that provide a service to either client applications or other cluster resources.

There are three different categories of resources in a cluster: non-shared, shared, and quorum. Each of these is defined and examined in the remainder of this section.

7.2.1. Non-Shared Resource Types

A non-shared resource is the stereotypical cluster resource. It derives its name from the fact that it can only be active in one location in the cluster at any given time.

Microsoft has defined nine types of non-shared resources. They are as follows:

- Internet Protocol (IP) address

- File share

- Generic application

- Generic service

- Logical disk

- Microsoft's Internet Information Server (IIS) virtual root

- Network name

- Physical disk

- Print spooling

These categories encompass an almost limitless variety of resources. They form the basis for controlling a resource's behavior in the cluster. As a resource is being defined in the Cluster Configuration Database, it is first identified as a member of one of these categories. Category selection brings up a resource profile of pertinent mandatory and optional parameters that must be set for each resource.

The actual resources can vary greatly from system to system. The one limitation is that any given resource can only exist in an online state, in one place in a cluster at any given time. Offline back up resources can exist, but they are only brought online in the event of the primary resource's failure. Each resource provides a different service through a Resource DLL.

Microsoft's Cluster Server

> **NOTE** There is one significant ramification of Cluster Server's recognition of "generic applications" as a distinct non-shared resource type. It would be quite logical to expect that cluster-aware, load-balancing applications that are developed specifically for Microsoft's Phase Two Cluster Server can be considered a resource. This type of application would simultaneously be active on all cluster nodes and dynamically redistribute workloads to maintain an optimal balance.
>
> Unfortunately, this contradicts the basic premise of a non-shared cluster resource. Defining such applications in the Configuration Database as a cluster resource, or even adding them to resource groups, creates a logic violation. Remember, cluster resources can only exist in one place in a cluster at any given time. Shared applications can be supported, but not actively managed, by Cluster Server. They must employ their own means of coordinating access to shared resources.
>
> Support for a generic application resource type is intended to provide a framework for defining a non-shared, nonload-balancing application in a multinode fail-over cluster.

In addition to the aforementioned types and their configurable parameters, cluster resources have seven distinct properties. The behavior of resources is also directly dependent upon how well these properties are defined. These properties include the following:

- Dependencies
- Group membership
- Online state
- Poll intervals
- Possible nodes
- Resource type
- Restart policy

Of these seven, three are directly related to the fail-over function. These are *group membership*, *online state*, and *dependencies*. Dependencies are functional interrelationships with other resources. These are described in more detail in section 7.3.

Resource type identifies which one of the types presented in the beginning of section 7.2.1 best describes the resource. *Possible nodes* is a listing of all nodes that could own the resource, should the original resource fail. Each of these possible nodes must have the resource and its associated group members already defined and inactive in anticipation of a failure.

One attribute that warrants further examination is the resource's online state, because there is a finite influence that an administrator can have on this property. Resources can exist in six different "states." The state is a highly volatile condition and describes the current status of a resource. Of the six states, four are considered stable, and the other two are distinctly transitory. The stable states include *online, starting, failed*, and *offline*.

> **NOTE** The status of a resource *is* highly volatile; however, within the context of this volatility are four *relatively* stable states. This note is offered to preempt any claims of oxymoronic descriptions.

Offline resources may be physically ready for service, but the node that they reside on does not own that resource on behalf of the rest of the cluster. Remember, a resource can only be online in one place at a time in a cluster. All other copies may remain ready but given an offline status until a fail-over necessitates migration of the ownership of the original resource.

Implicit in this definition of offline resources is the definition of an online resource. The *online* resource is the one that is owned by its hosting node on behalf of the cluster.

A resource may be somewhere between offline and online. During that brief transitory period of a fail-over, the ownership of a resource might migrate to a node whose resource is not physically ready. A disk drive might need to be spun up, or a file system mounted. Regardless, the resource is not physically ready, but ownership has already migrated. This resource is placed in a *starting* state. Even though this is clearly a transitory state, it qualifies as a stable state when compared to the two *really* unstable states.

The last stable state that can be attributed to a resource is *failed*. For whatever reason, the resource could not respond adequately to the Resource Monitor. The Cluster Service generated the fail-over request and removed the stricken resource from the pool of available, or potentially available, resources.

Resources can also be placed into two *pending* states. Its very name implies that its status is not stable. These states are known as *online pending* and *offline pending*. They are only used to define the state of a resource whose Resource DLL is transitioning from one of the stable states. A resource should be in a pending state only for a very short time.

7.2.2. **Shared Resources**

Shared resources can be supported in a cluster; however, they cannot be managed by the cluster. Shared resources can be active and executing on more than one node at the same time. An example would be a distributed application that is being load-balanced across the active cluster nodes. Such applications do not qualify for fail-over, nor do they require it. They can take advantage of most of the other Cluster Services, including synchronization and coordination across all active nodes. These distributed applications, however, must have some means, external to Cluster Server, to manage the sharing of their communal resources.

7.2.3. **Quorum Resources**

The last type of resource supported in Cluster Server is known as a *quorum resource*. Like any other cluster resource, a quorum resource can be any resource that can be arbitrated for, and owned by, only one node. It is a persistent record of cluster configuration changes. Change logs are kept in the *Quorum Database* of nodes that are not communicating. This use enables the quorum resource to provide two critical functions in a cluster:

■ The quorum resource is used to validate the Configuration Database of any newly active node that cannot establish communications with any other active nodes. Such nodes are considered the first active node in a cluster. In essence, they form a one-node cluster. If that node's Configuration Database is not an exact duplicate of the Quorum Database, it assumes the Quorum Database to be more up-to-date and updates its own database from it. This first active node owns the quorum resource for the cluster it just formed. This ownership may be arbitrated for and passed to other nodes as they join the cluster. Each such passing of ownership is recorded in each node's NT Registry.

■ The quorum resource is the mechanism that prevents hardware or network failures from splitting a cluster into two or more competing *cluster fragments*. Only the cluster fragment that owns the quorum will continue to function. The other, seeing that it cannot arbitrate ownership of the quorum resource, will release all its resources and cease operations. For more information on this aspect of the quorum resource's functionality, please refer to section 7.5.3 of this chapter.

It should be noted that only disk drives are currently capable of being a quorum resource. In the future, this may change because there are other I/O devices capable of persistent storage of volatile configuration data. The criticality of the quorum resource warrants its being mirrored to, or striped across, multiple drives.

In Cluster Server, SCSI is the standard technology for sharing peripherals. Each node in a small cluster can be physically connected to each SCSI bus. In this manner, the nodes are ensured access to the quorum resource without having to rely on the availability of other cluster nodes. Figure 7.5 illustrates this shared access to the quorum resource.

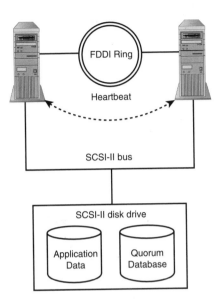

Figure 7.5.
Shared access to a quorum resource in a two-node cluster.

7.2.4. **Resource APIs**

Cluster Server uses Application Programming Interfaces (APIs) as entry points to all of its services. These APIs allow programmers to develop cluster-aware applications for Windows NT Cluster Server that can directly access the cluster's services. Such applications will be able to understand requests from the operating system and Cluster Server software and can respond appropriately. Applications that aren't cluster-aware probably won't behave properly and could compromise data during a fail-over.

Creation of cluster-aware applications requires the use of a set of Resource APIs. These APIs are an amalgamation of program entry points, callback functions, and miscellaneous other related devices that can be used to create Resource DLLs. Each cluster resource, including cluster-aware applications, must have its own Resource DLL. A basic set of Resource DLLs is included with Cluster Server, including one for generic applications. The Generic Applications DLL allows the creation of applications that can take advantage of the basic fail-over capabilities of a cluster.

There are many Resource APIs. Here are the most commonly used ones:

- Open API
- Close API
- Offline API
- Online API

- LooksAlive API

- IsAlive API

This basic set of Resource APIs enables monitoring and management of resources via their DLLs.

The Open and Close APIs are fairly self-explanatory. They are called by the Resource Monitor to open and close individual resources. Opening a resource allocates the system and process resources needed to support the opened resource. Once a resource is initialized, it can be activated. Closing a resource deallocates these system and process resources.

Online and Offline are used to activate and deactivate resources. Activation comes immediately after initialization and is necessary for the resource to be used. Deactivation can be done either automatically or voluntarily to remove a resource from an active state. Ostensibly, this is necessary to migrate ownership to another node.

LooksAlive and IsAlive are the two mechanisms employed by the Resource Monitor to actually monitor resources. LooksAlive is a superficial examination to determine if the resource is active. Typically, this API is called frequently by the Resource Monitor, although the polling interval can be manually set and even disabled. IsAlive is a more rigorous examination of the status of a resource. IsAlive attempts to determine whether the resource is behaving properly. This API is called routinely but with less frequency than LooksAlive. It is also automatically called by Resource Monitor if it appears that the resource has failed.

Figure 7.6 presents the basic architecture of monitoring cluster resources via the Resource APIs. These DLLs are accessed by the Resource Monitor in exactly the same manner as the basic Resource DLLs. The Resource Monitor access uses an entry point created using the Resource API and embedded into the newly created Custom Resource DLL.

Microsoft is using this API set to develop cluster-aware versions of its BackOffice suite of products. Microsoft has also formed alliances with other key manufacturers to ensure that there will be a wide selection of cluster-aware application software in the not-too-distant future.

Figure 7.6.
Resource monitoring via APIs.

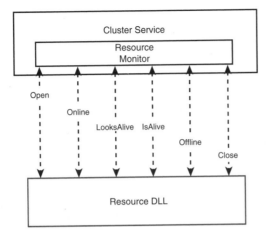

7.3. Resource Groups and Dependencies

Resources are frequently grouped together logically because of functional interdependencies. There are very few resources that are complete unto themselves. Such resources are called *optional resources* because they can fail without impacting the functionality of any other cluster resources. Optional resources are not valid in the first release of Cluster Server.

Typically, any given function requires the combined efforts of several resources. Such *resource groups* must always reside on the same cluster node. In the event of a fail-over, they *must* fail-over in unison. Although the resource is identified as the basic unit of fail-over in a cluster, in practical and implementable reality, the basic unit of fail-over must be the resource group. As such, the Fail-over Manager treats groups as the basic units of fail-over.

Groups are identified by a unique *network service name*. Resources can be added to a particular group by referencing this name as they are added to the Configuration Database.

> **NOTE**   It is imperative that the network service name of every group be defined on every cluster as well as be consistent across them. This permits one node to own an active resource group, while the other nodes maintain an inactive group and set of resources in anticipation of a fail-over.

7.3.1. Resource Dependency Hierarchy

Establishing groups permits interdependent resources to be failed-over together. In theory, this prevents unexpected interruptions in processing. Merely defining interdependent resources as a logical group is not quite enough to ensure smooth operations during a fail-over. There is usually a natural hierarchy to the interdependence that must also be adhered to. Proper functioning during a fail-over is contingent on recognizing this hierarchy and restoring the online status of the grouped resources in the right order.

Resources can have two types of relationships to other resources. A resource can *depend on* another resource. This is the basis for logical groupings of resources.

A resource group can *contain* one or more dependency trees. In such cases, the group is identified via the linkage to the topmost resource in the linkage. The linkages are transitive in nature, thus there is no need to specify all the subdependencies of interdependent resources. For example, if an application is dependent on a database, and that database is directly dependent upon another database, the application only needs to be identified as depending on the first database. The impact of the interdependence between the two databases on the application is automatically understood.

In either case, all interdependent resources must fail-over together. This hierarchy is illustrated in Figure 7.7. Please note the relationship among Resource Groups, DLLs, and actual resources. All resources *must* be called through their DLLs.

Figure 7.7.

Logical view of Cluster Server's resource dependency hierarchy.

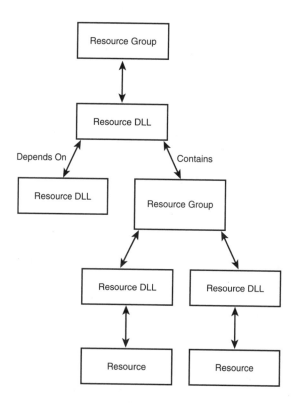

For example, an application can be dependent on the integrity and well-being of a database in order to function properly. This database, in turn, is dependent on the disk drive on which it resides. In this scenario, the application, database, and disk drive are all cluster resources. Their hierarchy is fairly clear: The application depends directly on both the database and the disk drive. The application also depends on the existence of an IP address. Each resource group in Cluster Server has its own IP address. This hierarchy of dependencies is illustrated in Figure 7.8.

Figure 7.8.

An example of hierarchical resource dependencies.

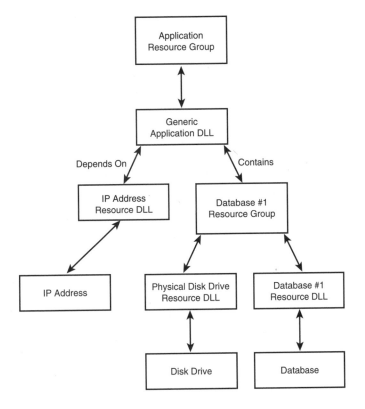

This interdependence must be made known to the cluster. The Cluster Administrator interface can be used to enter these dependencies into the Configuration Database. However, this is not enough! The nature, or hierarchy, of this interdependence must also be made clear so that the resources can be restored to an online status in the proper sequence. This hierarchy is known as the *resource tree* or the *dependency tree* in Cluster Server.

Failure to restore online status to failed-over resources in the proper sequence will defeat the purpose of the cluster. The users will experience a disruption in service. For example, if the application in the previous example were failed-over and restored to online status first before the disk drive was even spun up, any attempts to use the application would fail.

Microsoft's Cluster Server

Clearly, the disk drive is the most critical resource to restore to service in this example. It is dependent on no other non-shared cluster resources, yet many cluster resources are dependent on it. Until it is online, no other resources in its dependency tree can be restored. A resource in this situation is known as a *root resource.*

> **NOTE** The database in this example can also be considered a root resource even though it is physically dependent on a disk drive. Depending on the nature of the application and how the database was implemented, the database can migrate to other drives in the event of a disk failure.

Dependency trees can also be intertwined. Extending this example to include a second application and database yields the following set of interdependencies: Application #2 is directly dependent on Database #2. Application #1, in this example, is contained within the resource group of Application #2, even though it can also function as a self-contained group. Both databases reside on the same physical disk, thereby providing a second point at which the dependency trees interconnect. This hierarchy of interrelated dependencies is illustrated in Figure 7.9.

Figure 7.9.
Interrelated hierarchical resource dependencies.

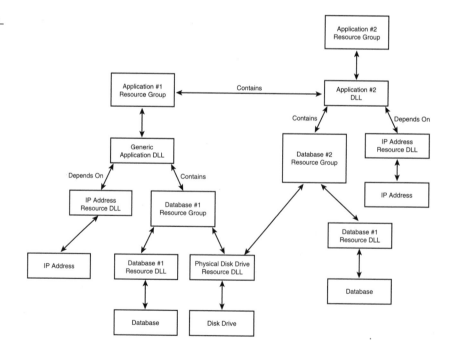

This example presents some of the complexities that are more typical of real-life situations than the cut-and-dried example presented in Figure 7.8. In Figure 7.9, there are two interdependencies. First, Application #1 Resource Group is contained by Application #2 Resource Group. Thus, any failure that forced a migration of Application #1 Resource Group would automatically necessitate the migration of Application #2 Resource Group. Second, both resource groups utilize a common disk drive. If this disk drive failed, both resource groups would be directly impacted. They would both be migrated even if one didn't contain the other. The effects of this failure on the hierarchy presented in Figure 7.9 are presented in Figure 7.10.

Figure 7.10.
Effects of disk drive failure on hierarchically dependent resources.

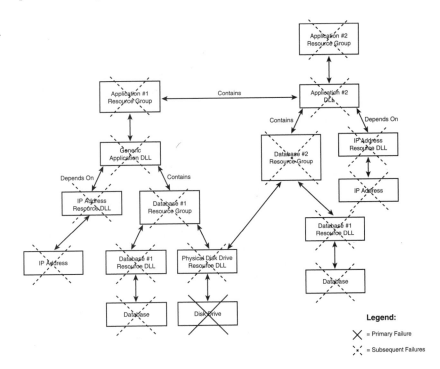

7.3.2. Group Properties

Groups, like their member resources, have many properties that can be customized to regulate their behavior. These properties are configurable by the administrator during the creation of the group via the Cluster Administrator interface. Here are the group property categories:

- `Contains`
- `PreferredOwners`
- `AutoFailbackType`

- ■ FailbackWindowStart
- ■ FailbackWindowEnd
- ■ CurrentState

These are the reserved words that are used to identify each property. Other properties were supported during the beta tests of Wolfpack, but it is not clear whether they will continue to be supported in the future. Consequently, they are not presented here.

Contains refers to the root resources of any dependency trees that the group might depend on. For example, in Figure 7.9, Application Resource Group #2 contains Application Resource Group #1. It only needs to reference the root (the group name), and need not know the details of the entire hierarchy.

AutoFailbackType specifies whether or not a group should automatically fail-back to its original node, as soon as all the necessary resources have been restored to an online status. Possible settings for this property are "0x00" to prevent an automatic fail-back or "0x01" to enable it.

> **NOTE** A *fail-back* is the opposite of a fail-over: resources are migrated back to their original node. This can occur either manually or automatically, depending on what triggered the fail-over resource migration.

FailbackWindowStart and FailbackWindowEnd are related parameters that define the time boundaries within a 24-hour period during which time a fail-back can occur. Failure to specify both a start and an end parameter results in no window. The default settings are for no window, which means that a fail-back happens immediately.

CurrentState identifies the current operational status of a resource group, and it is the only parameter that is stored in and updated to NT's Registry. This ensures that the status is persistent and can still be determined after a failure.

7.3.3. Group Fail-Over Policies

Fail-over policies are the key to successfully providing high availability in a cluster. These policies have but three components: *fail-over timing, preferred node,* and *fail-back timing.* These components are configured by the administrator through parameter settings in each group.

The *fail-over timing* parameter allows the administrator the latitude of selecting either an immediate or a delayed fail-over for any given resource group. The distinction between these options is made by selecting the number of times the

Fail-over Manager will *retry* to restore the resource to an online status before initiating a fail-over.

Critical functions should be failed-over immediately. Consequently, their retry value should be set to 0. However, it may be preferable to attempt restoration of less critical resources rather than failing-over their entire resource group. The Fail-over Manager can restart the resource's application and retry for a prespecified number of attempts before failing-over the entire group.

The next parameter in a fail-over policy is the *preferred node*. Although each node in a cluster is expected to be relatively fungible with every other node, some minor variations might exist. These variations might be based on slight configuration differences. Alternatively, the differences could be logical and temporary. For example, one node could own more resources during normal operation than another. For whatever reason, it might be preferable for any given resource group to fail-over to a specific node. This node is the *preferred node* for that group's fail-over.

The last aspect of a group's fail-over policy is *fail-back timing*. The last step in any fail-over is the restoration of ownership of the failed resource to the original node. This is known as a fail-back. Cluster Server supports both automatic and delayed fail-back through the use of this parameter. An immediate fail-back policy automatically and immediately restores the original resource ownership state, as soon as that resource has been restored to an online status. A delayed fail-back policy waits until a specified time to conduct the fail-back. This can be particularly advantageous if the resource group's fail-back will impact the client. Waiting until after the close of normal business hours will minimize the impact of the fail-back.

> **WARNING** Although fail-over policies are directly responsible for guiding the behavior of a fail-over, they use the resource attributes and group dependency trees as a foundation. They cannot overcome the handicap of poorly defined attributes, groups, and dependency trees.
>
> Successful fail-overs are the result of thoroughly thought out, well-implemented attributes, dependencies, groups, and fail-over policies. All are equally important to the success of a fail-over.

7.4. Cluster Service Architecture

Perhaps the single most important component of Microsoft's Cluster Server is its Cluster Service. This service is responsible for controlling all of the cluster's primary activities. It does so through the use of eight subcomponents. These

Microsoft's Cluster Server

subcomponents, known as *managers*, are focused on specific aspects of the cluster's functionality. They include the following:

- Communications Manager
- Configuration Database Manager
- Event Manager
- Fail-over/Resource Manager
- Global Update Manager
- Membership Manager
- Time Manager
- Node Manager

The simple box labeled Cluster Service in Figure 7.4, earlier in this chapter, is greatly expanded to reveal its internal architecture in Figure 7.11.

Figure 7.11.
Cluster Service architecture.

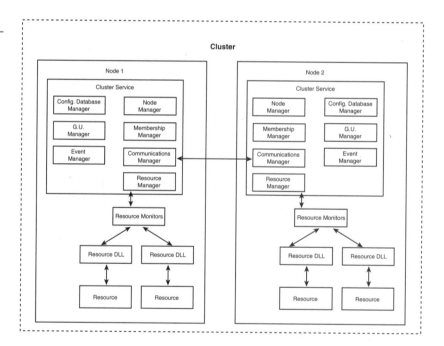

The functions of these managers are fairly self-evident. These managers and their functions within the cluster are explained in the remainder of the paragraphs in section 7.4.

7.4.1. Communications Manager

The Communications Manager is responsible for maintaining communications with all other cluster nodes. Any cluster activity that requires intracluster communications is the responsibility of this manager. Similarly, if a node-level failure occurs, the Communications Manager is responsible for identifying that failure (ostensibly via the loss of a heartbeat) and preventing further communications with that stricken node until the failure is rectified.

The wide range of responsibilities bestowed on the Communications Manager means that it requires an equal range of tools. Consequently, Communications Manager supports more than eight different types of internodal communications. The more common of these protocols are as follows:

- Database: The Communications Manager uses this protocol to update the Configuration Database.

- Enlist: This class of communications is used solely to establish the initial contact with a cluster, with the intent of joining it.

- Join: After the Communications Manager has used the Enlist class to initiate contact with a cluster, it switches to Join to perform the synchronization processes needed to become an active member of that cluster.

- Keepalive: The Keepalive protocol continuously monitors the status of the Cluster Service on the other member nodes in the cluster.

- Membership State Change: This protocol is used to negotiate with or inform other cluster nodes as a result of the detection of a change in the state of one or more nodes in the cluster. For example, if a system joins a cluster, leaves voluntarily, is forced out by the other cluster members, or experiences a system-level failure, the surviving nodes must ensure that they all know about that change in its status. These survivor nodes must then coordinate the redistribution of resources and processing responsibilities, but these activities are outside the scope of this protocol.

- Resource Group Push: The Resource Group Push protocol initiates the fail-over of resource groups to another node. This protocol is only valid for use in migrating resources to another node and cannot be used to pull resource groups away from other nodes.

- Resource Ownership Negotiation: When a node fails, the surviving nodes must negotiate for ownership of its resources. The essence of this negotiation is a comparison of each node's Configuration Database to determine whether or not a clear alternate owner has been prespecified for the resources from the failed node.

■ Resource State Change Notification: This protocol is used to track the active owner of resources and resource groups. Each change in the status of a resource is broadcast to all active cluster members. Tracking this ownership is useful to the other cluster members in the event of any given node's failure. Ostensibly, a major failure will take a system down without warning and, certainly, without giving the stricken node the opportunity to gracefully off-load its resources and processing. Consequently, the surviving nodes will have to surmise which resources were rendered unavailable and then negotiate among each other to determine the next owner.

7.4.2. Configuration Database Manager

The Configuration Database Manager is often abbreviated to "Database Manager." This abbreviation can be misleading and will be avoided in this book. Its function is to manage the cluster's configuration database. This database contains the physical and logical parameters that define the cluster, including its resources, the interdependencies of those resources (known collectively as *groups*), and contingency policies to implement upon the failure of any given resource.

7.4.3. Event Manager

The Event Manager is responsible for initializing the Cluster Service at start-up time. Initialization is a phenomenon that is internal to the node. Upon its completion, the node is still inactive from the other nodes' perspectives. To be recognized as active by the other nodes, the Event Manager must contact the Node Manager. The Node Manager, upon learning that the Cluster Service is active, can initiate the process of joining or forming a cluster.

> **NOTE**   Although they may appear similarly tasked, Event Manager and Communications Manager are not fungible. The Event Manager is focused inwardly and works closely with the Node Manager. Neither provides intracluster communications.
>
> Conversely, the Communications Manager is outwardly focused and works closely with the Fail-over/Resource Manager.

More importantly, the Event Manager notifies the cluster components about "events" that they need to be aware of. "Event" can be a broad, ambiguous term. Within the context of NT Cluster Server, an event is an activity. The Event Manager is the central point for almost all common services. It handles application requests for resources or actions, signals delivery of requested resources and completion of actions, and is even used to maintain *cluster objects.* A cluster object can be the following:

- Cluster nodes
- Resources
- Resource groups
- Types of resources

The Event Manager may interface with the Communications Manager, the Global Update Manager, the Fail-over/Resource Manager, and so on, to ensure the propagation of event notification throughout the cluster.

7.4.4. Fail-over/Resource Manager

The Fail-over/Resource Manager is, as the name implies, really two managers that are closely related. They are frequently referred to as a single resource with a compound name. In reality, the Fail-over Manager is a subcomponent of the Resource Manager. Together, they provide complete management of cluster resources.

The Resource Manager is primarily responsible for starting, stopping, failing, and restarting individual resources. Implicit with this responsibility is the monitoring of the status of those resources. The Resource Manager uses *Resource Monitors* to track the status of individual resources. These monitors are external to the Cluster Service and help insulate the service from being compromised by a problematic resource. Consequently, the Resource Monitor may fail with a resource, but not affect Resource Manager.

A node, typically, runs multiple Resource Monitors simultaneously. Resources can even be monitored simultaneously by more than one Resource Monitor. This provides even greater protection from the effects of a single resource failure. Each monitor can monitor the state changes of multiple resources and notify the Resource Manager of each state change detected, per resource.

Additionally, the Resource Manager is charged with the management of resource dependencies (that is, resource groupings). Tracking such interdependencies and treating groups as an indivisible unit are crucial to the successful operation of a fail-over cluster.

Whereas the Resource Manager is focused on individual resources and their interdependencies, the Fail-over Manager tends to be more of a group management tool. The obvious exception to this would be the optional resources described in section 7.3 of this chapter. Fail-over Manager has but two responsibilities. It arbitrates groups and determines ownership.

If the Resource Manager identifies a resource that has failed and either cannot or is not allowed to be restarted, it issues a fail-over request to the Fail-over Manager. The Fail-over Manager's response is to identify the impacted resource group, initiate contact with peer Fail-over Managers in the cluster via the Communications Manager, and migrate ownership responsibility to an alternate node. At this point, the Resource Manager broadcasts the resource state changes to the other active nodes.

7.4.5. Global Update Manager

The Global Update Manager, with the dubious acronym of *GUM*, provides a common interface for all global updates in a cluster. These global updates can be one of two extremes. First, global updates can require precise synchronization. This would be the case with sharing highly volatile information, such as state changes.

Alternatively, cluster components might need to broadcast information globally but not require the overhead of a traditional higher-level protocol that delivers reliably. The Global Update Manager provides a common mechanism for both these forms of global update.

7.4.6. Membership Manager

The Membership Manager, sometimes referred to as a *Node Manager*, is one of the three most important components of Cluster Service. Predictably, it is responsible for managing the nodal membership of the cluster. Each node, or system, in a cluster runs its own copy of Membership Manager. This symmetry enables each node to maintain its own current perspective of the cluster. Using a four-node cluster as an example, Figure 7.12 illustrates this node-centric cluster perspective that Membership Manager provides.

As is evident in Figure 7.12, Membership Manager maintains a list of members based on two criteria. These criteria are used in tandem, so there are only two possible membership states:

- Defined and active
- Defined and inactive

Members must be defined (that is, *persistent*). Nodes that are not defined as members of the cluster are just that—not members. The defined, or persistent, membership is established at Cluster Server installation. The various nodes that are a part of the cluster are defined in the Configuration Database. This is the basis of their defined membership.

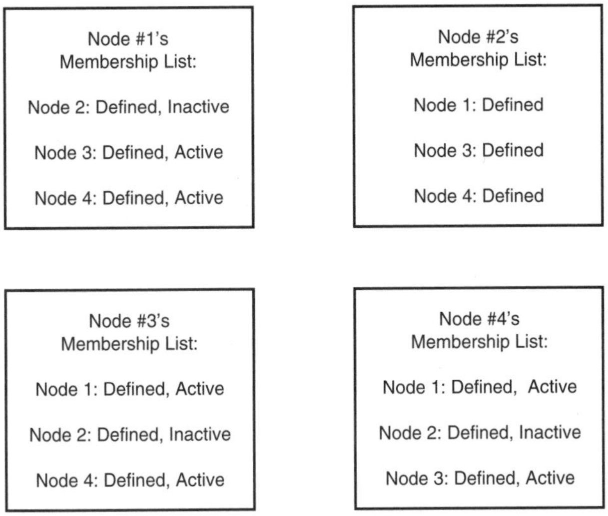

Figure 7.12.
Membership Manager's views of the cluster.

Node #1's Membership List:
Node 2: Defined, Inactive
Node 3: Defined, Active
Node 4: Defined, Active

Node #2's Membership List:
Node 1: Defined
Node 3: Defined
Node 4: Defined

Node #3's Membership List:
Node 1: Defined, Active
Node 2: Defined, Inactive
Node 4: Defined, Active

Node #4's Membership List:
Node 1: Defined, Active
Node 2: Defined, Inactive
Node 3: Defined, Active

Membership can also be dynamic. Defined members can either be active or inactive. The dynamic state of membership is established when the clustered node powers up, starts its Cluster Service, and synchronizes activities with other cluster members. Defined, but inactive, members have either powered down or suffered a service-impacting failure.

NOTE   The Membership List is stored in the "Cluster" part of NT's Registry.

It should be apparent from this description of Membership Manager's role in a cluster that it must communicate almost constantly with the other clustered nodes. Thus, it must interact with the Communications Manager. The Membership List is also the basis for both fail-over and resource management. The Fail-over/Resource Manager is notified of member nodes that become inactive, either voluntarily or involuntarily, through the Membership List. If any of the policies contained in the Configuration Database apply, based on the change, the Fail-over/Resource Manager implements them.

In Figure 7.12, Node 2 in the cluster is powered down. The Membership Managers of Nodes 1, 3, and 4 recognized that change in its status and updated their Memberships Lists accordingly. Each node's Fail-over/Resource Managers consulted the cluster management policies contained in the Configuration Database and arbitrated the new division of resource ownership. The Fail-over/Resource Managers, through the Communications Manager, coordinated this redistribution. These changes were also recorded in the Quorum Resource by the Resource Manager of the cluster that owned the quorum. All other active nodes also updated their NT Registry to reflect the changes in resource ownership.

7.4.7. Time Manager

Cluster Server's Time Manager, also referred to as *Time Services*, maintains a consistent and synchronized consensus of time throughout the cluster. The distributed nature of clustering's parallelism creates some interesting challenges. For example, each node is a stand-alone processor containing its own clock and timekeeping utilities. If each node in a cluster had its own date and time, the cluster could experience some unusual operational difficulties. Therefore, a single source of date and time is needed to establish and maintain a consistent date and time across all active cluster nodes.

> **NOTE** The function of the Time Manager is not, necessarily, to provide an *accurate* date and time. It is far more important for the clustered nodes to have a consistent group perception of time than it is to have an extremely accurate time.

The Membership Manager must elect a *TimeSource* for the cluster. Given that each node has its own Membership Manager, the successful election of a cluster TimeSource requires each Membership Manager to communicate and hold an *election*. Much like the political election, the results are the consensus of all active nodes. The results of the election are posted in NT's Registry under the parameter TimeSource. The TimeSource is the clock used by all active nodes.

If an extremely accurate time source is required, the administrator may manually select the TimeSource by directly editing the registry. Pointing this parameter at a system that has an external clock, such as a network-accessible atomic clock, ensures that the cluster has a consistent and highly accurate time.

7.4.8. Node Manager

The Node Manager is the Cluster Service component that is responsible for coordinating the activities within the node. Its most significant role is receiving inputs from the Event Manager, and relaying any pertinent news to the Resource Manager. The Resource Manager uses this information to make decisions about failing over resource groups.

7.5. Mechanics of Membership Change

Having explored the various components of Cluster Server, it is useful to examine their interaction in one of the most basic functions of a cluster: membership change. The membership of a cluster is dynamic. Active membership must be dynamic. Otherwise, an application's availability will be limited to the availability of a single physical platform.

Cluster membership can be changed in four significant ways:

- A node can form a cluster

- A node can join a cluster

- A node can exit a cluster

- A cluster can cease to exist

Each of these scenarios is both plausible and realistic. You can expect to encounter each during the normal operation of a cluster.

7.5.1. Forming a Cluster

The formation of any NT cluster begins with a single node. This node, upon powering up, should automatically start its Cluster Service as well as any local, non-cluster devices. Next, Cluster Service's Communications Manager launches its *discovery* process. This process is used to check whether any of the cluster's persistent members are active.

A cluster is formed if a node activates, but it cannot discover any other active members. The discovery process, conducted by the Communications Manager, must time out before the active node attempts to form its own cluster. When the discovery process times out, the active node checks its NT Registry to determine the last known location of the active, or owned, quorum resource. It then attempts to access that resource.

> **NOTE** Ostensibly, a cluster can be formed whenever a node becomes active but cannot find any other active peers. Successfully locating and securing ownership of the quorum resource in the absence of any active peer nodes constitutes the formation of a one-node cluster. A one-node cluster isn't really a cluster, but its Cluster Service will be active, and it will be able to assist other nodes as they activate and join the cluster.
>
> If a node cannot find any active peers, and also cannot negotiate ownership of the quorum resource, it will automatically disable itself. For more information on this, please refer to section 7.5.3.

Microsoft's Cluster Server

If the first active node is able to access the quorum resource, it verifies the contents of its Configuration Database against the contents of the quorum resource. If these two databases match, the active node takes ownership of that quorum resource and becomes an active one-node cluster.

If the two databases don't match, the active node assumes that the cluster configuration was updated since it was last active and updates its own database from the quorum. Then, it assumes ownership of the quorum and becomes a one-node cluster.

7.5.2. Joining a Cluster

Joining a cluster is very similar to forming a cluster. The differences begin with the newly activated node discovering at least one active node among its list of persistent members. Once this discovery is made, the joining node is authenticated by the discovered active cluster node.

Authentication is a simple process that compares the joining node's name with the list of persistent node names in the Configuration Database. If authentication fails, the attempt to join is rejected. The rejected node may either attempt to form its own cluster or release its resources and go offline. Its actions in such a situation will be determined by whether or not it can find and gain ownership of a quorum resource.

If the authentication attempt was successful, the new member of the cluster gets an updated copy of the cluster Configuration Database. This database, in conjunction with its own Registry entries, are used to find any cluster resources that need to be activated. Once its cluster resources are online, the node is a fully functional member of the cluster.

7.5.3. Leaving a Cluster

Leaving a cluster should be a fairly straightforward process. Unfortunately, when a node leaves a cluster, it is usually experiencing operating difficulties. This can make its departure from a cluster a bit messy. If it is able to leave gracefully, the surviving nodes can easily arbitrate ownership of the groups abandoned by that failed node.

This sequence begins with the Communications Manager of the departing node notifying its peers of its impending exit. Its Resource Manager issues an offline command to all of its Resource DLLs. This should result in the termination of all resource-based activity. Once they are inactive, the surviving nodes arbitrate new ownership of the offline resources and the cluster persists despite the loss.

A major failure, however, might alter this neat sequence of events. For example, a node can experience a sudden and catastrophic failure. In such cases, it is unlikely that it would be able to transmit a message to its peers warning of its impending departure. Their first notification of a problem will be when their Communications Managers lose the "heartbeat" from that failed node. In theory, they can then begin the arbitration process and develop a consensus on new ownership responsibilities. In actuality, this is fairly reliable.

One possible exception is if a failure somehow left two or more functional and active nodes unable to communicate. This is known as a *split cluster*. Split clusters are potentially dangerous situations because each cluster fragment might assume that it is the sole surviving node(s) of the original cluster. Cluster management policies would then dictate that its Resource Manager begin activating all necessary resources to fully assume responsibility for the "lost" resources. In this manner, the two fragments could actually be competing for resources that cannot be shared. The application and its data will suffer.

Cluster Server uses the quorum to prevent such confusion from happening. When a cluster is split, only the fragment that owns the quorum will continue to function. The other fragment, unable to arbitrate ownership of the quorum resource, will release all its resources and become inactive. Figure 7.13 illustrates how the quorum resource can prevent split clusters.

Figure 7.13.
Using the quorum resource to prevent "split clusters."

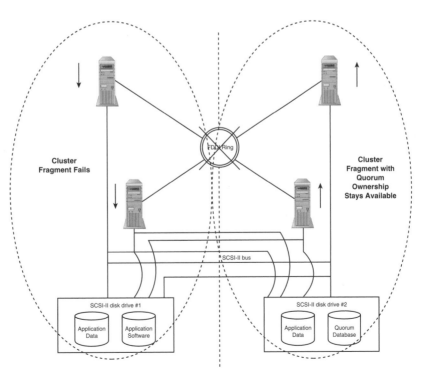

7.5.4. Destroying a Cluster

Destroying a cluster is the opposite of forming one. Whereas cluster formation begins with a single active node owning the quorum resource and waiting to be joined by other nodes, cluster destruction ends with a single active node that owns the quorum resource becoming inactive. In doing so, it releases all resources that it owns and becomes inactive. Thus, the cluster is really dormant but is functionally temporarily destroyed.

7.6. Summary

Microsoft's Cluster Server is designed to make clustering an open, affordable option on low-end computing architectures. It is tightly integrated with Windows NT and offers the ability to provide basic fail-over support for non-cluster-aware applications.

Cluster Server is an add-on product from Microsoft, designed specifically for the Windows NT Server network operating system. Cluster Server is different from most bolt-on modifications in that it does more than simply add new functionality to its platform. Cluster Server actually improves the performance of its host operating system, Microsoft Windows NT Server, in numerous ways. Two of these are rather obvious: Cluster Server improves on both the availability and scalability of NT Server. These are the tandem grails of clustering. The third improvement area might not be as intuitively obvious. This area is manageability.

7.6.1. Availability

Cluster Server improves the availability of any application that resides on an NT Server by enabling the clustering of multiple NT Servers. In effect, this eliminates the operating system as a single point of failure and provides automatic recovery from certain types of failures.

As discussed in Chapter 2, "Clustering for Availability," a large part of improving reliability and, consequently, availability is the elimination of as many single points of failure as possible. Typically, points of failure are usually regarded as hardware, not software. However, as reliable as NT Server is, it still requires downtime for maintenance, upgrades, and recovery from the occasional ill-behaved application.

7.6.2. Scalability

Cluster Server will assist in the development of scalable processing platforms using low-end computing architectures. As it matures, Cluster Server is expected to support up to 16 nodes in a cluster. Each node can be a symmetrical multiprocessor, thereby magnifying the increase in processing power available per additional node. This future expandability positions NT Server for supporting large or critical applications that were previously supportable only by UNIX systems or mainframes.

7.6.3. Manageability

Cluster Server offers host administrators an enhanced ability to manage clustered resources. In a more traditional, single-host NT Server configuration, hardware and software events typically result in operational downtime.

If those events were unanticipated (that is, a failure of some sort), the administrators are forced to react and manually rectify the situation. Anticipated events, such as scheduled maintenance, upgrades, and so on, offer the opportunity to forewarn the users and minimize downtime. Nevertheless, both types of events must be managed manually and individually. They both also diminish the availability of the application.

NT Cluster Server, however, greatly enhances the administrator's ability to manage the resources. Resources can be grouped together, and the administrator can set policies that automatically guide their behavior during hardware and software events, anticipated or otherwise. In this manner, management of the resources becomes proactive and automatic.

Microsoft's Cluster Server

Chapter

8

Building a New NT Cluster

Building a new NT Server–based cluster is slightly easier than trying to retrofit clustering capabilities to an existing system. All of the problems associated with legacy decisions about hardware, software, operating systems, vendors, and so on, are immaterial. You get to make your own mistakes!

Starting from scratch, however, is much more complicated than building a stand-alone NT Server–based application. Standard application development models can be used to develop a clustered application, provided they are flexible enough to allow for the distributed processing of the application.

Here are the two key success factors in the development of an effective cluster:

- The careful alignment of hardware, software, and networking in support of the application

- Absolute minimization of the network intensity of the application

> **NOTE**   Minimization of network intensity is particularly crucial for cluster management activities across the cluster area network (CAN). Selection of cluster management products should be based, at least in part, on the efficacy of their intracluster communications mechanisms.

Although easily described, these factors can be remarkably difficult to implement on a server-based platform. This chapter presents a basic methodology for satisfying these criteria when developing a new clustered application on the Windows NT Server platform. Also provided is a clustering checklist that should guide your cluster development efforts. Together, these tools should help you avoid some of the pitfalls of clustering. More importantly, these tools should help you maximize the performance potential of your clustered application.

If you are clustering an existing NT Server–based application, you might find Chapter 11, "Network-Friendly Clustering," more pertinent.

8.1. Cluster Development Methodology

Numerous formal models for developing client/server applications exist. Many more informal models are developed on-the-fly for a specific application and then discarded. The vast majority of these models fail to capture the significance of networking in a distributed processing environment. In a network-intensive, distributed-processing architecture like a cluster, this is a gross oversight!

Typical development models call for designing the supporting networks that interconnect the various physical components of the new clustered application *after* the research is done, the application (and/or objects) is designed, the client and server platforms are identified, and the application is under development. This is too late!

Many of the techniques for reducing the network intensity of the application (presented in Chapter 9, "Clustering an Existing NT Server/Application," and Chapter 10, "Programming for Parallel Environments," of this book) are rendered moot at this stage. Changes this late in the development cycle also tend to be disruptive to the development process and very expensive. Depending on your budget or time frame, the development effort may even be past the point of no return by the time the coding starts. Consequently, any changes, regardless of how important, cannot be accommodated without jeopardizing delivery dates and budgets.

A more effective methodology for developing clustered, server-based applications is presented in this section. The goals of this methodology are to align the clustered components with the application's requirements and to absolutely minimize the resulting cluster's network intensity. Before you dismiss this second goal as the mindless meandering of a bandwidth geek, remember that clustered systems consist of far more than just hardware and software. The three network functional areas described throughout this book bind together the cluster, its users, and possibly even its shared storage devices.

These networks also contribute to the users' perception of total system performance. Few, if any, users are sophisticated enough to discern the impacts of network performance from those of hardware or software performance. Therefore, it is in the best interests of everyone involved to ensure that the finished product delivers the highest possible performance levels for the users. This can only be done by incorporating the network ramifications into the early stages of system design.

This network-friendly methodology for developing clustered applications is illustrated in Figure 8.1.

8.1.1. Requirements Gathering

The first step in any application development methodology must, necessarily, be the gathering of customer requirements. Many long-standing techniques exist for collecting this data. These include the following:

- Interviewing users

- Examining performance benchmarks of any existing systems and databases that will either be replaced with the clustered application or that are functionally similar to it

Figure 8.1.
*Network-friendly,
clustered
application
development
methodology.*

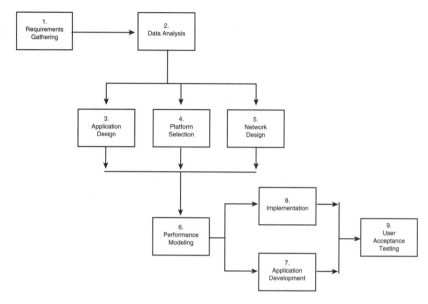

Figure 8.1.
Network-friendly, clustered application development methodology.

- Monitoring peak and sustained resource utilization rates on existing systems, by time-of-day increments

- Monitoring peak and sustained network utilization rates

- Working with technical support staff of cluster component vendors

This is by no means a complete list. It is, however, a reasonable starting point for developing user requirements. These will drive subsequent cluster and application design decisions. Therefore, any information gathered during this phase should be translatable into meaningful metrics.

8.1.2. Information Analysis

The result of the data-gathering exercise is the development of performance metrics as well as target values for those metrics. To convert the information into metrics and target values requires careful analysis. Here are some of the more common metrics:

- Round-trip delay

- Response time

- Processing time

- Data retrieval time

Some new metrics might also be appropriate for a clustered application. Metrics such as *fail-over times* and *load-balancing transfer times* might also be valuable to gauge the effectiveness of your completed cluster.

During this stage, it is also necessary to start identifying the various functions and processes that are required by the planned application. Data feeds, update mechanisms, and any other external resources that are needed by the clustered application should also be identified and mapped out in a system flow chart.

This flow chart should be used to identify relationships between existing systems and the planned clustered application, potential synergies, data flows, and so on. All of these can be used to make the new application as effective as possible.

8.1.3. Application Design

Next, the application must be designed in detail, using the information from the analysis stage. This includes the user interface screens, program logic, database structures, and anything else that might constitute part of your application.

The application design methodology used is immaterial. Conventional top-down structured programming, object-oriented programming, and so on, may all be used. The choice of design methodology can greatly impact the mechanics and reusability of the finished application. However, for the purposes of this book, methodology selection is considered a tactical choice and not strategic to the cluster's design.

8.1.4. Platform Selection

It might seem counterintuitive to begin designing the application without having first selected the physical platform that it will reside on. Platform selection can actually be done either before, during, or after application design. The important thing is to uncouple the application from the physical platform. The hardware should be disassociated from the operating system and any other layers of software utilities. Ideally, it should not matter to the application what the physical platform is (at least during the design stage!).

> **NOTE** Vendors of cluster management software products can supply lists of compatible hardware components and even recommend bundled platforms. Once you've selected a cluster management product, contact that product's vendor to obtain these lists. This will jump-start your platform selection process.

Armed with the knowledge of the number of clients and the type(s) of application(s) you need to support, you can begin evaluating the server and client platforms.

Building a New NT Cluster

8.1.5. Network Design

Network design in a cluster can consist of up to three distinct components. These components represent the network functional areas: client-to-cluster connectivity, cluster interconnect, and clustered host to peripheral devices. The network requirements for each area must be based on some reasonable estimate of the traffic load they'll support and the performance metrics they'll be measured by.

As part of the overall network design, each network functional area must have a network technology selected—Ethernet, Token Ring, FDDI, and so on. Vendors should also be carefully considered because many implement LAN technologies in different ways. Some may be more or less suited to your particular needs, so don't assume that Fast Ethernet (or any other LAN, for that matter) is a homogeneous commodity. It is not.

Lastly, network and transport protocols must be selected. It is quite likely that you will use different protocols for the different network functional areas. Each protocol should be carefully considered relative to the traffic load and performance requirements of each network functional area. For example, TCP/IP might be an ideal combination of network and transport protocols for communications between clients and the cluster, but it would probably be a poor choice for intracluster communications. The performance requirements are much more stringent in this network functional area.

8.1.6. Performance Modeling

Before finalizing the network and application designs, the last step must be performance modeling. Properly done, performance modeling enables the predictive assessment of the clustered application's potential performance. It is far less expensive to identify and correct potential performance problems before you deploy a system than it is after.

From an operational perspective, a cluster is a point-to-point system. The slowest component in the chain determines the entire system's maximum performance by creating a bottleneck. Consequently, it is imperative that the entire component chain be identified, and that each component's potential for performance be measured as carefully as possible. Every component, from the client station equipment and interfaces to the clustered application, as well as the various networks in between, should be modeled for individual performance and aggregate performance.

Performance models are little more than mathematical functions. To determine the throughput of a system, create a map of all the components and determine the performance potential of each, using the metrics and targets previously established. Identify any obvious mismatches in performance (latency, throughput, and so on) and focus your resources on this potential problem spot.

8.1.7. Application Development

Once you complete these activities (if you are custom developing the clustered application) it is time to actually develop it. At this point, you must make a few more decisions about tools, development methodologies, and programming languages.

When you finish building your application, you can test all aspects of the system. Software bugs and hardware glitches should be identified and corrected *before* the user finds them. This is an iterative process; you can return to any activity to make changes at any time. Designing a cluster is, to a large extent, a matter of trial and error.

When you finish testing, you can begin to move legacy data to the new system, if applicable. At this point, consider running the new system in parallel with the old, just to make sure you get the results you expect.

8.1.8. Implementation

If the application is being custom developed, you can start assembling the physical platform. The first step is to prepare the environment. Any environmental conditioning required should be installed before the cluster is built. This includes cooling and dehumidification, raised flooring, sound-deadening wall coverings, furnishings, electrical power, and possibly even a fire suppression system.

After the environment is prepared, the cluster can be installed. This goes beyond installing the cluster's nodes. It must include installing and testing all required networks, the cluster management software, and any other essential subsystems such as messaging, transaction processing, or database management. Ideally, by the time the application is completed, its platform will be completed, tested, and waiting for the application to be installed.

If the application is being purchased commercially, the implementation steps do not vary much, except that no parallel development effort is required. The shrink-wrapped software can be loaded as soon as the cluster's platform is completely built and tested.

8.1.9. User Acceptance Testing

The last step in any application development model is user acceptance testing. Prior to "live" use of the application, the customer must be trained and must actually conduct testing to ensure that every aspect of the application performs as expected. *Performs as expected* is the key phrase in the preceding sentence. It implies that the logic is sound, and that all components work harmoniously so that there are no obvious bottlenecks to impede performance.

During the training and acceptance testing, monitor the aggregate system performance and evaluate each component as a separate entity. Validate these individual components against your performance models, metric target values, and customer expectations. If any component fails to perform satisfactorily, identify the factors that impact its performance and attack. Minor problems can be remedied quickly and inexpensively by tuning parameters, load balancing, and so on. More serious problems indicate a flawed design process and can be the harbingers of lengthy and expensive reengineering.

8.2. Planning the Cluster

When it comes time to design the cluster, the obvious place to start is at the top of the "stack": the application. Everything else, from the physical layer, network, and processing platform, to the operating system, middleware, and so on, is nothing more than infrastructure that supports the application software and therefore subordinate to the application.

From the users' perspective, the finished cluster's performance is viewed in the aggregate. Distinctions in the performance of the various components are imperceptible. To them, the application isn't delivering the performance that they expect or require. This necessitates identifying the source of all performance mismatches in the cluster's components, from the user station to the cluster and everything in between. Consequently, it is important that the performance modeling be done as carefully as possible to ensure that all components are as accurately matched as possible. This may require several iterations of model/modify/re-model before you have a configuration that models smoothly.

Once you have ironed out all the potential performance mismatches, it is time to configure your cluster. This is a difficult task, and there is no single correct answer. There are, however, numerous limitations that face server-clustering pioneers. The most obvious one is the need for homogeneous configurations. This can be a significant limitation because Windows NT can run on quite a few different microprocessors, including the x86, Alpha, and PowerPC.

These microprocessors can also be configured with seemingly infinite variety, including the number of CPUs per host and the bus technology used. Subtle variations, too, such as the quantity and/or type of memory and storage available, offer additional flexibility. Normally, this flexibility is a feature. In early server-based clusters, the flexibility of the servers may prove more of a curse.

As cluster management products emerge and mature, their tolerance for mismatched physical platforms will improve. *Early cluster implementations should strive to maintain as homogeneous a distributed platform as possible.* This applies to processing technologies and configurations. If you try to develop a mixed technology cluster, it might not function. If it does, cluster management might be unreliable. Your results will vary based on the degree of disparity between the cluster nodes, the nature of the cluster's application, its topology, and its cluster management software.

Other limitations that should ease over time are scalability and functionality. Initial cluster products can be expected to be minimal and tentative offerings. As they mature, they can be expected to increase the number of supported nodes per cluster, improve fail-over times, and even add new features to the cluster.

A more significant limitation is the lack of available cluster-aware commercial applications. Slowly existing commercial applications will be made cluster-aware. However, anyone trying to develop a server-based cluster in the near future might find their options for cluster-aware applications severely limited.

Getting beyond these traps, the first thing that must be considered when sizing the cluster is the level of performance that is actually needed. The amount of memory, storage, and computational power can all be customized to the particular requirements of the application. The question is, "How many hosts should be in my cluster?"

Once you have established the technology base and performance requirements, sizing the cluster becomes a relatively easy task. There are three approaches that can be used for building a cluster of appropriate size for your application: minimum, maximum, or moderate density.

To illustrate the differences between these approaches, let's examine the possibilities for developing a cluster for an *online transaction processing* (OLTP) application. The workload is estimated to need 16 CPUs, a minimum of 256MB of memory (see note), and support a database that will grow to 40GB. Assuming that reusing the original machine is highly desirable, and that physical homogeneity is required by the cluster management software, each of the clustered nodes will be a symmetrical multiprocessor (SMP) that can support up to eight CPUs.

> **NOTE** The actual amount of memory, and maybe even CPUs, required to support any given application in a cluster may actually be higher than what is needed to support it on a single platform. This is a direct result of the inefficiencies of running multiple operating systems, instances of the application software, middleware, and so on. Consequently, in the example presented, the amount of memory required in the cluster must be *at least* as much as a stand-alone configuration.

8.2.1. Maximum Density

The first approach calls for absolutely minimizing the number of hosts in the cluster. This is done by opting for fewer, more powerful hosts, and by fully configuring them. Figure 8.2 shows a maximum density, shared nothing cluster of two nodes.

Figure 8.2.
Maximum cluster density.

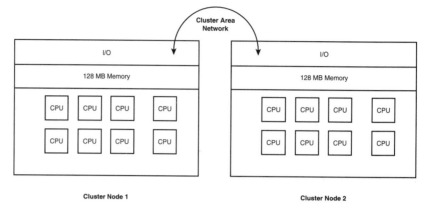

This approach is desirable because it can be built quickly and at a minimal cost. Only two hosts are needed to support the projected workload. Minimizing the number of hosts results in the need for less physical space in the computer room and is likely to require less administrative effort than a three or more host cluster.

The drawback to this approach is that any further scaling beyond the projected level requires an additional host to be added to the cluster. On the other hand, if the application isn't expected to grow beyond the projected limit, a maximum density cluster may be ideal.

8.2.2. Minimum Density

The second approach is the exact opposite of the maximum density approach. This approach is the minimum density possible within the cluster. Given the requirement of 16 CPUs worth of computational power, a minimum density approach would use 16 separate hosts with one CPU each. If we assume that the basic nodal platform will be an eight CPU symmetrical multiprocessor (SMP), each node in the cluster will have seven spare CPU sockets. Such a cluster could grow to a maximum of 128 CPUs without having to deploy another host. This approach is illustrated in Figure 8.3.

This approach offers the ultimate in low-cost scalability. It also offers the greatest protection from component failure because of the high degree of redundancy.

There are, of course, some drawbacks to this approach. The first is the tremendous increase in start-up, operations, and maintenance costs compared to the maximum density cluster. This approach requires a fourfold increase in processing platforms compared to a maximum density cluster. Consequently, it is reasonable to expect an incremental increase in the operations and maintenance costs of the minimum density cluster, relative to either a stand-alone SMP or a maximum density cluster.

Figure 8.3.
Minimum cluster density.

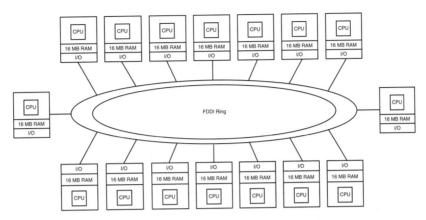

The second drawback to this approach is the increased complexity and overhead of distributing an application across such a large cluster. More clustered nodes directly equate to increased intracluster communications. This automatically renders the minimum density cluster a more resource-intensive configuration than a maximum density cluster.

8.2.3. Moderate Density

Of course, some compromise can be struck between these two extremes. For example, a cluster can be developed with moderate density. This is a tradeoff between the costs of starting up and the future costs of expansion. Figure 8.4 illustrates a moderate density cluster. Four hosts are clustered, each containing one-fourth of the required system resources.

This approach is capable of adequately supporting the hypothetical applications. Start-up costs are a bit higher than the maximum density solution, but much less than the minimum density solution. Additionally, it can grow with the applications at modest incremental cost.

8.2.4. What's the Right Approach?

All of the approaches described are valid solutions to the hypothetical scenario presented in section 8.3. They are simply different tradeoffs between start-up costs and future expansion costs.

The only way to determine which one is right for you is to broaden the base of decision criteria. For example, if business conditions indicate that budgets might tighten in the future, incurring a greater start-up cost may be preferable. In this case, a minimum density cluster would be preferable. This would let you acquire hardware to more than adequately support the application's projected growth. Future expenses would be limited to the incremental costs of acquiring and installing whatever internal system resources are needed.

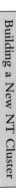

Building a New NT Cluster

Figure 8.4.
Moderate cluster density.

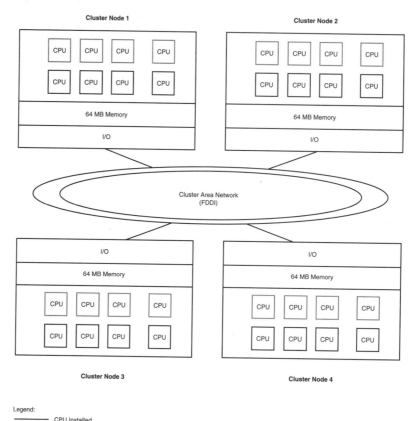

If existing business conditions are such that every dollar spent is carefully scrutinized, but the forecast for the future looks better, you may want to defer large expenses. A maximum density cluster would satisfy the projected requirements with a minimum investment in such circumstances.

Moving beyond the costs associated with the physical platform itself, other issues such as hardware budgets, maintenance, support costs, and even physical space constraints, might dictate the selection of one approach over the others.

The key is to develop a cluster that is well suited to the application it supports in terms of current and future requirements. This means that everything must be aligned and well matched. The application and its performance requirements must be reflected in every facet of the cluster. These facets include the following:

- Client-side technologies
- Various networking technologies

- Cluster topology
- Processor technologies
- Middleware technologies
- Cluster management software

Even the intangibles must be well aligned. These include:

- Current versus future budgets
- Platform vendor reliability
- Current versus future administrator workloads
- Physical space constraints
- Technopolitics

If these items are not synchronized with each other, the performance of the entire cluster will suffer.

When sizing your new cluster, try to think of external and internal scalability as coarse and fine-tuning tools, respectively. Adding external capacity, that is, more hosts to the cluster, is a way of coarsely tuning the processing platform to the application. Expanding internally, for example, adding CPUs to an existing multiprocessor, allows you to fine-tune the cluster platform.

In time, another way of tuning the platform may be to use different processing technologies, that is, mixing CPU types across the cluster nodes. For the time being, server-based clustering is still too immature for this to be practical, much less supportable.

8.3. Cluster Networking

Data networking, both local and wide area, has grown in functionality and significance with respect to application performance. This is generally true of distributed processing, but it's particularly applicable to clusters. By using network resources effectively, one can directly improve user perception of the overall clustered application's performance.

Unfortunately, there are no panaceas. Using network resources effectively encompasses a wide variety of tactics. Some tactics are specific to new application development, and some are general resource management principles. Those that are specific to new application development can enable new levels of system performance, as perceived by the users, and reduce network congestion for other users.

Building a New NT Cluster

To develop network-friendly clustered applications, you must consider bandwidth-reducing options during the design stage. Such options offer the ability to minimize both the quantity of bandwidth required and the number of components in the network require this bandwidth. Clearly, the greater these two numbers, the greater the impact on network performance, causing more users to be impacted.

Therefore, the system design stage must address all of the resources that will be balanced against each other in the system. Typically, it is easier and less expensive to incorporate new requirements such as network considerations at design time than it is to try to reduce the network intensity of the system after the user acceptance testing demonstrates performance deficiencies.

Application design and development processes that integrate network planning in the early stages will optimize total system performance by introducing a rich palette of performance-enhancing options. These options aren't new; they just haven't been given much consideration in the past. Nor have they been integrated into any formal design methodology.

It is critical that network design be integrated into the early stages of application design to ensure that total cluster performance is optimized. Given that clusters have three distinct network functional areas, each one must be examined individually to determine the optimal networking solution for it. The three functional areas are

- Client to cluster

- Cluster host to external storage device

- Cluster interconnectivity

8.3.1. Client to Cluster

Any server must somehow be connected to the users. Therefore, the first network functional area, client to cluster, is probably already present. Before the cluster is developed, this area should be examined to determine whether it will withstand the projected increased volume. It is likely that much, if not all, of the network connecting clients to the cluster will also be used to transport data from other applications, possibly even bandwidth-intensive applications such as the World Wide Web or multimedia communications. It would be worthwhile to investigate this aspect of the cluster's network infrastructure to ensure that it would continue to support the clustered application processing as it scales upwards.

8.3.2. **Cluster Host to External Storage Device**

Depending on the cluster's configuration, the second network functional area, cluster host to external storage device, might have to be developed. If the cluster being developed is a shared nothing cluster, then nothing needs to be done, except for ensuring that each node in the cluster has its own connectivity to any external storage devices.

If, however, the cluster is to be a shared disk cluster, then something must be done to extend this network functional area to all cluster nodes. There are two possible ways to provide connectivity to external storage devices throughout a cluster. The first way is to use a single, robust bus technology to interconnect all hosts to their shared storage devices. This approach is illustrated in Figure 8.5. It is only viable in a shared disk cluster configuration.

Figure 8.5.
Providing connectivity to shared storage devices.

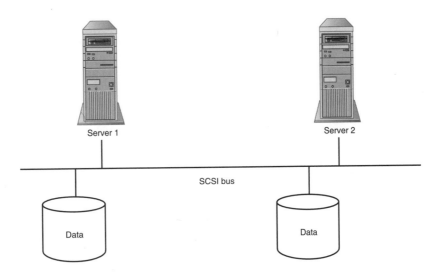

The second way is to deploy fully separate and redundant buses. This topology is illustrated in Figure 8.6. Redundant buses would be most useful in fail-over clusters that do not support a common application.

8.3.3. **Cluster Interconnectivity**

The functional area that would likely have to be added as the cluster is built is the cluster interconnectivity networking. This network will be responsible for transporting the cluster management protocols. Functions such as "heartbeats" or status messages, fail-overs, and load balancing all require intracluster communications. The efficiency with which this network supports these functions directly determines the aggregate efficiency of the entire cluster. It is in your best interest to design and implement the most robust network technologies possible for this area.

Building a New NT Cluster

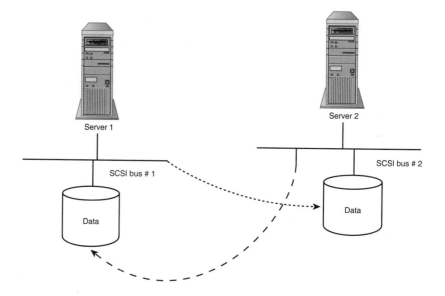

Figure 8.6.

Fail-over connectivity to shared storage devices.

Here are the attributes to look for in a network technology:

■ Fast transmission rate, preferable 100Mbps (megabits per second) or higher

■ Low latency Layer 2 protocol

■ Well-regulated media access methodology

■ Robust and error-free transmission media

■ Network interface cards (NICs) that are supported by the clustered hosts' platform

Selecting a network technology that satisfies these criteria will all but guarantee a successful cluster area network. These criteria are for selecting a cluster area network technology only. Implicit with this concept is that the NORMA I/O model will be used. If either the NUMA or ccNUMA I/O models are used, it is possible that traditional network technologies will not be used.

> **NOTE**   The use of a "well-regulated media access methodology" as a criterion does *not* necessarily preclude the use of any of the Ethernet technologies. Ethernet uses a Carrier Sense/Multiple Access with Collision Detection (CS/MACD) access methodology. Ordinarily, this is a chaotic media access methodology that would not be acceptable for use in a cluster area network. However, Fast Ethernet is available in both full duplex and port-switched varieties. Full duplex uses different physical wires to transmit and receive. Thus, there can be no contention or collisions.
>
> The emerging Gigabit Ethernet, which appears to be a good candidate for the cluster area network, is a full duplex technology.

8.4. Application Issues

Having determined the appropriate physical composition of your cluster, it is time to return to the application layer. It is important that the application, operating system, and any middleware be cluster-aware. If any, or all, of these software products are not cluster-aware, the cluster might not be able to deliver the expected benefits. In fact, one could expect several different types of errors to occur.

Here are the typical fail-over errors:

- The inability of the application to respond to the operating system's requests to cease operations prior to the fail-over

- The inability of the operating system to replicate the application's state and data to the fail-over node

Here are the typical errors in a dynamic load-balancing cluster:

- Application-level errors caused by the inability to cope with the operating system's attempt to dynamically balance load

- Data corruption

If the clustered application is a commercially available software package, chances are that it will be made cluster-aware in the not-too-distant future. You might want to verify roll-out schedules with your software vendors.

If the clustered application is to be homegrown, the issues become more complicated. The first thing that you'll need to determine is whether or not the application's functionality lends itself to clustering. If it can be clustered, you will also need to identify any limitations that it might impose on the functionality of the cluster. For example, does the application's functionality automatically dictate a shared disk cluster, or can you implement it successfully on a shared nothing cluster?

The application's specifications should also be scrutinized to determine how well it can take advantage of parallel execution. Can it be parsed out to different CPUs for concurrent execution in an SMP? More importantly, can tasks be distributed across multiple nodes? If the answer to either of these questions is affirmative, then the next hurdle is technical expertise. It is highly unlikely that in-house developers will have the necessary expertise to begin developing cluster-aware applications—they will require training. Alternatively, new hires or temporary workers who are already trained can be used.

Building a New NT Cluster

Perhaps the greatest hurdle facing anyone attempting to custom develop a cluster-aware application is which API to use. In this age of open computing, openness has become the front door to propriety. Once inside, you'll find yourself (again) locked into a single vendor because of the desirability of certain features that are not part of the open standard technology set that you selected. APIs will become the battleground over which "open" cluster management software wars are fought in the future. Select your API carefully! You'll probably have to live with the choice for a long time.

8.5. New Clustering Checklist

The following checklist should help you get started with developing a new NT Server cluster.

Research
Gather user requirements
Analyze data
Establish performance metrics and goals
Cluster functionality? (Availability, scalability, load balancing, combination?)

Application Design
Design user interface screens
Design logic modules
Design database structures
Define data feeds (Inbound and outbound)
Application functionality versus cluster functionality? (Availability, scalability, load balancing, combination, limitations?)

Platform Selection
Select computing platform technology
Cluster size? (Maximum, minimum, or moderate density)
Cluster topology? (Shared disk, shared nothing, complex)
Operating system selection (Must be cluster-aware)
API selection
Cluster-aware middlewares
Cluster management software selection

Network Design
Select I/O model (NORMA, NUMA, ccNUMA)
Select technology and topology for client-to-cluster networking
Select technology and topology for cluster host to storage device network
Select technology and topology for intracluster communications

Application Development
Iterative performance modeling until satisfactory results
Application development

Implementation
Physical environment preparation (Electric, raised floor, AC, and so on)
Hardware installation
Software installation (OS, middleware, cluster management, and so on)
Network installation
Application installation

Testing
Systems testing
User acceptance testing

8.6. Summary

Clustering is an extremely useful and valuable concept. Its worth has already been proven over the past two decades in the mainframe and midrange computing markets. Thus, it might appear to be a "no-brainer" in the low-end computing market. However, clustering is a complicated and potentially dangerous undertaking that shouldn't be taken trivially. It requires careful planning and execution if the expected benefits are to materialize.

Properly planned and executed, clustered NT Servers can blur the distinctions between the low-end and midrange computing architectures. The checklist provided in this section is intended to guide you as you develop and deploy new NT Server clusters.

Building a New NT Cluster

Chapter

9

Clustering an Existing NT Server/ Application

Retroactively clustering an existing NT server is a bit more complex than simply adding hardware and cluster management software. A cluster is a complex structure composed of hardware, software, and networking. Each component must be well-suited to the performance goals of the cluster and to each other—a challenge inherent to clustering. Retrofitting an existing NT server and its applications presents other challenges, too. This is because retroactively clustering an existing server and applications is more difficult than designing a cluster from scratch.

This chapter describes some of the challenges you'll face when you're attempting retroactive clustering. To guide you through these potentially difficult challenges, this chapter also provides a basic approach and a clustering checklist. These tools are designed to maximize the performance potential of your completed cluster. Depending on your particular circumstances, some of the recommendations in this chapter may not be viable.

If you are developing a cluster from scratch, you might find Chapter 8, "Building a New NT Cluster," more appropriate.

9.1. Where Should I Start?

The obvious place to start is at the top of the "stack": the application. Everything else, the physical layer, the network, the processing platform, the operating system, and so on, is nothing more than infrastructure that exists only to support the application software. They are subordinate to the application.

Different application types require very different types of performance. That you are investigating clustering as an alternative to a *present method of operation* (PMO) indicates that there is some aspect of performance that is not currently being satisfied. If you are going to reinvest in a server-based application, you should do it right. Any and all deficiencies must be identified and corrected because if the customers aren't going to be happy with the clustered solution, it isn't a solution.

These deficiencies can be either real or perceived, or they can be current or looming. They can also be driven by either hardware or software. From the user's perspective these distinctions are imperceivable and, therefore, inconsequential. To them, the application isn't delivering the performance that they expect or require, period. Your job as a system administrator or cluster architect is to separate fact from fiction and figure out how to improve the customers' perceptions.

This necessitates identifying the sources of all deficiencies—real or anticipated, hardware or software—before the clustering overhaul begins. In fact, these deficiencies must be identified before you can accurately determine whether or not clustering is an appropriate solution. Otherwise, the clustered solution becomes a more complex and expensive means of emulating the previous method of operation. Given that the clustering initiative was probably driven by some perceived deficiency with the original configuration, it is unlikely that the users will be any happier.

9.2. Current Deficiencies

Performance deficiencies that are currently being experienced can be caused by almost anything. The trick is figuring out the culprit. There are two primary sources of information that can be used to diagnose the source of a performance problem.

The first is the application's users. From the users' perspective, any constraint, regardless of its type and nature, will result in similar application behaviors. Typically, users describe the application as "slow." This information doesn't provide any insight at all into the cause of the performance deficiencies. If you can, try to have the users provide some clarification. Perhaps only some of the application's functions are slow. Depending on which functions are slow, you may be able to determine whether there is an I/O bottleneck, a dearth of CPU cycles, or insufficient memory. Don't count on this, however.

User complaints should not be your first indication of application performance trouble. By the time they complain, you already have a problem. If additional resources are needed, the problem will likely persist (and get worse) for quite some time before it gets better. This is not the way to run an IS shop.

A better approach is to proactively monitor the "health" of the various servers by continuously monitoring the usage levels of their systemic resources. This will enable you to identify and resolve resource constraints before they become obvious to the users. Ideally, there should be enough mechanisms already deployed to automatically track system resource utilization. The reports generated from these mechanisms, whether online or batched, should be reviewed routinely for early warning signs. Unlike user complaints, these reports will pinpoint exactly which resources are constraining the performance of the application itself.

The most common categories of performance deficiencies are physical capacity, features and functionality, availability, and accessibility. Many factors could contribute to a perceivable deficiency in any of these categories. Any remediation, clustered or otherwise, should address all of the contributing factors.

9.2.1. Physical Capacity

The first of the demonstrable deficiencies is the physical capacity of the hosting platform. All processing platforms have a finite internal capacity for memory, storage, and even compute cycles. As an application's or server's usage increases, these system resources become constrained, usually unevenly.

Once the resource constraints are identified, the next question is, "How much more of that resource is needed?" In many cases, adding a fixed quantity of hardware will "fix" the problem. For example, adding a 16-megabyte memory module or 10-gigabyte disk drive should go a long way toward relieving most performance-impacting resource shortages. You can continue to incrementally grow the server in this manner up to the maximum supported by that device. Previously, you had to upgrade the server to a larger model. This has changed with the introduction of clustering technologies in the server arena.

Today, your choices are either incremental growth within the confines of the existing platform, rehosting to a more powerful platform, or clustering. Obviously, clustering is a more expensive solution in the short run because it requires acquiring and supporting additional machines. In the long run, however, clustering will provide additional functionality and scalability that may prove to be more economical than any of the alternative solutions.

If you feel that clustering would be a better approach, you should partner with the user community and the application's administrators. Their input is necessary for you to determine if the constraint you are witnessing is an temporary aberration, the result of normal incremental growth, or just the beginning of a major increase in activity. If it is either of the first two, incremental internal expansion might be preferable, provided that adequate expansion capacity is available.

If external expansion is a necessity, some hard decisions must be made. The traditional form of external expansion is rehosting the applications to a larger, more powerful processing platform. This is still a viable means of providing expansion, and should be at least a part of the basis for evaluating clustering as a potential solution.

9.2.2. Features and Functionality

It's no secret: Commercial software manufacturers continuously "leapfrog" each other's technology through constant innovation and addition of features and functions. Thus, it is entirely probable that a perceived performance problem may be resolved by upgrading to the latest release of whatever commercial software is being used.

Alternatively, there may be no actual performance problem with the application. Rather, it may be showing its age and just not have all the bells and whistles that the users are becoming aware of. Some features and functionality can be added to an application simply by retro-clustering it. And, as has been described throughout this book, clustering is a potentially valuable technique that can be used to provide the reliability and availability in a low-end computing architecture that is prerequisite to supporting mission-critical applications.

Clustering can also be used to separate an application's various functions onto different tiers of clustered processors. This enables each tier to be customized to the specific function (like transaction processing) that it supports. Although this won't necessarily add any features or functionality, it enables you to fine-tune the application's performance. This may serve to forestall the need either to replace the application with a newer one, or (if home-grown application software is used) to rip open the source code and modify the existing one.

These last two options should be considered the last resorts for adding features and functions to an application. However, as will be discussed in section 9.5 of this chapter, some modification of the application's source code may be necessary to successfully cluster it. Consequently, clustering may provide the incentive to upgrade a software package to the most current release level, thereby providing users with new features and functionality, even though they might not be directly related to clustering.

9.2.3. Availability

An application's availability has everything to do with how well it sustains the vicissitudes of operations and maintenance. One characteristic of availability that has not yet been addressed in this book is the potential for clustering to enable software upgrades to the operating system, middleware, and even application software without disrupting the availability of the application.

Historically, this type of maintenance had to be scheduled in advance. This is especially true for mission-critical applications. Contingency operations and "back-out" plans must be developed before the upgrade can begin. Usually these are done during the off-hours when backups or other system maintenance functions are performed. As cluster management software matures, it is reasonable to expect support for "n and $n+1$" release levels. In other words, multiple release levels of software can be supported simultaneously in the cluster. Thus, the nodes can be upgraded one at a time without compromising the application's availability.

This level of availability far surpasses the now familiar and basic fail-over cluster capability. This should not be misconstrued as saying that fail-overs are not an important tool for maintaining high application availability. On the contrary, fail-overs are essential for maintaining availability *in case of a failure*. By its very nature, fail-over protection is a reactive measure. Support for "n and $n+1$" is a much more proactive means of providing high availability rates. Together, these tools should enable low-end computing architectures to rival the availability rates of well-pampered mainframes.

9.2.4. Accessibility

In this age of network-centric computing, the actual location of a cluster is moot. The ubiquity and performance of the network compensates for geographic distances between users and clusters. The key word in the preceding sentence is "performance." If the network is heavily laden, users will experience problems either with accessing or with using the cluster. From their perspective, the cluster is having problems. Thus, the accessibility of an application (clustered or otherwise) must be considered one of the prime suspects responsible for the client's perception of an application's performance.

If the network is causing the performance degradation that users are experiencing, system resource monitoring tools that may be used on the host will not reveal a problem. In fact, they will usually demonstrate a smaller than usual workload. This directly reflects the difficulties encountered in the network that connects the users to the application's host.

This example underscores the need for cooperation between all parties responsible for the health of the application. Everybody—whether they are responsible for the LANs, WANs, server administration, or the application or databases and other subsystems—must participate in the identification of performance problems.

9.3. Cluster Configuration

Once you have identified all the existing and potential application performance constraints in the present method of operation, it is time to configure your cluster. This is a particularly difficult task, and there is no single, correct answer. Your goal should be to establish a cluster configuration that can satisfy performance requirements, both for today and for the future.

After you have committed to clustering an existing application, you must make an important decision: Do you keep the existing platform, or change it? If you intend to change the platform, what will it be? One limitation that faces clustering pioneers is the need for homogeneous configurations. This can be a significant limitation because Windows NT can run on quite a few different microprocessors, including the x86, Alpha, PowerPC, and so on.

These microprocessors can also be configured with seemingly infinite variety, including the number of CPUs per host and the bus technology used. Subtle variations, too, like the quantity and type of memory and storage available, offer additional flexibility. Normally, this flexibility is a feature. However, in early server-based clusters, flexibility may prove to be more of a curse.

As cluster management products emerge and mature, their tolerance for mismatched physical platforms will improve. Early cluster implementations should strive to maintain as homogeneous a distributed platform as possible. This applies to processing technologies and configurations. If you try to develop a mixed technology cluster, it might not function. If it does, cluster management might be unreliable.

It is also important to see the addition of cluster management capabilities to an existing server/application for what it is: a new variable. Thus, if you are intent on migrating to a new platform *and* adding cluster management, you may wish to minimize your risks and perform the technology migration first, and then build the cluster.

After getting beyond these traps, the first thing that must be considered when sizing the cluster is the level of performance that is actually needed. The amount of memory, storage, and computational power can all be customized to the particular requirements of the application. The question is, "How many hosts should be in my cluster?"

Once you have established the technology base and performance requirements, the sizing of the cluster becomes a relatively easy task. There are three approaches that can be used for building a cluster of appropriate size for your application: minimum, maximum, or moderate density.

To illustrate the differences between these approaches, let's examine the possibilities for developing a cluster for an online transaction processing (OLTP) application. The current workload is severely taxing an 8-CPU host with 128 *megabytes* (MB) of memory, and 20 *gigabytes* (GB) of stored data. The application is expected to continue growing over the next year. Then it will plateau at approximately twice today's workload.

Clustering would be a better approach than simply migrating to a single multi-processor that's twice as large because of the redundancy and load balancing that could be achieved. The clustered solution must have 16 CPUs, a minimum of 256 MB of memory (see note), and support a database that will grow to 40 GB. Assuming that reusing the original machine is highly desirable, and that physical homogeneity is required by the cluster management software, each of the clustered nodes will be a *symmetrical multiprocessor* (SMP) that can support up to 8 CPUs.

> **NOTE** The actual amount of memory, and maybe even CPUs, required to support any given application in a cluster may actually be higher than what is needed to support it on a single platform. This is a direct result of the inefficiencies of running multiple operating systems and instances of the application software, middleware, and so on. Consequently, in the example presented, the amount of memory required in the cluster must be at least as much as the stand-alone configuration, and probably a bit more.

9.3.1. Maximum Density

The first approach calls for absolutely minimizing the number of hosts in the cluster. This is done by opting for fewer, more powerful hosts, and by fully configuring them. Figure 9.1 shows a maximum density, shared nothing cluster of two nodes. The existing multiprocessor is retained. A duplicate machine has been deployed to support the anticipated growth.

Figure 9.1.

Maximum cluster density.

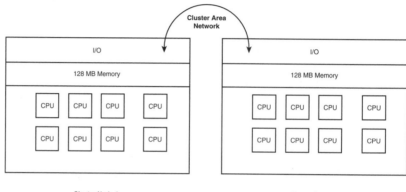

This approach is desirable because it can be built quickly, and at a minimal cost. Only one more host is needed, and the existing node is retained intact.

The drawback to this approach is that any further scaling beyond the projected level requires an additional host to be added to the cluster. On the other hand, if the application isn't expected to grow beyond the projected limit, a maximum density cluster may be ideal.

9.3.2. Minimum Density

The second approach is the exact opposite of the maximum density approach. This approach strives for the minimum density possible within the cluster. Given the requirement of 16 CPUs worth of computational power, a minimum density approach would use 16 separate hosts with one CPU each. Assuming the retention of the original platform, each of the 15 new hosts would be an 8 CPU symmetrical multiprocessor with 7 spare CPU sockets. This cluster could grow to a maximum of 128 CPUs without having to deploy another host. This configuration is shown in Figure 9.2.

Figure 9.2.
Minimum cluster density.

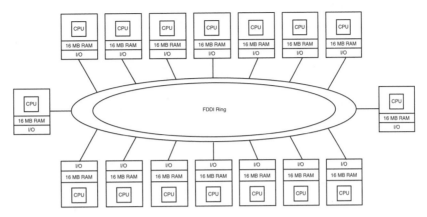

This approach offers the ultimate in low-cost scalability. It also offers the greatest protection from component failure because of the high degree of redundancy.

There are, of course, some drawbacks to this approach. The first is the tremendous increase in start-up, operation, and maintenance costs compared to the maximum density cluster. The second is the increased complexity of distributing an application across such a large cluster. A minor point is that, although all of the components of the original host were retained, a considerable amount of effort would be needed to redistribute its resources among the eight clustered hosts.

9.3.3. Moderate Density

Of course, some compromise can be struck between these two extremes. For example, a cluster can be developed with moderate density. This is a tradeoff between the costs of starting up and the future costs of expansion. Figure 9.3 illustrates a moderate density cluster. Four hosts are clustered, each containing one-fourth of the required system resources.

This approach is capable of adequately supporting the hypothetical applications. Start-up costs are a bit higher than the maximum density solution, but much less than the minimum density solution. Additionally, it can grow with the applications at modest incremental cost.

Figure 9.3.
Moderate cluster density.

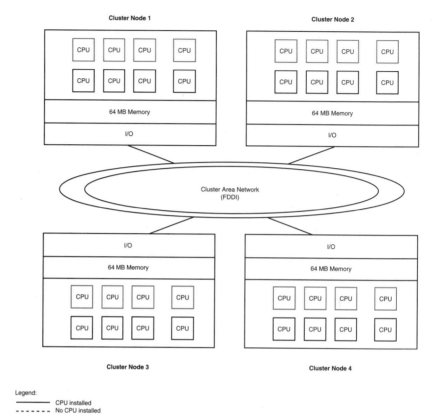

9.3.4. What's the Right Approach?

All of the approaches described are valid solutions to the hypothetical scenario presented in section 9.3. They are simply different tradeoffs between start-up costs and future expansion costs.

The only way to determine which one is right for you is to broaden the base of decision criteria. For example, if business conditions indicate that budgets might tighten in the future, incurring a greater start-up cost could be preferable. In this case, a minimum density cluster would be preferable. This would let you acquire hardware to more than adequately support the application's projected growth. Future expenses would be limited to the incremental costs of acquiring and installing whatever internal system resources are needed.

If existing business conditions are such that every dollar spent is carefully scrutinized, but the forecast for the future looks better, you may want to defer large expenses. Thus, a maximum density cluster would satisfy the projected requirements with a minimum investment.

Moving beyond the costs associated with the physical platform itself, other issues like hardware budgets, maintenance and support costs, and even physical space constraints may dictate the selection of one approach over the others.

The key is to develop a cluster that is well suited to the applications it supports, in terms of current and expected requirements. This means that everything must be aligned and well matched. The application and its performance requirements must be reflected in every facet of the cluster. These facets include

- Various networking technologies

- Cluster topology

- Processor technologies

- Middleware technologies

- Client technologies and platforms

- Cluster management software

Even the intangibles must be well aligned. These include

- Current versus future budgets

- Current versus future administrator workloads

- Physical space constraints

- Technopolitics

If all these items are not synchronized to each other, the performance of the entire cluster will suffer.

When sizing your cluster, try to think of external and internal scalability as coarse and fine tuning tools. Adding external capacity, that is, more hosts to the cluster, is a way of coarsely tuning the processing platform to the application. Expanding internally, such as adding CPUs to an existing multiprocessor, allows you to fine tune the cluster platform.

In time, another way of tuning the platform might be to use different processing technologies. That is, mixing CPU types across the cluster nodes. For the time being, server–based clustering is still too immature for this to be practical and implementable, much less supportable.

9.4. Cluster Networking

Retrofitting a cluster around an existing server and its applications also introduces some networking requirements that previously did not exist. It is likely that the present method of operation contains two of the three network functional areas described in Chapter 12, "Cluster-Friendly Networking." These three functional areas are client to cluster, cluster host to external storage device, and cluster host to cluster host.

9.4.1. Client to Cluster

Any server must somehow be connected to the users. Thus, the first network functional area, client to cluster, is already present. Before the cluster is developed, this area should be examined to determine if it will withstand the projected increased volume. It is likely that much, if not all, of the network connecting clients to the cluster will also be used to transport data from other applications, possibly even from the World Wide Web and multimedia communications. It is worthwhile to investigate this aspect of the cluster's network infrastructure to ensure that it would continue to support the clustered application processing as it scales upwards.

9.4.2. Cluster Host to External Storage Device

Depending on the server's configuration, the second network functional area, cluster host to external storage device, may also exist. If the cluster being developed is a shared nothing cluster, then nothing needs to be done, except for ensuring that each node in the cluster has its own connectivity to all external storage devices.

If, however, the cluster is to be a shared disk cluster, then something must be done to extend this network functional area. There are two possible ways to extend connectivity to external storage devices throughout a cluster. The first way is to use a single, robust bus technology to interconnect all hosts to their shared storage devices. This approach is illustrated in Figure 9.4. It is only viable in a shared disk cluster configuration.

The second way is to deploy fully separate and redundant buses. This topology is illustrated in Figure 9.5. Redundant buses are most useful in fail-over clusters that do not support a common application.

Figure 9.4.
*Extending
connectivity to
shared storage
devices.*

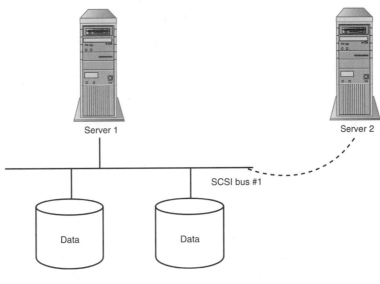

Figure 9.5.
*Fail-over
connectivity to
shared storage
devices.*

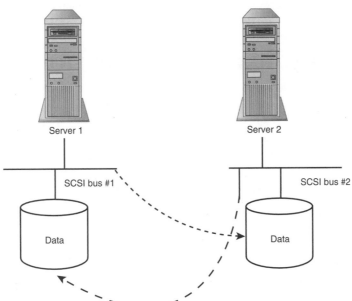

9.4.3. Cluster Host to Cluster Host

The functional area that would likely have to be added as the cluster is built is the cluster host to cluster host networking. This network will be responsible for transporting the cluster management protocols. Functions like "heartbeats" (or status), fail-overs, and load balancing all require intracluster communications. The efficiency with which this network supports these functions directly determines the efficiency of the entire cluster. It is in your best interest to design and implement the most robust network technologies possible for this area.

Attributes to look for in a network technology are the following:

- Fast transmission rate, preferably 100Mbps or higher

- Low latency Layer 2 protocol

- Well-regulated media access methodology

- Robust and error-free transmission media

- Network interface cards (NICs) that are supported by the clustered hosts

9.5. Application Migration Issues

Having determined the appropriate physical composition of your cluster, it is now time to return to the application layer. Migrating the application itself to a cluster requires far more than simply porting the code to a clustered configuration. It is highly unlikely, for example, that an existing server-based application will be able to communicate with a cluster-aware operating system via a cluster management *Application Programming Interface* (API). Any attempt to port an application that is not cluster-aware to a cluster will likely result in less than complete success.

Typical fail-over errors are

- The inability of the application to respond to the operating system's requests to cease operations prior to the fail-over

- The inability of the operating system to replicate the application's state and data to the fail-over node

Typical errors in a dynamic load-balancing cluster are

- Application-level errors caused by an inability to cope with the operating system's attempt to dynamically balance load

- Data corruption

Thus, a decision must be made about whether the application should be re-written or replaced with a newer, cluster-aware application. If these potential errors are deemed acceptable, then existing applications may be clustered post haste!

If the clustered application is a commercially available software package, chances are that it will be made cluster-aware in the not too distant future. You might want to verify roll-out schedules with your software vendors.

If the clustered application is homegrown, the issues become more complicated. The first thing that you will need to determine is whether or not the application is suited for clustering.

If the application is designed for parallel execution, the next hurdle is technical expertise. It is highly unlikely that in-house developers will have the necessary expertise to begin developing cluster-aware applications. They will either have to be trained, or augmented with new hires or temporary workers who are already trained.

Perhaps the greatest hurdle facing anyone attempting to custom develop a cluster-aware application is which API to use. In this age of open computing, openness has become the front door to propriety. Once inside, you will find yourself (again) locked into a single vendor because of the desirability of certain features that are not part of the open standard technology set that you selected. APIs will become the battleground over which "open" cluster management software wars will be fought in the future. Select your API carefully! You'll probably have to live with the choice for a long time.

9.6. Retro-Clustering Checklist

If you are still determined to retro-cluster, the following checklist should help you get started.

Cluster Design
    Identify performance deficiencies
    Assess need to cluster versus performance deficiencies
    Computing technology upgrade or migration
    Cluster size (maximum, minimum, or moderate density)
    Cluster topology (shared disk, shared nothing, complex)
    Cluster functionality (availability, scalability, load balancing, combination)

Cluster Technologies
    Operating system selection (must be cluster-aware)
    Cluster-aware middlewares
    Cluster management software selection
    API selection

Cluster Networking
     Viability of client to cluster networking
     Viability of cluster host to storage device network
     Technology selection for intracluster communications
     I/O model (NORMA, NUMA, ccNUMA)

Application
     Application suited for parallel execution
     Application type suited for clustering
     Load balancing (static, dynamic, or none)
     Rewrite or replace application for cluster-awareness

9.7. Summary

Retro-clustering may appear to be a "no-brainer" on the surface. However, it is a complicated and potentially dangerous undertaking that shouldn't be taken lightly. It requires far more than simply installing cluster management software on a pair of servers.

When it's properly planned and executed, clustering NT servers and their applications, can rejuvenate the old promise of distributed computing. From an application perspective, well-constructed clusters will blur the distinctions between the low-end and mid-range computing architectures.

Poorly planned and executed clusters, however, will create an uncomfortable and untenable situation from which the best way out is a quick change of scenery.

The checklist provided in this section isn't intended to be an exhaustively complete, step-by-step process. Rather, it is intended to stimulate thought every step of the way through the retro-clustering process.

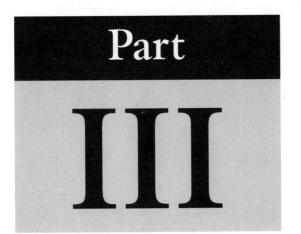

Part

III

Implemen-
tation Issues

Chapter

10

Programming for Parallel Environments

Parallel computing environments, regardless of whether they are internal, external, or both, are very different from uniprocessing environments. The fundamental difference is that in a uniprocessor, there is no competition for system resources. Consequently, programming is greatly simplified.

In a parallel processing environment, application programmers must anticipate and provide for the inherent competition for system resources. This chapter examines the differences between uniprocessors, parallel processors, and the distributed parallelism of a cluster. This is the context for identifying the challenges that await anyone attempting either to develop a new cluster-aware application, or to port an existing application to a clustered platform.

10.1. What's a "Parallel Environment"?

All computers process instructions in one of two ways—either in serial or in parallel. Serial processing is the sequential processing of instructions, one at a time. Parallel processing is the simultaneous processing of more than one instruction. This distinction holds tremendous implications for program execution and, therefore, design. Proper programming for parallel environments requires you to have an understanding of those environments.

10.1.1. Serial Processing

Computers that process instructions serially usually do so for lack of alternatives. For example, uniprocessors are a class of computers with a relatively simple architecture and one central processing unit (CPU). In addition to its single CPU, a uniprocessor also features input/output (I/O), RAM, and a system bus. This architecture requires that all instructions be processed serially: each one must finish processing before the next one can begin. It has only one CPU, so all instructions must be processed one at a time. Figure 10.1 illustrates this serial sequencing.

Developing programs for serial execution is fairly straightforward. There is no need to break the program down into sub-tasks that can be processed independently of each other: With certain exceptions for multitasking, they will execute serially anyway.

Figure 10.1.
*Serially
processing
instructions.*

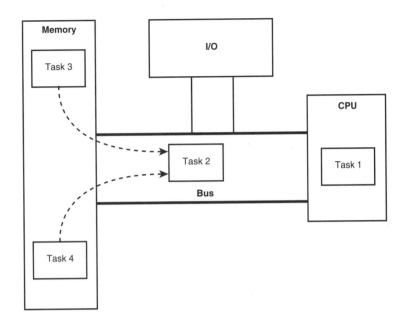

10.1.2. Parallel Processing

Parallel computing is the integration of multiple CPUs in a single "system". As you will see later in this chapter, this definition is not as cut and dry as it might appear. A system can be either completely self-contained, or it can be externally distributed among multiple computers. In either case, having more than one CPU enables the system to process multiple instructions concurrently (in parallel). In addition to being either internal or external, parallelism can be either symmetric or asymmetric.

An asymmetric parallel processing architecture can take many forms. The example presented in Figure 10.2 does not qualify as a symmetric architecture because only one of the CPUs can perform I/O functions.

Though one could argue that the architecture presented in Figure 10.3 appears symmetric, it is not. It contains a visually balanced, hence "symmetric," design by virtue of having private memory available to each processor. This is not, however, a symmetric architecture. Symmetry is determined from the perspective of the processor. If the rest of the system looks exactly the same from the perspective of each of the processors, then the system is symmetric. The architecture in 10.3 is not symmetric because each CPU has its own private memory. Consequently, functional symmetry is compromised although visual symmetry is preserved.

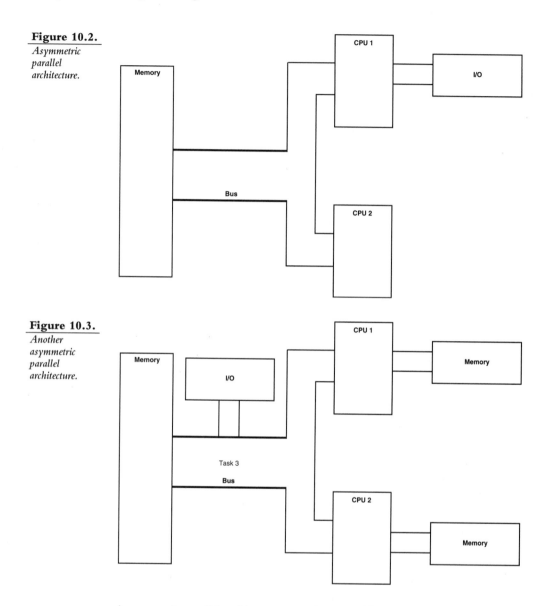

Figure 10.2.

Asymmetric parallel architecture.

Figure 10.3.

Another asymmetric parallel architecture.

A symmetric parallel architecture contains several key attributes. First, obviously, it must contain more than one CPU. Second, all other system-level components must be shared by all CPUs. This enables the third attribute: each CPU must be completely *fungible*. That is, each of them must be equally capable of the following:

- Accessing all RAM and storage addresses

- Performing all I/O functions

- Processing any instruction

A symmetric parallel processing architecture can have from two to hundreds of processors. Its architecture, however, does not change. Any processor is capable of performing any task. An example of a symmetric parallel architecture is presented in Figure 10.4.

Figure 10.4.
Symmetric parallel architecture.

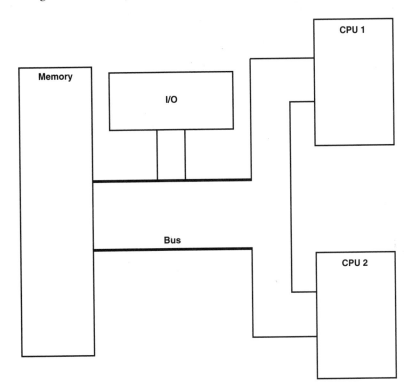

A symmetric, parallel architecture is more commonly referred to as a Symmetric Multiprocessor (SMP). In an SMP, the operating system is "aware" of the multiple processors and automatically distributes tasks to them. If one of them fails, the operating system should be able to detect the failure and not direct any other tasks to that processor. All CPUs share common memory, disk, I/O, and other hardware resources. These represent several *single points of failure* (SPOF). If any of these shared resources fail, the entire system is affected and may fail completely. This limitation can be overcome by developing clusters of SMPs.

In both symmetric and asymmetric parallel architectures, parallel processors can be purchased with as few as two, or as many as hundreds of CPUs in a single machine. These processors can also be any brand, and either Reduced Instruction Set Computer (RISC) chips, or Complex Instruction Set Computer (CISC) chips. Regardless of their size or type, the CPUs work in parallel to process instructions. This requires programs to be developed specifically for concurrent, or parallel, execution of instructions. Developing applications for parallel execution requires the use of a programming model that enables the application to benefit from the capabilities of its environment.

10.2. Programming Models

A programming model, for the purposes of this book, is a computer's architecture as perceived by an application. It is important to note that operating systems and high-level programming languages shield the application from much of the physical platform. This shielding effectively uncouples the hardware from the application software and is one of the hallmarks of open computing.

Depending on how the cluster is constructed and what functions it provides, one of two programming models can be used: the *symmetric multiprocessing* model and the *message-passing* model.

10.2.1. Symmetric Multiprocessing Model

The model used for developing applications for execution in a symmetric multiprocessing environment is known as multiprogramming. Multiprogramming is an old concept. Early multiprogrammed applications took advantage of the differences in speeds at which I/O and the processor operate. While one instruction was waiting for its I/O request to be fulfilled, thousands, if not millions, of other instructions could be executed by the same processor! Rather than waste CPU cycles, the waiting instruction is cached in memory, and additional instructions are processed. Once the original instruction's I/O request is fulfilled, it is taken out of memory and continues its operation. Today, this is more commonly referred to as *multitasking*.

> **NOTE**   A similar concept is known as *multithreading*. Multithreading enables two or more different instructions from the same application to execute concurrently on the same CPU. This is possible because of the speed mismatches that exist between the CPU, memory, and the various I/O devices. Essentially, while one program's instruction is awaiting the completion of an I/O request, it is preempted by an instruction from the other program.

In a symmetric multiprocessing environment, multitasking is still a highly desirable feature. It maximizes the performance of any CPU. However, an additional layer of complexity is added by the presence of multiple CPUs. Taking full advantage of each processor in a multiprocessor requires the operating system to monitor the status of each instruction executing, waiting to be executed, or waiting for I/O requests to be fulfilled.

Beyond the operating system, the application itself must be developed using a multiprogramming method that enables it to be processed in parallel. Multiprogramming techniques focus on uncoupling the serial nature of instructions to be executed, breaking them into independent tasks. This saves time because several of them can be run simultaneously. Control within each application must be able to be passed to these different parts of the application. This is the essence of multiprogramming.

Of course, there will be tasks that are directly related to other tasks immediately following or preceding them. Running these out of sequence can have disastrous results for the application's users.

When they're properly designed, multiprogrammed applications run significantly faster than old applications "ported" to a parallel computer. The nonlinear tasks can be distributed among the CPUs by the operating system. Providing operating system-level support for multitasking provides even more efficient processing in a multiprocessor.

Using a multiprogramming technique enables jobs that would have to be run as separate jobs on a serial processor to run as a single job on a multiprocessor. Applications that are written for serial processing on a uniprocessor will not benefit much, if at all, from a multiprocessing platform.

Figure 10.5 demonstrates the operating system distributing an application's tasks to its CPUs. Multiprogramming is invaluable for expediting application processing, provided that the application resides and executes within the confines of a single computer system.

Figure 10.5.

Parallel processing in a symmetric multiprocessing computer.

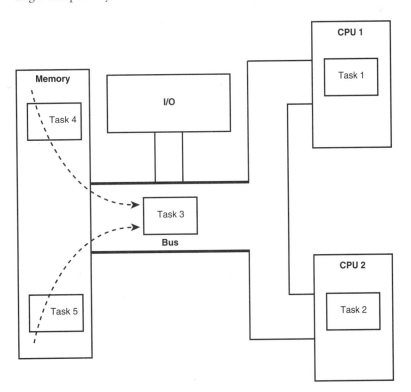

10.2.2. Message-Passing Model

Message-passing, unlike the previous multiprogramming model, assumes that the data does not reside within a single computer system. Rather, the data is distributed among two or more completely separate machines, each with its own data storage facilities. Therefore, to obtain the necessary data, messages must be transmitted from computer to computer.

Figure 10.6 illustrates the passing of a message to another computer. This message requests the receiving host to fulfill an I/O operation on the originator's behalf.

Figure 10.6.

Message-passing in a shared nothing cluster.

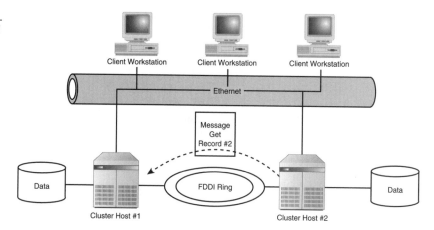

This model brings with it some unavoidable quandaries. First, shipping I/O requests to external hosts to access the distributed data requires that there be some mechanism that can be used to track the locations of data. Second, and more seriously, shipping I/O requests is an extremely time-consuming activity. I/O is already the most expensive function within a computer because of the differences in speed between the CPU and sundry I/O devices. Distributing the recipient of the I/O request requires an even slower network than computers use internally.

Typically, a computer would use a fairly robust bus to interconnect its system resources. Output devices like disks are no exception, and having them in close proximity allows very high speed, but very short distance, buses to be used. As fast as these buses are, CPUs are much faster—so much so that it makes sense to move any instructions that are awaiting fulfillment of an I/O request to memory and start working on the next instruction(s).

Distributing data across multiple external hosts usually necessitates using an even slower network: a local area network (LAN). LANs tend to operate at ten, or maybe even one hundred, megabits per second. This is standing still in comparison to the transmission rates of some internal computer buses. Predictably, the application that generated the I/O request will experience some significant performance degradation as a result of this extremely time-consuming activity.

To make matters worse, a message passed to another system can be subject to the vicissitudes of local area networking. Depending on the type of network in use, collisions can occur that can destroy the request. Alternatively, it can take quite a few milliseconds to gain permission to begin transmitting the message on the LAN.

At this point, a fair question to ask is "Why bother?" For many applications, particularly those with stringent performance requirements (like *online transaction processing* (OLTP) systems), shipping I/O might be unacceptable. Still, there are some benefits to be gained.

Distributing data across multiple, fully redundant computer systems eliminates the fundamental vulnerability of parallel and uniprocessors. All the single points of failure are effectively eliminated through distributed redundancy. This breeds a host of other logistical issues that must be resolved. An SMP needs to be concerned with locking access to records so that undesirable and counterproductive competition from multiple CPUs is eliminated, but a series of loosely coupled hosts (that is, a cluster) that shares the data and processing load for a single application severely aggravates that problem.

10.2.3. Multiprocessor Operating Systems

The key to success in a multiprocessor environment is the operating system. The operating system is responsible for insulating the application software from the physical platforms. If it were not capable of this, applications couldn't be ported from one platform to another. They might not even be portable from one brand of hardware to another.

Implicit in this notion is that the operating system "hides" the hardware from the application. The application doesn't know, nor does it need to know, about how much memory is available, or how many processors exist in the computer it runs on, and so on. The operating system automatically provides whatever functions are necessary to execute the application's instructions within the context of the physical platform. Typically, global queuing is used to buffer much of what would otherwise be chaotic data transfer within the computer. Queues are used to buffer instructions that are waiting for an I/O request to complete, or are waiting their turn for processing, or are waiting for a file to be unlocked for them, and so on. These functions are essential to the success of a multiprocessor. If they are not provided by the operating system, the multiprocessor would not operate efficiently.

Therefore, for an application to execute successfully in a multiprocessor environment, it must have an operating system that is intrinsically designed for multiprocessing.

Figure 10.7 shows a typical small SMP, with two CPUs sharing common I/O, RAM, and system bus. As illustrated, an application written for serial processing must be processed by the same CPU, regardless of whether the system and operating system are capable of parallel execution.

Figure 10.7.
Serial processing in a symmetric multiprocessing computer.

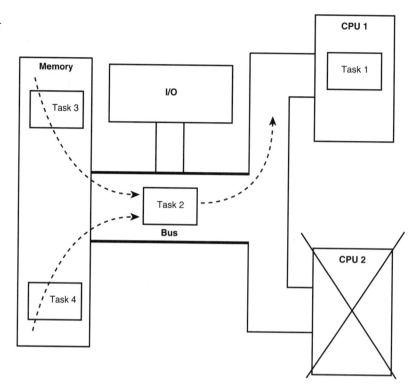

An application's failure to benefit from a multiprocessing platform is a relatively benign failure. A more serious side effect of implementing a serial processing application on a parallel, multiprocessing platform is abnormal termination of the application's processing. An application designed to execute serially might find its instructions being spread across multiple CPUs in a multiprocessor by the operating system. If its instructions are parsed out to multiple CPUs, the application might "bomb out" if it does not know how to re-integrate the output of instructions processed in parallel. This can result in the abnormal termination of the application because the operating system's actions will be interpreted as an error for which no contingency has been defined.

10.2.4. Communal Data Access

Parallel operating environments, regardless of type, present a fundamental issue that must be resolved: communal data access. Uniprocessors don't have this issue. There is only one CPU, so there is no competition for a common data set. In parallel environments, there are multiple CPUs competing for access to a common set of data. This creates the need to manage access to files.

Figure 10.8 illustrates a two-CPU SMP that uses a *database management system* (DBMS) to regulate access to data. The DBMS uses a technique known as *lock*ing to prevent CPUs from accessing data that is already being modified by another CPU. Only unlocked records can be accessed and modified.

Figure 10.8.
The database management system "locks" records that are in use.

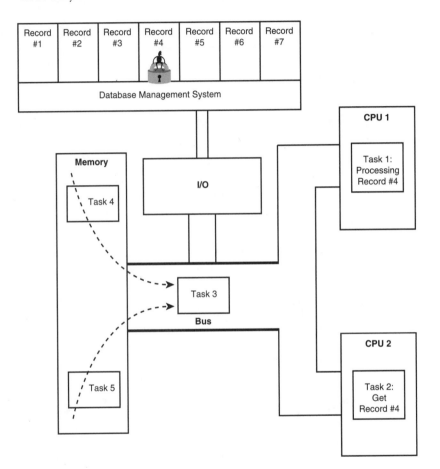

If a CPU receives an instruction needing data that is already locked, that instruction is typically buffered until the needed data is unlocked. Then the buffered instruction is sent back to the CPU for completion.

Failure to implement a mechanism to regulate access to data in a parallel environment can have disastrous results. At the least, the data will quickly become corrupted and unreliable. At the worst, the application can unexpectedly terminate if it can't resolve the conflict for data access.

10.3. Internally Parallel versus Clustered Parallel Processing

There is a strong correlation between the relative complexity of an SMP compared to a uniprocessor, and the relative complexity of a cluster compared to an SMP. Clusters, even those developed on uniprocessing platforms, are a loosely coupled, external form of parallelism. Thus, all the issues that are associated with internal parallel processing apply to clusters.

10.3.1. Programming Models

Depending on the physical platform on which a cluster is implemented, as many as three different programming models can be used. One that is pervasive among uniprocessors is the Von Neumann model. The symmetric multiprocessing model can also be used (either in lieu of or in addition to the Von Neumann model) in a cluster that mixes uniprocessors and multiprocessors.

Because they are externally parallel processing environments, clusters require some form of communication to coordinate activities across the clustered machines. This in turn requires that the message-passing model be present.

Regardless of the model chosen, it is imperative that applications use industry standard application programming interfaces. Otherwise, the cluster will pay the consequences. These can range from it becoming a proprietary kludge that is onerous to maintain, to a failure to benefit from the full functionality of the cluster's management features.

10.3.2. Multiprocessor Operating Systems

As was true with internally parallel systems, one of the keys to success is the operating system. It is absolutely essential to have a cluster-aware operating system. Microsoft's NT Server is being updated to provide cluster-awareness. This refresh might well launch a new client/server revolution by providing highly desirable functionality in a relatively low-cost, easy-to-administer platform.

Depending on the type of cluster, additional software might be required to perform some of the highly specialized cluster management tasks. Several network operating system vendors are already rushing to bundle this level of support into their products, so it is likely that this will not be an issue for long.

The cluster-aware operating system and cluster management software should be capable of hiding the cluster from the application. This does not mean that the application should not be aware of the cluster. Much like the serial program that can successfully execute on a parallel platform, applications that are not cluster-aware can execute with an equivalent degree of success on a clustered platform.

10.3.3. Cluster Management Software

Cluster management software resides between the clustered application and the clusters' operating systems. It is a utility that provides the benefits of the cluster like fail-over and scalable growth. This software has to use APIs to communicate with the applications it supports.

Some more common cluster management features are continuous monitoring of, and load balancing between, clustered neighbors, varying degrees of automated recovery from failures, replication of states of failed machines, and so on.

Because some operating system vendors are trying to incorporate cluster management support into their products, it is likely that these will be fairly general offerings. Additional functionality will likely continue to be available through application-level software packages that focus on very specific market niches.

10.3.4. Communal Data Access

A cluster has all the same problems as an internally parallel processor when it comes to sharing access to data, and then some! Clusters developed on SMPs must worry about data sharing on two levels. First, access must be regulated internally in each SMP, and then coordinated externally between all the SMPs in the cluster.

Given the tremendous speed mismatch between I/O and CPUs, coordinating the sharing of common data becomes a performance bottleneck that requires some innovative thinking to resolve. One approach might be to develop an asymmetric cluster—a cluster in which only one host controls data access. All the other hosts would be responsible for user interface and application processing. All requests for I/O would have to be shipped to the I/O controlling host. Although this resolves the complexities of sharing data, it also imposes performance penalties. The extent of these penalties, and whether or not they are acceptable, will vary by application and cluster platform.

10.4. What Does All This Mean?

Building successful clusters requires far more than simply purchasing a couple of servers, grafting on the appropriate cluster management software, and porting an application over to this new cluster. Just as operating systems that are not SMP-aware cannot use the power of that platform, operating systems and applications that are not cluster-aware will not be able to use the capabilities that the cluster would otherwise afford.

Programming for Parallel
Environments

Microsoft is already developing a cluster-aware version of its Windows NT Server operating system. NT will also have cluster management functions bundled in, as well as at least a subset of the proposed industry standard cluster APIs. This is the easy part.

The difficulty is in developing cluster-aware applications! Existing applications might run nicely on whatever platform you've selected for your cluster. That is, they would run nicely until they needed (or the operating system tried to use) a cluster service. For example, consider a cluster of three SMPs developed for fail-over protection of a mission critical application.

Because they're part of a fail-over system, these three machines might well support three completely unrelated applications. They share disks and have adequate spare capacity to support the load of either of the other two applications. When one of the servers fails, everyone expects that the fail-over will take place automatically. Because of the shared disks, even data and application replication isn't an issue. So where's the problem?

The problem is that, unless the applications are cluster-aware, the operating system will be unable to conduct a graceful shutdown and transfer of control to the backup server. In addition, the operating system won't be able to replicate the stricken server's state. Thus, although the transition will occur, any processing in the failed server will be lost. The fail-over won't be smooth; it will be quite noticeable to all current users.

The applications simply won't understand any of the cluster services and will not respond to shutdown and state replication attempts by the operating system/cluster management software.

The goal of any cluster should be the absolute transparency of that cluster's particular features to the applications and their users. Using a cluster-aware operating system like Windows NT Server is only the first step in developing this transparency. The next essential step is developing, or using, applications that are cluster-aware, too.

10.4.1. Developing Cluster-based Applications

Developing a cluster-based application is not a trivial task. Many variables must be carefully balanced to ensure that the migrated application performs as expected in its new environment. For example, the processing platform and its operating system are the logical candidates to evaluate first. Once the platform is established, other variables (like which brand of cluster management software and application programming interfaces) must be considered.

The next important decision is about the physical cluster topology. This must be established before you can consider the local area networks, wide area networks, and even the cluster area networks that will be implemented.

Once the physical platform is selected, and the necessary topology developed, the application itself must be made as acutely aware of the cluster and its functions as possible. This can be quite challenging if the application is homegrown. This can also be an exercise in patience (or futility) if the application is vendor-provided.

The challenge, especially in this nascent stage of this technique's life, is to maintain as open a platform as possible. Given the proliferation of cluster product and API announcements, it might not be feasible to develop a cluster-aware application without tying it to a single vendor's products.

10.4.2. Migrating Existing Applications to a Cluster

Migrating an existing application to a cluster, serial or parallel, is even worse. As happens with the development of a new cluster, there are certain decisions that must be made regarding the cluster's physical platform, management software, supported APIs, and physical topologies. There is no escaping these basic decisions.

A far greater challenge is retrofitting an existing application with cluster awareness. If the application was homegrown, this might require ripping open its source code in a major redevelopment effort. This rework can be particularly acute if the application was previously executed serially on a uniprocessor!

Shrink-wrapped applications, however, might be somewhat easier to migrate. If the vendor has stated its intention of supporting clusters, and it provides maintenance upgrades, cluster-awareness might be a maintenance release away. Of course, this is the idyllic scenario. It is more likely that the vendors either will not commit to supporting cluster awareness quickly, or that the upgrade won't be as trivial as a maintenance patch.

Other problems to watch for with migrating commercial application software to clusters are compatibility with the physical platform, cluster management software, and APIs that you've implemented on your cluster. Selecting Windows NT Server as your cluster's operating system does not necessarily dictate your choices in this arena. Many vendors are developing competitive products for the NT Server operating system.

In short, there are some significant issues to consider before migrating existing applications to clusters. The right answer might well be either waiting until the technologies stabilize and industry standards emerge, or simply not porting pre-existing applications to clusters. Instead, whenever possible, applications you select should be designed and developed to be cluster-aware from the start.

Only if you are willing to accept the limited subset of a cluster's functionality will porting cluster-unaware applications to a clustered architecture be acceptable.

10.5. Summary

Programming for parallel environments, whether clustered or self-contained, poses some interesting challenges. To overcome them you should understand the capabilities and potential hazards of the platform relative to the performance requirements of the application. This chapter introduced you to some of the pertinent issues that face the programmer in a parallel environment.

The remaining chapters of this book build on the basic concepts presented in this chapter. They delve into more of the complexities of cluster-aware applications and present ways to maximize the performance of your clustered application. Chapters 11, "Network-Friendly Clustering," and 12, "Cluster-Friendly Networking," continue to develop your command of the fundamental issues by exploring the interrelationships between the cluster infrastructure and application performance. Chapter 9, "Clustering an Existing NT Server/Application," and Chapter 8, "Building a New NT Cluster," present approaches that can be used when preparing to cluster an application.

Chapter

11

Network-Friendly Clustering

Networking is an integral part of any cluster and a major factor in its aggregate performance. Unfortunately, networking is almost always an afterthought in application development, if it is considered at all.

This chapter explores the significance of effective bandwidth utilization. Specific recommendations are made for improving the overall performance of clusters and their applications, recognizing that bandwidth utilization should be a fundamental part of the application's design.

11.1. Overview

Business processes are becoming increasingly dependent on information technology. Information technology, in turn, is becoming increasingly dependent on networking. Paradoxically, current application and system design methodologies, whether structured, client/server, or object-oriented, typically treat network design as an afterthought. The network is designed *after* the application and its platform have been designed.

This demonstrates and reinforces an increasingly problematic separation of data networking skills and application design/development skills at a time when the technology is requiring their integration. Worse, it fails to optimize the performance of applications created in this manner because it excludes the network from the application design stage. This stage determines the appropriate balance between resources and costs that will satisfy user requirements.

Data networking is an integral component of the platform that applications run on. As such, it should be an integral part of the application design and development processes. This will enable a more efficient use of the existing infrastructure, forestall the need to add capacity, and increase customer satisfaction with finished applications.

11.1.1. Network-centricity

The new distributed computing paradigm is called *network-centric* computing. This describes the "anytime, anywhere" access to information in a seamless, transparent, and real-time manner. The locations of processors, or clusters, are immaterial. Their actual location is subordinated by the ubiquity and performance of the network. Network-centricity is presented, conceptually, in Figure 11.1.

Figure 11.1.

The conceptual perspective of network-centricity.

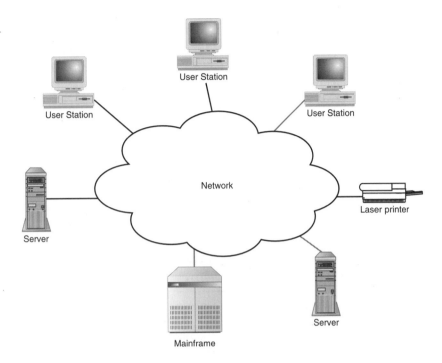

Many factors contribute to this ever increasing reliance on network bandwidth. These include the following:

■ The convergence of many network protocols onto a single enterprise-level network—for example, migration of "legacy" networks to IP.

■ The technological advances in network technology, including LAN hardware and protocols, as well as WANs, that increase the functionality and performance of networks.

■ The technological advances in computing hardware and software that require network connectivity—for example, collaborative groupware, multimedia MIME types and applications, and distributed server-grade clusters.

■ The increasing richness of network-attached resources.

This last item is, perhaps, the most compelling evidence of the ubiquity of the network-centric paradigm. The commercialization of the Internet, mass deployments of IP-based intranets, and, now, the development of semiprivate extranets are all undeniable proof that network-centricity is here to stay!

Network-Friendly Clustering

11.1.2. The Language Barrier

One of the key barriers to achieving optimal cluster performance, or any network-centric application, is overcoming the language barrier that divides two communities of information technologists. This barrier arises from the two communities' separation by a common protocol stack, as shown in Figure 11.2. The Open Systems Interconnection (OSI) Reference Model can be used to dramatize this point.

Figure 11.2.
The Open Systems Interconnection Reference Model.

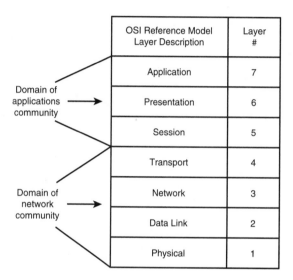

OSI Reference Model Layer Description	Layer #
Application	7
Presentation	6
Session	5
Transport	4
Network	3
Data Link	2
Physical	1

Domain of applications community →

Domain of network community →

Although the OSI protocol has fallen into disuse, its reference model continues to serve admirably as a means of decomposing an otherwise complex topic into more understandable components.

Of the two communities, one group (the networkers) lives and breathes at the bottom-most layers of the stack: the physical, data link, and network (or Internet) layers. They might even venture so far as the transport layer, but no farther.

The development community preoccupies itself with the top-most layer: the application layer. This layer is abstracted in the sense that operating systems, application programming interfaces, and open standard communications protocols insulate applications from hardware-level details.

In one camp are the system analysts, developers, and project leaders. This community thinks in terms of bytes, fields, records, files, databases, and so on. To them, the network is a pipe that they can funnel these structures into for safe passage to their destinations. Figure 11.3 illustrates this perspective.

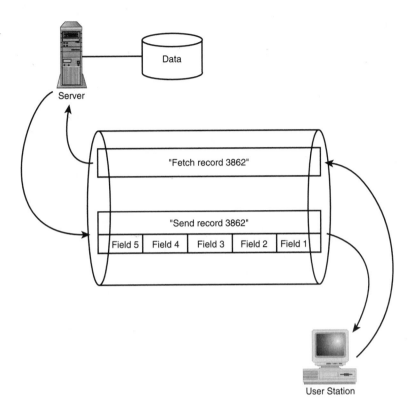

Figure 11.3.
The applications perspective.

In the other camp are the data network technologists. This community thinks in *octets*. Octets are simply data structures that contain eight bits. No distinction is made between data, instructions, check point records, or anything else that traverses the network in this structure. All the aforementioned structures become a homogeneous part of the same octet-oriented bit stream. Figure 11.4 demonstrates this bit stream perspective.

Realizing that not everyone in the networking community is intimately familiar with the hardware layer, Figure 11.5 demonstrates the layer 2, or link layer, perspective. This perspective provides recognizable details of the layers 2, 3, and 4 transport mechanisms. Consequently, it is more representative of the context within which the network community operates. The network frames used in Figure 11.5 are typical—that is, they do not represent any specific LAN technology. Rather, they include familiar elements of the IEEE 802 family of specifications.

Network-Friendly Clustering

Figure 11.4.
The bit stream, or layer 1 perspective.

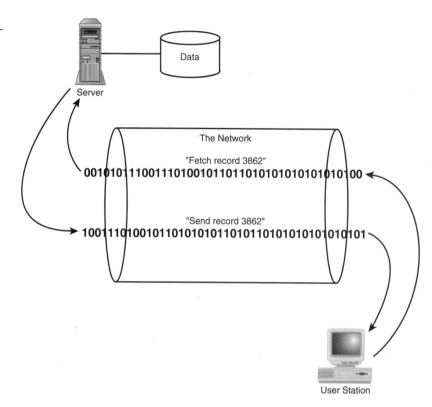

Figure 11.5.
The layer 2 perspective.

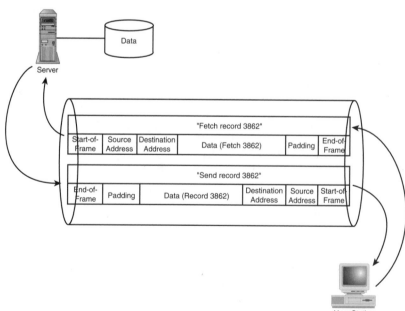

Although the differences between the layers 1 and 2 perspective are fairly extreme, the gap between the layers 2 and 7 perspectives remains substantial. At layer 7, the more complex data structures are obvious and useful. These structures can be shipped fairly transparently using the appropriate network utility and addressing.

At layer 2, however, the overheads of layers 2, 3, and 4 are more accessible. The data structures have been encapsulated into data fields of either fixed or varying lengths. They are no longer visible, or material. Where individual records stop or start, or even what they contain, is of no consequence to the protocols in these layers.

These figures demonstrate the separation of data networking skills and application development skills. This separation comes at a time when the network-centrism is driving the integration of both skill sets. Typically, however, network engineers and designers are usually handed a complete application design and asked to develop a network that will support it. This should come as no surprise. All application design methodologies, whether structured, client/server, or object-oriented, call for network design that provides connectivity after the application has been designed.

11.1.3. The History

The reasons for these behaviors are fairly simple. Before PC networks and client/server architecture came into vogue, there were fairly rigid boundaries between the technical skill sets. Companies retained staffs of programmers, either through contracts or as salaried employees. Among this universe were team leaders responsible for coordinating design and development activities. In this era of proprietary hardware, expertise on that hardware could be obtained free of charge from the hardware vendors.

Networks were simple. After the platform was selected, and applications were designed, the network vendor was given the system's requirements. They then designed the network. This was an apparently easy task: bandwidth was available only in fixed increments. If a 9.6-*Kbps* (thousands of bits per second) circuit was too small, then a 56-Kbps circuit was prescribed. If this wasn't enough, the next size up was a T1 that offered 1.544 *Mbps* (millions of bits per second) on a single circuit.

Local Area Networks (LANs) followed this pattern. Initially, LANs were available only in 1-Mbps Ethernet or 4-Mbps Token Ring formats. In time, these were supplanted by 11-Mbps Ethernet or 16-Mbps Token Ring products. If these became inadequate, bridges and routers were often used to segment the LAN into smaller components. Breaking the LAN into smaller interconnected pieces created a theoretical improvement in performance by reducing the number of users sharing the bandwidth.

Network-Friendly Clustering

These "one size fits many" selections reinforced the notion that networking wasn't a critical factor in the design of a new application. Once the network was in place, the costs of the network (purchase, installation, and recurring facilities charges) were regarded as sunk costs. The money was already spent or, at least, budgeted to be spent. Therefore, spare bandwidth was "free" to new users and applications, provided they didn't overrun the capacity of the existing network's components.

11.1.4. The Not-Too-Distant Future

The fact that Information Technology (IT) is being used to drive a competitive advantage in the marketplace today heightens the importance of using it efficiently and effectively. As computing continues its move towards network-centrism, the business risks of inefficient network usage will increase exponentially.

In the not-too-distant future, developing applications that are anything less than optimal in their design and execution will be a competitive disadvantage. This is especially true with respect to network bandwidth utilization. Inefficiencies designed into clusters, and other network-centric applications, are multiplied by the expected lifespan of the application, the frequency of its use, and its network intensity. Under the right circumstances, even minor inefficiencies can quickly demonstrate painful results.

Given this, it is time to accept that data networking is an integral component of the platform that applications run on. As such, it can no longer be relegated to a back-end function in application design and development processes.

Data communications and networking must be addressed as part of the complete end-to-end system and not used to link together already defined components. Treating them as integral parts of the cluster and application will enable the design team to distinguish between necessary and unnecessary network traffic. Keeping network traffic to a minimum will enable existing network resources to more effectively service the necessary traffic. This might even forestall the need to add capacity to the network infrastructure, and probably even improve the customer's perception of the cluster's overall performance.

11.2. Network Performance Definitions

Before any rational exploration of optimizing total system performance can begin, it is necessary to define *performance*.

The performance of a network can be measured in a wide variety of ways. Specific metrics, such as round-trip time, utilization rates, transmission rates, and so on, have been developed. Despite this variety of metrics, there are three that should be considered critical to success during application design. These three are

- Transmission time

- Response time

- Network latency

The users' requirements will determine which of these are appropriate measurements of the cluster's end-to-end performance. Their definitions are presented below.

11.2.1. Transmission Time

Transmission time refers to the total duration of transmission, or the total time on the network. This measurement is usually applied to bulk data transfers. Such transfers are characterized by predominantly "one-way" transmissions between two hosts or between a user and a host.

Because transmission time is an aggregate metric of a network's performance, it is important to understand all the components that can be contributors. As it is only measuring time on the network, factors like the application's execution time, disk latency, I/O, and a cluster's other internal components do not count as part of the transmission time. The clock starts running after the data is put onto the transmission media.

Devices that do contribute to transmission time are all LANs, routers, WAN transmission facilities, and any other transmission devices or facilities that might exist between the transmitting host and its destination.

11.2.2. Response Time

Response time is distinctly a metric of the performance of *on-demand* computing. On-demand computing is characterized by the need for immediate processing at the time of the request. In most cases, some form of response is delivered back to the requester. The "requester" can be either a live user or another application.

In those cases where the requester is a live user, he or she is usually watching the computer's monitor and waiting for the response. Although users cannot assimilate information, or process it, as fast as a computer, they are more demanding because they are impatient. Lengthy response times are a source of aggravation.

Network-Friendly Clustering

The requester can also be another application. Applications—at least in theory—suffer a greater opportunity cost from lengthy response times. This is because they are capable of doing far more "work" than their human counterparts in any given amount of time. Unfortunately, they are currently incapable of complaining. Thus, they suffer in silence.

Regardless of whether the requester is carbon-or silicon-based, response time includes the network's aggregate transmission time, the host's I/O and processing times, and the transmission time back to the requester.

Response time, by this definition, is critical to the success of any system, clustered or otherwise. The greater the response time, the longer the requester is kept either idle or diverted to other tasks. In either event, lengthy response time directly translates into increased processing costs.

The sum of the trade-offs between customer requirements and the performance delivered by each of the cluster's components is critical to the success of the entire cluster. If any one of the cluster's components, including its supporting network, is aggravating response times, the performance of the entire cluster is adversely affected. Given that networks typically deliver only a fraction of the speed with which a computer's internals operate, they will automatically be a constraining factor on response time.

Users will probably not be astute enough to discern which of the components is the source of dissatisfaction. They will simply be dissatisfied with the entire system. Thus, as applications and clusters become more network-centric, the customer's satisfaction with the cluster will increasingly depend on the capability of the networking to deliver the needed performance. Therefore, network design must be incorporated into the overall system design and not relegated to a back-end function.

11.2.3. Latency

Latency is a measure of the waiting time that occurs between the time a device seeks access to a transmission channel and the time that access is actually granted.

This definition implies that very little can be done to alter latency after the network components are purchased. Latency can be used as either an individual component metric, or an aggregate metric of an end-to-end network and cluster configuration.

Regardless of which way it is used, it is important to remember that it is an innate attribute of individual network components. For example, an Ethernet hub can have a fairly high latency because access to the transmission channel is regulated in a rather haphazard, contention-based manner. A switched Ethernet port, however, has a much lower latency for the following two reasons:

- First, the chaotic access method is reduced to a minimum of two devices: the hub port and the device that it connects to the LAN.

- Second, a switch tends to operate at much higher internal speeds than conventional repeaters or bridges.

Both of these characteristics contribute to a switched hub's lower latency compared to a traditional broadcast hub of the same protocol.

The network's link level protocol, too, has much to do with the innate latency of its hardware. Ethernet, continuing with the previous example, uses variable length frames to transport data. Access to the LAN's transmission channel can be increased somewhat if the bulk of the traffic consists of 1500-octet frames. Asynchronous Transfer Mode, the epitome of low latency networking, uses fixed length cells of 53 octets in length. Obviously, if both protocols were implemented in a switch that operated at the same transmission rate, the ATM switch would still have a lower latency because devices seeking access to its transmission channel wouldn't have to wait for up to 1500 octets to breeze past.

Latency requirements are fairly nascent and are often confused with response time. Real-time interactive systems can have stringent response time requirements and no significant latency requirements. Latency requirements are imposed only by time-sensitive applications like live, interactive voice or video conferencing. These applications are radical departures from traditional networked computing applications because they are much more concerned with timeliness of delivery than with the data's integrity on delivery.

The technologies that enable these time-sensitive applications are still emerging. Few, if any, of today's applications have real latency requirements. This definition is included solely to demonstrate that network performance metrics are still emerging and will continue to evolve.

There are different ways to measure network performance. The application design team must understand the customer requirements and then decide what level of network performance is necessary as well as which performance metrics are appropriate. Once this is accomplished, they can begin designing an integrated hardware/software/network clustered system that will optimize aggregate performance and satisfy the customer's requirements.

The next section introduces options for reducing the network intensity of clustered applications. These options are intended to facilitate the optimization of cluster performance.

Network-Friendly Clustering

11.3. Network Intensity

Network intensity is a nonspecific term that describes the total networking requirements of any given network-centric activity or application. It includes

- The amount of bandwidth required relative to the amount of bandwidth available

- The amount of time that this bandwidth is required

- The efficiency of the network protocols used

> **NOTE** Inefficient protocols will have either a lower transmission rate or a greater overhead-to-payload ratio, or they'll simply generate excessive network traffic by being "chatty." Any of these circumstances will increase network intensity by increasing either time on the network or the bandwidth required or both.

- The quantity of network components, both LAN and WAN, for which the bandwidth is required. This includes hubs, routers, switches, and leased transmission facilities.

The most commonly used measurement of network requirements is bandwidth. Bandwidth is typically expressed in either thousands (Kbps), millions (Mbps), or even billions (Gbps) of bits per second. This, however, is only one facet of an application's or system's network intensity. It does not discern how those bits are utilized, over what distance the bandwidth is utilized, or how much of the network's infrastructure is engaged in the transmission. It also does not provide any indication of how well the user's requirements are being met.

Each of the network components listed above has a cost associated with its ownership and operation. These costs, and the performance they purchase, must be included in the economic balancing of cost versus performance that is usually, if only tacitly, considered during an application's design stage. Reducing the network intensity of an application also reduces its hidden operating costs.

11.4. Network Intensity Reduction Techniques

Although applications are becoming more network-intensive, one should recognize that there are still ways to minimize time "on the net." This is done by distinguishing between essential network traffic and avoidable network traffic.

The following suggestions should increase awareness of the types of avoidable network traffic. When implemented, they will reduce the network intensity of applications. Reducing network intensity to its absolute minimum requires a bipartisan effort, so these tips are categorized by IT community. They are targeted at the otherwise separate IT communities of application and network personnel that are being joined at the hip by the network-centric computing paradigm.

11.4.1. Tips for the Layer 7 Crowd

The layer 7, or application, personnel can do much to reduce the network intensity of a clustered application through the design and management of that application.

Clustered application design considerations include the following:

- Bias toward cluster architectures and products that are simultaneously scalable and reliable. Shared disk clusters tend to be limited in both respects.

- Cluster architectures that avoid having to use data lock management tools. Such tools tend to become constraining factors as the cluster's use scales upwards.

- Using geographically dispersed shared nothing clustering as a disaster recovery mechanism only. Do not try to support load balancing of a single application across a WAN.

- Considering that LAN and WAN bandwidth (two of the clustered application's resources, like CPU cycles, memory and disk space) should be balanced against costs to satisfy user requirements.

- Using compression when possible. This is intended primarily for use with time-sensitive and bandwidth-intensive applications. Examples include the transmission of graphic files and either voice or video communications. There is a tradeoff to consider with compression: Compression techniques consume more CPU cycles, so you should consider the balance between bandwidth savings and CPU expense.

- Matching the block sizes used for data transmission to the network. Use large blocks of data for transmission across relatively low-use networks. This improves the payload-to-overhead ratio and helps improve the rate of network utilization. Use small blocks for transmission across heavily trafficked networks that are likely to discard any eligible packets. This minimizes the amount of data that must be retransmitted for any lost packets.

- Trying to minimize the physical network distances designed into applications. Network mileage often varies from geographic distances because networks seldom reflect geography. The dynamic nature of switching might also mean that no reliable way to determine network mileage exists.

Network-Friendly Clustering

Therefore, it is generally wise to consider the networking ramifications when deciding on physical locations for databases, applications, and objects relative to the user's location.

> **NOTE**   Technologies like fiber optic cabling, and products like Frame Relay that feature distance-insensitive pricing, might give the impression that network distances have no impact on system performance. There is, however, a positive correlation between the physical network mileage and the number of components needed to drive the network's bandwidth. This translates directly into network intensity, regardless of the underlying technologies.

- Reducing data redundancy as part of the application design. This reduces the amount of traffic generated across networks for the express purpose of preserving the integrity of data stored in multiple locations.

- Reducing the amount of network traffic by using distributed databases and objects. Placing them close to the customers keeps traffic on networks to a minimum. Tradeoffs between the networking and processing costs of distributing data exist and should be carefully balanced.

- Writing applications using standard APIs. Do not write directly to network protocols. This will facilitate later technology migrations and help to prevent the creation of new legacy networks.

- Reducing the amount of data requested to only what is necessary. Transmission of extraneous data that is of no value to the requester serves only to waste resources.

- Avoiding clustered application designs that require routinely shipping I/O requests to other cluster nodes.

- Bias towards transmitting instructions, not data. This includes

  - Performing table searches and joins on the remote host. Transmit only the minimal and necessary output data back to the local station or server.

  - Making SQL queries as specific as possible. Pull down only the data required rather than the entire table.

  - Not sending complete "screen dumps." Train users to use instruction sets that send data and any commands necessary to build the screen to be displayed on their workstation, rather than sending the entire screen. This reduces the overall traffic load on both the WAN and the LAN. You can use Java, JavaScript, Inferno, or any of the other programming languages that use the browser as a runtime environment.

■ Refreshing only screen display pixels that have changed rather than updating the entire screen display. For video transmissions, MPEG format will automatically do this.

■ Transferring only the data required. Although transferring excessive data might save CPU cycles on the host (because files are not sorted or processed to extract the necessary data), this consumes more bandwidth.

■ Scheduling jobs carefully. Do not build large data transfers into production schedules that coincide with peak interactive usage periods or other sources of large bulk data transfers.

■ Using efficient file transfer software. This efficiency is composed of numerous components, the first of which are "checkpoint records." In the event of a transmission failure, these restart the transmission at the last successful checkpoint rather than at the beginning of the file.

■ Compressing files before transmission. Ideally, the file transfer software will offer user-selectable compression types (string, character, pattern, and so on). Matching the compression type to the characteristics of the data being transmitted can optimize the effects of compression.

■ Scheduling file transfers for times when interactive traffic is not likely.

11.4.2. Tips for the Layers 1–4 Crowd

Network personnel, too, can directly affect the network intensity of a clustered application or system. The following tips present additional techniques for reducing the network intensity of new applications through network design and management techniques.

■ Use *firewalls* to reduce unnecessary incoming traffic originating outside company facilities. This is also an excellent way to maintain the security and integrity of data assets. Firewalls can, and should, discriminate on the basis of network addresses and network protocols to prevent unsecured ingress to the internal WAN and its network-attached resources.

■ Utilize address filtering, activity logs, and so on to ensure that network traffic is limited to legitimate business activities.

■ Implement fully separate, high speed networks in the cluster area network (CAN) role. Do not use those LANs that are used for cluster access for intracluster management functions.

■ Select efficient physical networks and protocols that are well suited to a cluster's network requirements.

Network-Friendly Clustering

- Use a network protocol with flexible size transmission packets for transporting bulk quantities of data blocks.

- Bias against LANs that feature contention-based media access, whenever possible.

- Minimize the number of *hops* that a communications session encounters. This will directly reduce the network intensity.

> **NOTE** A hop is defined as passage through a router (a layer 3 packet forwarding mechanism). Hop counts refer only to the number of routers in a path and ignore the layer 2 switching devices and other transmission facilities that comprise the underlying network fabric. This is because the network fabric is the domain of the commercial service provider. IP tools like ping and tracert are incapable of detecting devices below layer 3. Thus the commercial network fabric remains invisible. Nevertheless, switching devices add milliseconds to the round-trip time of a packet, just like routers do.

- Engineer the network to accommodate peak traffic loads.

- Minimize competition for local area network bandwidth by segmenting the user base. This might include deploying new, high-speed or low-latency network technologies like switching hubs instead of software driven routers.

11.5. Summary

Not all these options for reducing the network intensity of a clustered application are feasible, or even desirable, for all applications. For example, business conditions might force the consolidation of processors into key locations. Distributing processors to a small number of locations that are close to the users, rather than at each user location, offers the opportunity to leverage administrative expertise. Fewer administrators can manage more processors without necessarily causing an unacceptable increase in the network intensity of the application. This example should demonstrate just one of the countless ways that you can balance network intensity against available operational expertise, system resources, and other factors without compromising the effectiveness of the applications.

The goal of developing network-friendly clusters is not to avoid network-intensive applications. The entire industry is moving applications towards network-centric, therefore network-intensive, computing platforms. The goal should be to differentiate between appropriate types of network-intensive activities and unnecessary bandwidth-consuming activities, as dictated by the user's requirements. By restricting network usage to legitimate and necessary traffic, the cluster's network performance will be improved. This will directly translate into an improved customer perception of overall cluster performance. A pleasant side-effect will likely be some measure of cost containment.

The only way to achieve this is to consider network bandwidth as part of the cluster's resources during application design. This creates a wealth of opportunities for increasing overall cluster performance.

Network-Friendly Clustering

Chapter

12

Cluster-Friendly Networking

Network-centricity is the proverbial double-edged sword. As important as it is to develop network-friendly clustered applications, it is equally critical to develop cluster-friendly networks. A cluster-friendly network is one carefully selected to maximize the performance characteristics of your particular clustered application. Taking this a step further, a cluster-friendly network also must be implemented in a way that reinforces the performance requirements of its cluster.

12.1. Cluster-Friendliness

Because interhost communications are an integral part of a cluster's performance, you shouldn't begin developing your cluster-friendly network without a thorough understanding of the cluster's mechanics and its performance requirements. This understanding forms the context for examining the potential of the various network technologies' performance specifications. If you fail to use the right networking tool for the job, the performance of your cluster will be adversely affected.

Clustering typically requires network connectivity for one or more of three network functional areas:

- Client to cluster

- Cluster host to cluster host

- Cluster host to shared storage device

Figure 12.1 illustrates these network functional areas in a typical shared nothing cluster.

There is a fourth network functional area: intracomputer communications. The choice of technology for this function lies with its manufacturer. Beyond selecting a vendor, there is nothing you can do to impact this communications arena. Therefore, internal bus technologies will not be addressed in this chapter.

12.1.1. Client to Cluster

Client to cluster networks provide connectivity between the clients and their cluster. This connectivity depends a great deal on where the clients are located relative to the location of the cluster. For example, if they are all in the same location, wide area network (WAN) technologies are immaterial. On the other hand, if the clients are geographically dispersed, a combination of local area network (LAN) and WAN technologies will be required.

Client to cluster networks are likely to be LAN or WAN based. Figure 12.2 illustrates both of these in a typical, shared nothing cluster.

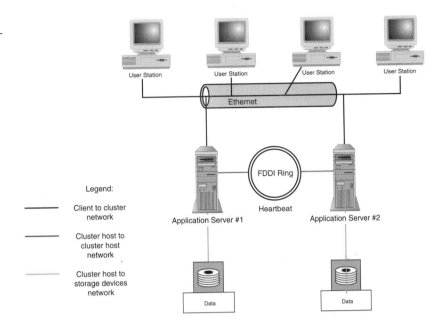

Figure 12.1.
Network functional areas in a typical shared nothing cluster.

Legend:

—————— Client to cluster network

—————— Cluster host to cluster host network

---------------- Cluster host to storage devices network

User Station   User Station   User Station   User Station

Ethernet

FDDI Ring

Heartbeat

Application Server #1   Application Server #2

Data   Data

Fortunately, for the purposes of clustering, this is likely to impose the least stringent network performance requirements. This network will probably support direct requests from users, so response time is the most appropriate metric to evaluate the effectiveness, or potential effectiveness, of any network technology for this functional area.

12.1.2. Cluster Host to Cluster Host

Cluster host to cluster host networks provide the vehicle for coordinating and managing activity within a cluster. Load balancing, I/O shipping, status monitoring, and even fail-over activities are conducted over this network. Thus, the performance of this network functional area is critical to the internal operations of the cluster.

> **NOTE**   This is the network fuctional area responsible for interconnecting a cluster's nodes. It is described more succinctly as cluster interconnect throughout the rest of this book.

This area is the glue that binds the cluster together. It is as integral to the cluster as any of the clustered nodes or shared disks. For this reason, it is identified explicitly as a *cluster area network* (CAN). Figure 12.3 illustrates the CAN within a typical, close proximity, shared nothing cluster.

Cluster-Friendly Networking

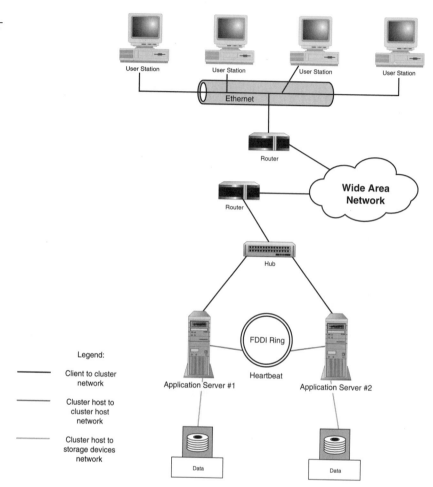

Figure 12.2.

Client to cluster networking in a typical shared nothing cluster.

The importance of the CAN requires any network technologies used in this capacity to be robust and well matched to the cluster's functionality and its processing platforms. CANs should not be considered to be an optional component of a cluster. Although you could construct a cluster without implementing a separate network for cluster management activities, this is almost always a mistake. CANs should be robust—and dedicated to cluster management activities.

The one possible exception to this rule involves geographically dispersed, shared nothing clusters. Unlike most cluster topologies (those that require close physical proximity of the clustered nodes), this specialized cluster topology disperses the clustered nodes geographically. Consequently, this cluster's CAN must include WAN components. The CAN components of a geographically dispersed cluster are depicted in Figure 12.4.

Figure 12.3.
Cluster area networking in a typical, close proximity, shared nothing cluster.

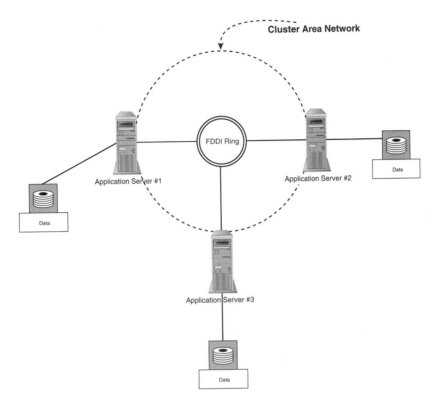

The vast majority of WAN transmission facilities and components are significantly slower than those for LANs. Consequently, the ability of a geographically dispersed, shared nothing cluster to perform normal cluster management activities is inferior to that of a close proximity shared nothing cluster. This performance degradation usually limits geographically dispersed clusters to disaster recovery roles.

Typically, disaster recovery clusters do not share applications, which minimizes their cluster management activity. I/O shipping and load balancing, two of the most resource-intensive cluster management activities, are obviated in such scenarios. The only activities remaining are data and application software updates, status monitoring, and fail-overs. With the possible exception of data updates, these are much less network-intensive functions, and could be successfully shared with other application traffic on lightly loaded WANs.

The performance requirements for this network component depend directly on the nature of the cluster. For example, fail-over clusters will require this to be a high speed, noncontention based network that is dedicated solely to interhost communication. This will enable the quickest possible identification of a failed host and, subsequently, the quickest autorecovery.

Figure 12.4.

Cluster area networking in a typical, geographically dispersed, shared nothing cluster.

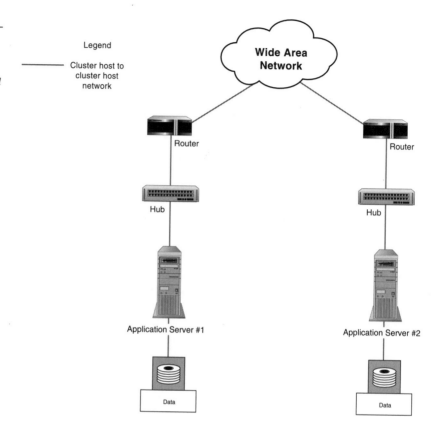

Depending on the actual implementation, scalable clusters would typically impose more demanding performance requirements for I/O than they would for intracluster host communications. As a result, scalable clusters might be able to use the same network used for client to cluster host connectivity for all intra–cluster communications. As a general rule, however, intracluster communications should always be conducted using network facilities that are dedicated to this function.

12.1.3. Cluster Host to External Storage Devices

The networking that interconnects cluster hosts to their storage devices imposes some of the more stringent performance requirements of any of the network functional areas. This functional area is present in shared disk and shared nothing clusters alike. It is typically satisfied via bus technologies instead of LAN or WAN technologies. Of course, there are some exceptions to this rule, but not many.

It is safe to assume that this network functional area will always require high speed connectivity. Thus, the distances between the cluster hosts and the storage devices, as well as the expected number of hosts that will comprise the cluster, will dictate the choice of network technology.

12.1.4. Network Functional Areas and Bandwidth

The unique demands and constraints of each of these functional capacities must be evaluated relative to the performance characteristics and limitations of each network technology. Improperly matching network technology to network function will compromise the aggregate performance of your cluster. The impact on its performance might be slight and unnoticeable, but it might also be quite severe and intolerable.

You should begin the process of selecting network technology by developing an estimate of the bandwidth demanded for each network functional area.

> **NOTE**   Although bandwidth is frequently confused with throughput, you should remember that they are separate and distinct. Bandwidth is, literally, the width of the communications channel. The term's meaning is derived from the definition of unguided transmission bands, or channels, in the electromagnetic spectrum. Bandwidth is rather like an EPA mileage estimate: Under ideal circumstances, and without any overhead, this is the maximum potential you can expect. Throughput is the actual sustainable data rate that you are likely to experience.
>
> Throughput is only one of the essential network performance metrics. Others, like response time and latency, are equally important. The appropriate metrics must be determined for each network functional area in a cluster.

12.2. Estimating Bandwidth Demands

Estimating the amount of bandwidth demanded at each of the network functional areas is an easy task to define, yet it is almost impossible to execute. To make matters worse, the process used to estimate necessary bandwidth will vary with those areas.

12.2.1. Client to Cluster Bandwidth Estimation

You must locate and identify the cluster's potential users. They must be accurately counted, and that count must be correlated to their physical location. Estimating their need for bandwidth will be difficult, especially if the cluster is to support a completely new application for which no historical usage data is available.

Cluster-Friendly Networking

If a historical precedent to the clustered application exists, then a good way to estimate the cluster's client to cluster bandwidth requirements is to examine that precedent application. If there are existing networks being used (like X.25, asynchronous networks, or even other LANs and WANs), they can be invaluable sources of information. They should be monitored to determine the following:

- Type of communications session (for example, bulk data transfer, online transaction processing, database query, and so on)

- Average number of octets generated by each type of incoming request

- Average number of octets generated by fulfilling each type of incoming request

- Frequency of use (that is, how many of each type of request per minute, per hour, and per day)

- Peak utilization times

- Peak utilization volumes

From these basic data, it should be relatively easy to develop an understanding of the aggregate traffic patterns between the clients and the cluster. Typically, these patterns can be expected to shift at different times of day. By examining the peak traffic volumes and the normal, sustained volumes, you can begin to select appropriate network technologies and transmission facilities to accommodate the projected loads.

An important piece of information you should determine during the data collection phase is the type of network performance needed. The best way to approach this is to understand the functionality supported by the cluster over each of the network functional areas. The client to cluster network is likely to support on-demand processing—either transactions or queries. If this is the case with your cluster, the various on-demand types of processing indicate that response time is an appropriate network performance metric. It is essential that this performance metric be factored into the network design.

Another important piece of data is the projected aggregate traffic flow. This is especially important if the client networks, or any piece of the networking that comprises the client to cluster network functional area, is also used to support other applications concurrently with the clustered application. In such instances, the cluster's aggregate performance will be directly impacted by the network traffic of other applications.

In addition to existing traffic supported by client networks, other details might prove useful, too. Important details are

■ The type and transmission rate of each LAN

■ The number of users connected to it

■ The number of hosts connected to it

■ Existing traffic loads and collision rates (if appropriate)

■ Routed protocols (such as IP, IPX, and so on)

■ Transmission control protocols (for example, TCP, UDP, T/TCP, SPX, and so on)

These selection criteria are not perfect or complete, but they are an excellent start. Unfortunately, collecting this data won't be quick or easy. You will probably have to substitute "guesstimates" for hard facts, because such facts rarely, if ever, exist.

12.2.2. Cluster Host to Cluster Host Performance Requirements

The network functional area that presents the most stringent performance requirement is the cluster host to cluster host networking. It is a well recognized fact that I/O is the most expensive operation that a computer can perform because of the tremendous disparities between the clock rates of the CPU and the various I/O mechanisms.

Local area networks can be one of the slower of the I/O mechanisms available to the computer. Therefore, using a LAN to communicate the commands that coordinate activity between cluster nodes imposes a performance limit on the entire cluster. The more sophisticated the cluster, the more cluster management functions will be transmitted across this network functional area. Thus, the choice of LAN used to interconnect the nodes or hosts of a cluster directly impacts the performance of the cluster more than any of the other network functional areas.

Unfortunately, the type of machine-generated requests that traverse this network functional area make it almost impossible to determine its bandwidth requirements. However, the importance of this network to the performance of the cluster means that response time, not bandwidth, is what the network should be engineered to deliver.

As a rule, minimizing response time means deploying the fastest possible network technology in this capacity. Among the steps you can take to minimize the impact of a LAN are avoiding a LAN that uses a contention-based media access method (for example, the Ethernet family of LANs) and implementing a per-port switched high-speed LAN, or both.

12.2.3. Cluster Host to Storage Device Bandwidth Estimation

Estimating the bandwidth required between the hosts in a cluster and their storage devices may seem to be an odd task. Many computer systems come with a standardized technology, like one of the *Small Computer Systems Interface* (SCSI) variants. While the manufacturer's choice of technology may serve admirably for the vast majority of applications, it is in your best interest not to leave anything to chance when designing your cluster. Remember: Any I/O mechanisms are substantially slower than the CPUs that generate I/O requests!

Though not a complete list, the following items will help you estimate your cluster's bandwidth requirements for this network functional area. These requirements can then be used as a simple metric for evaluating the suitability of the alternative technologies. Among the things to consider are

- Types of requests—that is, queries, transactions, and so on

- Quantities of each type of request per day, hour, and minute

- Average number of octets received per request type

- Average number of octets transmitted per request

- Peak utilization times

- Peak utilization traffic volumes

This information will help you to develop a clearer understanding of the disk intensity of the clustered application.

12.2.4. Bandwidth Estimation Summary

Bandwidth estimation should be done for each of the cluster's network functional areas. This is a critical first step you must take when you're selecting appropriate network technologies for your cluster, and appropriate network technologies are essential for successfully developing a cluster that meets or exceeds your expectations.

12.3. Network Technologies

Among the many network and bus technologies that can be used in a cluster are 10-Mbps Ethernet, 100-Mbps Ethernet, FDDI and CDDI, ATM, ESCON, SCSI-2 and III, and Fibre Channel. Each has its own peculiarities, and you must consider how well these will meet the clustered system's performance requirements. A quick survey can reveal just how different network technologies can be, and their strengths and weaknesses should highlight the importance of network technology selection for each of your cluster's network functional areas.

Each network technology strikes a different balance between speed and distance, a balance that varies with the physical media on which it is implemented. Two other differences between network technologies that also serve as key metrics for comparison are sustainable throughput and latency. Both of these are a function of the network's protocols for media access and packet handling. These are the metrics that should be applied to assess each technology's viability in the cluster. This is true for any network technology, regardless of whether it is listed here.

12.3.1. Ethernet (10 Mbps)

10-Mbps Ethernet is an extremely mature and stable technology. As defined in the Institute of Electrical and Electronic Engineers' (IEEE) specification numbered 802.3, there are four different physical layer specifications for transmission media. Table 12.1 presents the distance limitations and the data rates that can be achieved with each of the physical layers.

Table 12.1. Ethernet's physical specifications.

Physical Media	Max. Distance	Data Rate
10Base-2 Thin Coaxial Cable	up to 185 meters	10 Mbps
10Base-5 Thick Coaxial Cable	up to 500 meters	10 Mbps
10Base-T Unshielded Twisted Pair	up to 100 meters	10 Mbps
10Base-FL Fiber Optic Cable	up to 2000 meters	10 Mbps

Ethernet uses a variable length packet to transmit data that can vary from 64 to 1500 octets. This is an extremely efficient means of transporting bulk data, because the packet-to-payload ratio can be automatically optimized. Ethernet's effectiveness in bulk data transport makes it incapable of providing consistently low latency levels for time-sensitive traffic.

Cluster-Friendly Networking

For its access method, Ethernet uses *Carrier Sense, Multiple Access with Collision Detection* (CSMA/CD). This is a contention-based media access method. Devices connected to the LAN must compete for empty packets. This competition can cause packets to collide—especially if the network is heavily utilized. Packets that have collided are retransmitted.

The net effect of Ethernet's flexible packet sizes and competition for bandwidth is a protocol incapable of gracefully accommodating heavy traffic volumes. At over 20% utilization, performance begins to degrade quickly. Sustainable throughputs are therefore limited to less than 3 Mbps. However, utilizing switched Ethernet will bolster the performance of this technology by increasing the amount of bandwidth available to switch-connected devices, and by reducing the competition for available packets to an absolute minimum of two devices. These two devices are the network-attached device and the hub port it is connected to.

12.3.2. Fast Ethernet (100 Mbps)

100-Mbps Ethernet is a recent extension to the 802.3 specification. It presents a graceful migration path from (and ready interoperability with) its slower sibling. Unfortunately, it also retains all of Ethernet's shortcomings, albeit at a faster transmission rate. The physical layer, and its attendant distance limitations and data rates, are presented in Table 12.2.

Table 12.2. Fast Ethernet's physical specifications.

Physical Media	Distance	Data Rate
62.5 micron multimode fiber optic cabling (100Base-FX)	up to 412 meters	100 Mbps
Category 3 Unshielded Twisted Pair (100Base-T4)	up to 100 meters	100 Mbps
Category 5 Unshielded Twisted Pair (100Base-TX)	up to 100 meters	100 Mbps

With an order of magnitude faster clock than its predecessor, Fast Ethernet is capable of sustaining approximately an order of magnitude more throughput—that is, about an aggregate of 20 to 30 Mbps—before it begins experiencing performance degradation. Implementing port-switched Fast Ethernet effectively reduces competition for packets on a segment to just two devices: the hub port and the computer that it serves. This means that each switch-connected device can use at least 40 to 60 Mbps, rather than competing for that bandwidth with all the other devices and their respective hub ports on the LAN.

12.3.3. FDDI and CDDI

FDDI and CDDI are 100-Mbps token passing local area networks that use a ring topology. Network access is highly deterministic because it is governed by a "token" that passes around the FDDI loop. Decreasing network latency is easily accomplished by reducing the size of the ring. In other words, the fewer devices connected, the more frequently each device gets the token.

FDDI also features a dual, counter-rotating, ring topology that can "splice" together logically to heal a broken cable. The drawback to this self-healing capability is a sudden increase in propagation delay in the event of a cable break. However, this is a minor price to pay for a network that can autorecover.

Table 12.3 presents the distance limitations and data rates supported by FDDI and CDDI's physical transmission media.

Table 12.3. FDDI/CDDI's physical specifications.

Physical Media	Max. Distance	Data Rate
62.5 micron multimode fiber optic cabling	200 total kilometers (100 per "ring")	100 Mbps
Category 5 Unshielded Twisted Pair	Greater than 100 meters	100 Mbps
Type 1 Shielded Twisted Pair	Greater than 100 meters	100 Mbps

FDDI, and its wire-based sibling CDDI, are designed to provide high levels of sustainable throughput, approximately 60 to 80 Mbps. This is largely due to the regulated media access method.

12.3.4. ATM

Asynchronous Transfer Mode (ATM's proper name) was originally developed as an asynchronous transfer mechanism for Broadband Integrated Services Digital Network (B-ISDN). It is a high bandwidth switched protocol that uses a 53-byte packet: 48 bytes of payload with a 5-byte header.

Although essentially a connectionless protocol, mechanisms have been implemented that enable it to function in a connection-oriented mode. ATM was initially touted as a grand unifier in the world of networking, capable of seamlessly integrating LANs and WANs. Predictably, ATM was implemented in numerous data rates that were designed specifically for a LAN environment. For example, data rates as low as 25.6 Mbps were developed for client connectivity.

The full rate of 155.52 was intended for hub interconnectivity, as well as server and high-end client connectivity.

In theory, this protocol is scalable up to approximately 2.4 Gbps, although LAN products are currently only available up to 622 Mbps. The norm for host connectivity is the 155.52 Mbps interface. ATM's more common data rates, distance limitations, and physical media types are given in Table 12.4.

Table 12.4. ATM's physical specifications.

Physical Media	Distance	Data Rate
Category 3 Unshielded Twisted Pair	up to 100 meters	25.6 Mbps
Category 3 Unshielded Twisted Pair	up to 100 meters	155.52 Mbps
Category 5 Unshielded Twisted Pair	up to 100 meters	155.52 Mbps
62.5 micron multimode fiber optic cabling	up to 2 kilometers	155.52 Mbps

Given that ATM is an inherently switched technology, its sustainable throughputs should be fairly close to its data rate. ATM also uses a fixed-length packet. This makes it a low latency protocol, ideally suited to time-sensitive applications. Conversely, it has a high overhead of packet frame to payload. Thus, it might not be as efficient at bulk data transport as a protocol with a flexible length packet, yet it operates at a higher data rate than either Fast Ethernet or FDDI.

12.3.5. ESCON

ESCON (Enterprise Server CONnectivity) is an IBM channel technology. It provides 17.1 Mbps sustainable throughput. Due to its protocol and packet structure, ESCON excels at bulk data transfer. It does not handle short transactions or interactivity well at all. Attempts to use ESCON for a high volume of small transfers will result in a premature deterioration of its performance well short of its potential.

Table 12.5. ESCON's physical specifications.

Physical Media	Distance	Data Rate
9 micron single mode fiber (LASER driven)	20 kilometers	200 Mbps
50/100 micron multimode fiber optic cabling (LED driven)	up to 2 kilometers	200 Mbps

Physical Media	Distance	Data Rate
62.5/125 micron multimode fiber optic cabling (LED driven)	up to 3 kilometers (9 km with repeaters)	200 Mbps

12.3.6. SCSI-2

Small Computer Systems Interface, version 2 (known as SCSI-2), is a moderately high bandwidth bus technology. It was designed for peer-to-peer connectivity of peripheral devices and at least one host. Its major limitations are the number of devices that can be connected, and the short distance that the bus can span. These limitations make SCSI-2 useful only for connecting cluster hosts to storage devices.

Table 12.6. SCSI's physical specifications.

Physical Media	Max. Total Distance	Data Rate
Single-ended cable (16-bit SCSI-2)	6 meters	10 MBps
Differential cable (16-bit SCSI-2)	25 meters	10 MBps
Single-ended cable (32-bit SCSI-2)	1.5 meters	40 MBps
Differential cable (32-bit SCSI-2)	25 meters	40 MBps

The actual data rates achieved in asynchronous transmissions will be a function of the aggregate cable length and implementation. Synchronous transmissions are a function of cable length and SCSI implementation. For example, 32-bit SCSI-2 buses are capable of transmission speeds of up to 40 MBps and 16-bit SCSI-2 can transmit up to 10 MBps.

12.3.7. Fibre Channel

Fibre Channel was originally developed by IBM as an optical channel technology for mainframes. Its specification provided for a transmission rate of one gigabit per second! Because mainframes were (and are) not likely to support time-sensitive applications like voice and videoconferencing any time soon, flexible length packets were used.

Cluster-Friendly Networking

Fibre Channel has since been implemented as a LAN technology. The physical layer specification for this technology provides for a variety of speed and distance trade-offs over most common transmission media. These are presented in Table 12.7.

Table 12.7. Fibre Channel physical specifications.

Physical Media	Distance	Data Rate
9 micron single mode fiber optic cabling	up to 10 kilometers	800 Mbps
50 micron multimode fiber optic cabling	up to 1 kilometer up to 2 kilometers	400 Mbps 200 Mbps
62.5 micron multimode fiber optic cabling	up to 500 meters up to 1 kilometer	200 Mbps 100 Mbps
Video coaxial cabling	up to 25 meters up to 50 meters up to 75 meters up to 100 meters	800 Mbps 400 Mbps 200 Mbps 100 Mbps
Miniature coaxial cabling	up to 10 meters up to 15 meters up to 25 meters up to 35 meters	800 Mbps 400 Mbps 200 Mbps 100 Mbps
Shielded Twisted Pair	up to 50 meters up to 100 meters	200 Mbps 100 Mbps

This technology provides for automatically scaling back the clock rate if it begins to experience transmission errors. Thus, the values listed in Table 12.7 should be considered maximum data rates that will be supported. Your mileage will vary.

12.3.8. Matching Network Technologies to Functional Areas

Matching these network technologies to functional areas may seem trivial. After all, it is relatively easy to examine network technologies from an academic perspective and select the ideal candidates for each network component of a planned cluster. This is especially true if the comparison is based on a limited number of obvious criteria, such as the distance limitations and transmission speeds for various physical media. These are good, tangible, criteria for a "paper" evaluation that can be used by anyone with a passing familiarity with data networking.

However, network selection criteria cannot stop there. There are many more subtle, yet significant, criteria to consider. For example:

- Is the network's maximum sustainable throughput capable of accommodating the peak traffic load?

- How well do the selected network technologies scale upwards? Can they meet the projected growth of the cluster, or will they have to be replaced—requiring reinvestment?

- Are there any hardware or software dependencies dictated by your cluster's platform (such as the availability of *network interface cards* (NICs) and software drivers) that would preclude the use of any network technologies?

- How constraining is your budget? The idealized networks may be too expensive either to purchase and install, or to administer and maintain once they are up and running.

- Is the network capable of living up to the cluster's expected availability and scalability rate?

This last item is often overlooked. It should be obvious that a chain is only as strong as its weakest link. Clusters—a "chain" of technologies—are no exception.

12.4. Did We Miss Anything?

Once you have identified the network technologies for each functional area, you must be equally diligent about their implementation. Consider the network a functional extension of the cluster. As such, it is critical that the technology be implemented to reinforce the intended functionality of the cluster.

12.4.1. Fail-overs

For example, if the cluster supports a mission critical application that is designed for 100% availability, the network, too, must be capable of 100% availability. This means selecting hardware that supports circuit board hot-swapping, protecting all the network's electrical components with Uninterruptible Power Supplies (UPS), and having fully redundant network paths to all clustered hosts. Otherwise, the cluster may find itself experiencing service outages that it cannot fix with a fail-over.

Another important implementation issue is addressing. This is of particular importance in switched implementations of broadcasting LANs. Many of the network technologies mentioned are available in a switched form. *Switching* is a technique that improves network performance by segmenting the LAN into smaller segments, thereby providing greater overall bandwidth across the network. This performance gain brings with it additional cost and complexity in addressing. You must ask yourself if switching is necessary or desirable in terms of the cluster's projected network requirements.

Switches work like high speed bridges. They use tables to collate physical ports with addresses. Host naming and addressing that can support the functionality of the planned cluster must be worked out. For example, you should ensure that when a fail-over occurs, all network routing and switching tables are updated automatically to reflect the failed host's unavailability. Ideally, clients will access the cluster using a single mnemonic name and will not need to know any specific addresses. If it's properly planned and implemented, the network will automatically route or switch around failed hosts without the clients even knowing a failure occurred.

A slightly more subtle networking issue in fail-over clusters is the impact on aggregate traffic flow across WANs during a fail-over. This is of particular concern with geographically dispersed clusters implemented for disaster recovery, although it could affect close proximity clusters, too. For example, if the planned-for disaster occurs, and the fail-over is automatically implemented, what happens to the WAN and the traffic it supports? Will some links that previously were only lightly loaded suddenly find themselves dropping packets? Is this acceptable under the circumstances? Before you dismiss these questions as irrelevant because you aren't building a cluster for disaster recovery purposes, think again. Any cluster, even those self-contained within a single work location, can be impacted by changes in aggregate WAN traffic flows, if that WAN is used in any of the three cluster network functional areas! This includes the client to cluster functional area.

12.4.1. Scalability

If a cluster is designed primarily for scalability, the network must be designed to scale upwards as gracefully and easily as the cluster. Ideally, the networks would be over-engineered relative to the cluster's initial loads. Thus, additional ports for connectivity and bandwidth would be available in advance to support the cluster's growth as it happens.

Failure to build an appropriate degree of scalability into the network functional areas of a scalable cluster is tantamount to failing to build scalability into the cluster itself. It may take precious time to procure and install the necessary network expansion components. This could be time that the cluster's users do not have, especially if NT Server–based clustering lives up to its promise and becomes the cluster platform for mission critical applications.

12.5. Summary

The answers to many, if not all, of the questions raised throughout section 12.4 will vary from situation to situation. It is important, however, that you have thought about them and have answers ready before a crisis occurs.

In real life, many other variables, including subjective or nontechnical issues, must also be factored into the selection of network technologies. Existing skill sets, training costs, budgetary constraints, vendor relationships, and so on, all are important constraints that must be considered when you're selecting technology.

This may begin to resemble an impossible dilemma—and in fact that's partially true. There is no single correct answer. The correct answers will vary from project to project, and company to company. Don't despair. To find them, start with a fundamental appreciation for the business goals and performance requirements of your cluster. Identify the expected intensity with which the cluster's resources (CPU cycles or I/O) will be consumed by each cluster component.

Next, identify all the network technologies that may be appropriate for each network functional area required. Then use the realities of your particular situation, including the local technopolitics and all the other soft criteria, as the final criteria for matching your "short list" of network technologies to your cluster's performance requirements.

Cluster-Friendly Networking

Chapter

13

Clustering
for
Competitive
Advantage

Information technologies (even clusters of symmetrical multiprocessors) are commodity items that are readily available to all competitors for about the same price. Merely purchasing such technologies does not impart competitive advantages. Rather, competitive advantages are derived from the manner in which information technologies are used to reinforce core competencies and support business goals. Within this context, it is important to apply information technologies well.

This chapter assumes that the application itself is well aligned with the organization's goals. Similarly, it is assumed that the platform choices are well suited to the skill sets found within the organization. This chapter focuses, therefore, on describing some of the ways that clustering can be applied to deliver competitive advantages for each application type.

Some of the more common types of applications in today's business environment include Online Transaction Processing (OLTP), Decision Support Systems (DSS), Executive Information Systems (EIS), and Office Automation (OA).

These application types have distinct characteristics and resource requirements that must be reflected in their physical configurations. Their strengths, weaknesses, and resource requirements are identified. This serves as a context for exploring potential ways to optimize a cluster for a particular application type.

13.1. Data Storage Structures

An enterprise tends to store its data in structures that are directly tied to the applications that create and maintain them. Thus, before examining specific application types, it is useful to first examine some of the more common of today's data storage structures.

Implicit in this notion is that the databases will be structured to maximize the operational efficiency of the particular applications that created them. Whenever a database is pressed into double duty—that is, whenever it is used for a secondary purpose—its structure may impede the effectiveness of that secondary application.

Some of the more common of these structures are examined in the remainder of this section. They are relational databases, data warehouses, and data marts.

13.1.1. Relational Database

A relational database is organized by the relationships between its data elements. Within the typical relational database are files. Each file contains tables of rows and columns. Each table is related to the others through at least one common field. This relationship forms the basis for data retrieval. It usually results in the relational database being limited to a single function or application.

13.1.2. Data Warehouse

A *data warehouse* is a database, or a collection of databases, designed to support decision making. Data warehouses typically contain enormous amounts of data. They are designed to provide quick responses to online queries. Implicit in this definition is that data warehouses are *Decision Support System* (DSS) tools.

A data warehouse is not simply a collection of databases that support other applications. Such databases may serve as primary information sources for a data warehouse, but they are not the data warehouse. Analyzing the data in support of business decision-making processes requires a DSS to gather the information it needs and aggregate it to an appropriate level of detail. This aggregated data is then stored for future use in its own specialized environment, one that is optimized for decision support purposes. This environment is a data warehouse. A data warehouse is a specially designed, fully separate environment into which an enterprise's data is consolidated for use by a DSS. Figure 13.1 illustrates this concept of aggregating data into a warehouse.

Figure 13.1.
Enterprise data is aggregated into data warehouses.

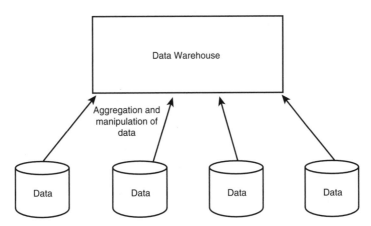

Therefore, data warehouses are a highly specialized form of database. They are not merely historical collections of transactional data. Nor are they simply the raw data from any other application type, although such data may be used to develop the appropriately detailed warehoused data.

13.1.3. Data Mart

A *data mart* is a mini-data warehouse. It is a subset of a data warehouse, and is usually limited to a single subject, user community, or function. The data is still manipulated into the appropriate level of detail, including time series, trends, and other useful types of data—it is just a much more limited set of data.

13.2. Overview of Decision Support Systems

Decision Support Systems (DSS), sometimes referred to as *Decision Information Systems* (DIS), are information and planning applications that support focused business decision-making processes. Typically, ad hoc queries are made that generate an automated data analysis used to predict the outcome of decisions before those decisions are actually made. This predictive modeling can be extremely cost-beneficial by eliminating some of the risks inherent in managing a business in a dynamic environment.

It is important to note that DSS is not just another modeling technique. It transcends the abilities of standard modeling tools. A DSS is a comprehensive and tightly integrated series of programs that move, modify, share, and enable automatic data analysis without restriction.

Over the past two decades, decision support-type systems have evolved continuously. Original DS systems were little more than predefined query facilities in mainframe systems.

During the mid-1980s, they took on the form of stand-alone *personal computer* (PC) tools. During the early 1990s, they evolved yet again into a client/server query facility. Each succeeding generation brought expanded flexibility, functionality, and ease of use. Each, however, tended to suffer from the same limitation: it analyzed the data stored in databases designed for other purposes.

Today, decision support systems are no longer an afterthought to a mission critical application. They are discrete applications unto themselves. They must be extremely robust and provide analysis at the enterprise level. In a contemporary DSS, databases are a source of information that directly guide business decisions, rather than just a repository of historical data.

13.2.1. DSS Characteristics

The DSS analysis process is initiated through ad hoc queries. Business decisions, typically, are complex and nonrepetitious. This prevents the use of predefined queries and report generation facilities. Such mechanisms may be useful, but in a different context. They are more typical of *Executive Information Systems* (EIS). Clustered EIS applications are covered in section 13.3.2.

DSS queries must be given the flexibility to examine as much, or as little, of a database as possible. Queries must also be able to examine data in multiple databases, regardless of where the data may be physically located. Constraining the capabilities of queries directly translates into diminished capacity of the DSS to support dynamic business decision making. Though this point is obvious, effective implementation is deceptively difficult, especially in a clustered server configuration.

One legacy of DSS's history is that the databases they use still tend to be specifically designed to support other applications. They can be from external information sources, databases that are updated "live" by OLTP systems, or databases that contain historical data. Regardless of the original reason for developing the database, one of the problems facing DSS is that database systems tend to be optimized for their original purpose.

Another significant problem is that, even today, the query requirements of DSS are relatively poorly understood. This is true of DSS users and suppliers alike. As evidence of this, commercial database systems support queries in a highly inconsistent manner. The effects of this can be observed by measuring response times for queries of varying complexity, across different relational database products. Given the hardware intensity of queries, this performance disparity directly translates into operational cost disparities across different DSS platforms.

For example, an *Online Transaction Processing* (OLTP) system's database is usually designed to facilitate data entry. Each transaction is logged in a new record, and there is seldom a need to do anything but write new records to the database. Thus, it makes sense to develop a structure that optimizes the speed with which new records can be added.

If this OLTP database is later used by a DSS, the DSS performance will likely suffer because the database won't have been structured to gracefully accommodate queries for fine levels of detail. Frequently, DSS users make queries that require the DSS either to have, or to calculate on demand, aggregate numbers or time-series trend data. Neither of these is available in an OLTP system. Asking the DSS a question concerning trends or aggregates forces the DSS to first develop those data, and then to analyze them. Even if all the necessary data were resident in a single database, this would take an unacceptable amount of time.

These factors, combined with the notorious lack of consistent query performance across the generally available commercial products, make data mining activities one of the more challenging tasks to implement effectively. As a result, a DSS typically requires its own highly specialized data storage structure.

13.2.2. Data Warehousing and OLAP

As explained in section 13.1.2, data warehouses anticipate the need for aggregated data, and even time-series data, and gather the necessary raw data in advance. This data is manipulated until it is better suited for decision support, and then stored in a data warehouse. This aggregation is both I/O and CPU intensive.

Warehoused data can be either accessed directly by DSS users, or through another form of highly specialized processing engine for a more thorough analysis. This engine, known as *Online Analytical Processing* (OLAP), or *data mining,* uses multidimensional database techniques to produce a more comprehensively analyzed result than can be achieved with standard database query tools. OLAP engines are well suited to the level of detail developed by data warehouse products. OLAP is simultaneously I/O and CPU intensive.

13.2.3. DSS on a Cluster

Given the historical difficulties of developing effective data mining systems, implementing them on a clustered platform can be extremely challenging. DSS already suffers from being I/O intensive. Implementing it on an almost equally I/O-intensive platform like a cluster can be punishing if not done properly. Rather, a way must be found to match the strengths and weaknesses of a cluster to the resource and processing requirements of DSS.

The benefits of a cluster consist of two distinct categories: operational performance and application performance. Operational benefits can be anything that improves or enhances the administrator's ability to operate the processing platform. Application performance benefits are anything that improves some aspect of the application's execution.

It should be obvious by now that clustering can bring several operational benefits to a DSS system. First, any SMP will contain numerous single points of failure that are antithetical to high availability. A cluster, through its distributed redundancy of otherwise singular components, is capable of extremely high availability rates.

Application performance benefits may, however, be tougher to derive. Merely supporting intraquery parallelism on a cluster will not improve the cost-performance of DSS queries. Symmetrical multiprocessors (SMPs) can also provide this exact form of parallelism. Supporting intraquery parallelism across clustered nodes adds the overheads of shipping I/O. This would slow down the application's runtime. Again, an SMP might be a better choice if your cluster's DSS functionality was limited in this way.

This shouldn't be misconstrued. Intraquery parallelism should be a necessary feature of a clustered DSS, assuming that the clustered nodes are SMPs. Additional performance gains can be realized by using the distributed parallelism of a cluster to run the application nonlinearly. For example, any given query might result in an expansion to dozens of activities. Some of these activities can be run in parallel to others, while others are contingent upon the successful completion of other activities.

A cluster can expedite the application's runtime by identifying those activities that can run in parallel, and shipping them off to a less busy node. These nodes have their own dedicated system resources. Consequently, any processes farmed out to another node won't have to compete for I/O, RAM, CPU, or anything else with other processes. They will execute in parallel on separate machines that are only logically tied together.

13.2.4. DSS on Layered Clusters

The database queries in a DSS are typically very long, read-only events that require lots of I/O. Because of the extreme mismatch in speed between I/O buses and devices and the CPU, I/O is the single most expensive operation that any computer can perform. Forcing DSS queries and users' online demands for processing to cohabit on the same physical computer can be punishing for the users.

The concept of layered clusters, introduced in Chapter 4, "Complex Clusters," may be used to effectively resolve this quandary. A layered cluster, sometimes referred to as a client/server/server topology, can utilize two layers of clusters to segregate a DSS's different functions.

Figure 13.2 demonstrates how a DSS can be split functionally across two layers of a cluster. Depending on how you configure your NT cluster, these layers may be completely separate clusters, or just two levels of integration within a single cluster. The first server layer is responsible for user interface and for responding to queries. This includes the execution of all business logic.

The second server layer is responsible for all database management functions. This includes any data gathering and manipulation required to support the DSS.

> **NOTE** Because of the extreme differences between the various data warehousing products, this example must be considered illustrative only. It may or may not be feasible to develop this topology in your particular circumstances.

In this fashion, much of the I/O and CPU intensity of the DSS application is relegated to a back-tier that users do not log on to. Thus, their chance of experiencing an unacceptable response time because of the resource intensity of gathering and manipulating data is eliminated.

Figure 13.2.
*DSS functions
separated across
layered clusters.*

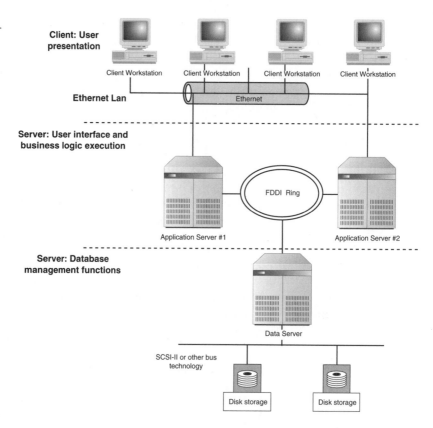

13.3. Overview of Executive Information Systems

Whereas a DSS is designed to facilitate making business decisions, *Executive Information Systems* (EIS) are more concerned with providing information about how the business is performing. As indicated by its name, the intended users of this type of application are executive managers. Generally speaking, executive managers tend not to be very technically proficient. Thus, it is essential that it be extremely user-friendly.

Typically, an EIS consolidates and summarizes all transactions that have occurred within the organization. This summarized data might or might not be augmented with data from external sources before being presented to the users as a synopsis of the current state of the organization's operations.

The distinction between EIS and DSS systems is blurring. EIS applications are currently providing some limited modeling of hypothetical extensions of trends.

This "what if" modeling is, so far, just a limited form of the modeling capabilities available in a DSS. However, even this limited modeling results in an increase in the computational intensity of this type of application.

13.3.1. EIS Characteristics

An EIS exhibits many of the characteristics of a DSS in that it aggregates and summarizes data from many data sources. One of the key differences is that, typically, the majority data used by an EIS comes from databases that are updated in real-time. Additional data sources can be DSS aggregate data, and even sources of "soft" data such as that coming from humans.

All inputted data is summarized, and then subjected to a fairly rigorous analysis based on user-specified criteria. As a result of this, an EIS is inherently I/O and CPU intensive.

Another difference between an EIS and a DSS is the nature of the queries that are made of the data. An EIS demonstrates a smaller range of potential queries and, therefore, a greater possibility of repetitious queries. This creates the opportunity for predefined queries, and relieves the need for extremely complex index structures on the summarized data.

The last key difference between these two application types is their focus. Managers use a DSS to facilitate the business decision-making process and executives use an EIS to determine the success of both their policies and their managerial decisions.

13.3.2. EIS on a Cluster

The nature of an EIS is such that scalability is much less important than availability. There are two key factors driving this bias:

- There are far fewer executives than there are managers in the typical organization.
- Executives can adversely impact your IT budget.

Consequently, it is in your best interest to select a platform that provides the highest possible degree of availability. Fortunately, any cluster topology can increase an EIS's availability relative to any stand-alone computing solution.

A sample cluster topology for an EIS is presented in Figure 13.3. This topology stresses high availability and maximum application performance through support for cascading fail-over across multiple nodes, redundant disk arrays, and load balancing of the application across all active nodes.

> **NOTE**   Please note, this is a sample topology and does not necessarily reflect
> the capabilities of any particular cluster management product, nor of
> any hardware products. It is presented solely to demonstrate some of the ways that the
> requirements of an application can be reinforced through clustering.

Figure 13.3.

EIS in a cluster.

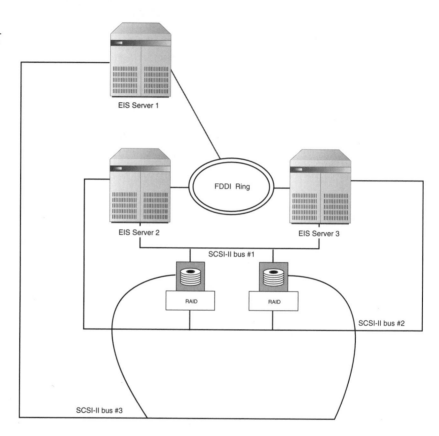

In this solution, scalability can be provided either internally by using less than loaded symmetrical multiprocessors, or externally by adding nodes to the cluster.

It is possible to take performance maximization a step further by separating the database management function from the client interface and logic execution functions across separate layers. This was the recommended solution for a DSS solution and is depicted in Figure 13.2. However, the smaller number of users should mean that logic execution and client interface is a much smaller pair of tasks. Similarly, the limited and potentially repetitious nature of queries should also translate into a less resource-intensive database management function.

13.4. Overview of Online Transaction Processing

Online Transaction Processing (OLTP) is a generic term that describes the immediate processing of transactions. The alternative is buffering, or saving, the transactions until a certain time or quantity threshold is reached, and then processing the entire batch at once.

A transaction can be any event that requires a change to the data contained in the master files. Although the word "transaction," for many people, has a commercial connotation, a transaction can be any data event that results in a real-time update of the master files. The nature of the event is immaterial; it can be a sales transaction, updates to an employee's personnel file, or anything else.

The processing of data events in real-time makes it possible to extract up-to-date information about the business. Thus, OLTP databases are more than simply historical repositories of business activity—they are prime sources of information for DSS and EIS type systems.

13.4.1. OLTP Characteristics

Historically, OLTP has been the most important application type in any company. This was ostensibly because it is used to support the customer-facing functions of the business including sales, customer care, and other functions of the day-to-day operations of the business. In a commercial organization, these functions must be mission critical. Consequently, the demands on OLTP systems tend to be great. They must remain highly available and reliable throughout normal business hours.

An OLTP system's database is usually designed to facilitate data entry. Each transaction is written as a new record in the existing file structure. The typical OLTP transaction is a short read/write action. A very strict locking strategy is essential to ensure that the database structure is not damaged by having multiple parties capable of writing records simultaneously.

13.4.2. OLTP on a Cluster

Developing a cluster that can effectively support OLTP applications is fairly easy. In fact, the nature of clusters lends itself readily to this task: Distributed redundancy coupled with fail-over capability does wonders for providing the high availability that OLTP requires.

Two tricks are sizing the cluster to the application's processing requirements and providing the distributed locking mechanism (DLM) to safeguard the data.

Sizing the cluster is a matter of understanding the number of transactions per second that the application is expected to support, and then selecting a processing platform that can support it.

Lock management offers two options in an NT cluster. First, as the initial releases of NT Cluster Server do not support a native distributed lock manager, it is necessary to find a database vendor that supports this feature in an NT cluster. Figure 13.4 illustrates a two-node, shared disk cluster with distributed lock management for OLTP.

Figure 13.4.

Distributed lock management in a cluster for OLTP.

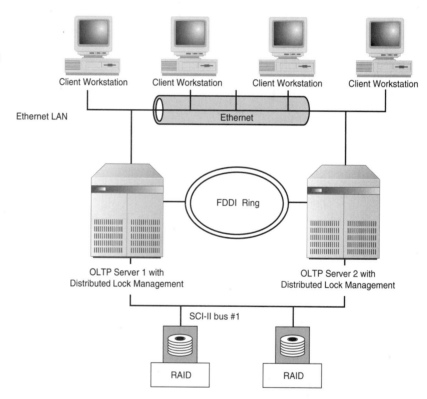

A much more scalable solution is to employ the client/server/server topology described in Chapter 4. In Figure 13.5, an OLTP application is split into two functional layers of a cluster. The first layer is responsible for client interface and executing the application's logic. Transactions can be buffered temporarily in a message-oriented queuing system for transmission to the second layer. The second layer is a nonclustered computer that is solely responsible for database management functions. This obviates the need for distributed lock management by centralizing that function onto a single system.

Figure 13.5.

Avoidance of lock management in a client/server/ server cluster topology.

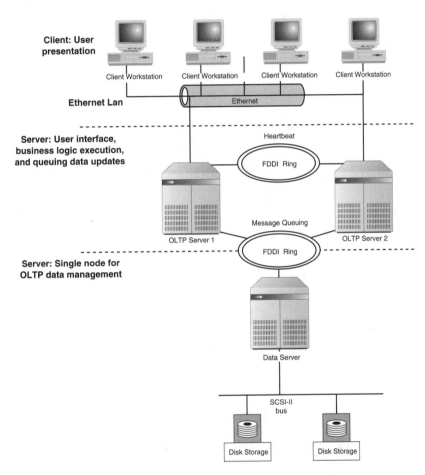

A further refinement of this concept is presented in Figure 13.6. The second layer in this scenario is actually a second cluster. Clustering the database management function increases the start-up costs of the cluster, but achieves an increased availability for this function. Please note, this configuration re-introduces the need for distributed lock management across the clustered nodes in the second layer.

Figure 13.6.

Lock manage-ment in a client/server/server cluster topology.

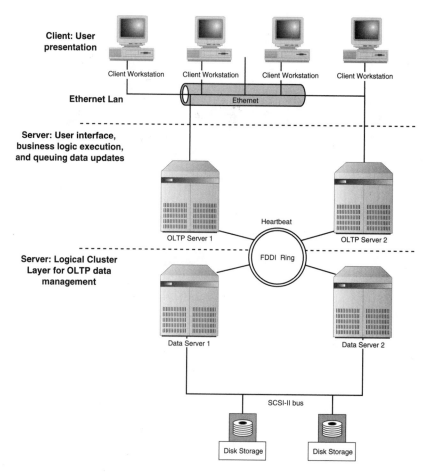

Client: User presentation

Client Workstation   Client Workstation   Client Workstation   Client Workstation

Ethernet Lan   Ethernet

Server: User interface, business logic execution, and queuing data updates

OLTP Server 1   Heartbeat   OLTP Server 2

Server: Logical Cluster Layer for OLTP data management

FDDI Ring

Data Server 1   Data Server 2

SCSI-II bus

Disk Storage   Disk Storage

13.5. Overview of Office Automation Applications

Office Automation applications are generic functions such as word processing, spreadsheets, calendars and time management, and electronic mail that automate many of the tasks found in an office environment. Supporting *Office Automation* (OA) applications is not a stretch for Windows NT. It was designed to support this class of applications, and it isn't difficult to find applications designed specifically for NT.

These functions are easily supported by traditional client/server networked computers. Substituting a cluster for the server can be done in a number of different ways, each with its own combination of performance enhancements.

13.5.1. OA Characteristics

OA applications can be categorized into two arbitrary classes, based upon where they execute:

- The first group are those applications that are downloaded and executed at the client.

- The second group are those applications that remain on the server, execute there, and provide a common data store for all users.

Each of these groups impose very different performance requirements on their host. Consequently, they must be treated differently in a clustered environment.

13.5.2. Clustering OA Applications

The first group can include virtually any application that is run in a stand-alone manner. Copies of a word-processing spreadsheet, for example, can reside on a server but be downloaded to the client for execution. This type of application is easily supported in a cluster, but would only benefit from having an alternate node to fail-over to. This scenario is illustrated in Figure 13.7.

The second group includes collaborative groupware and electronic mail. These applications, by virtue of executing on the server, stand to gain more of a cluster's benefits. This group, too, can benefit tremendously from a cluster's fail-over capabilities. More importantly, the performance of these applications can be enhanced through either static or dynamic load balancing across the cluster's nodes.

Figure 13.7.
*Shared nothing
fail-over support
for downloaded
OA applications.*

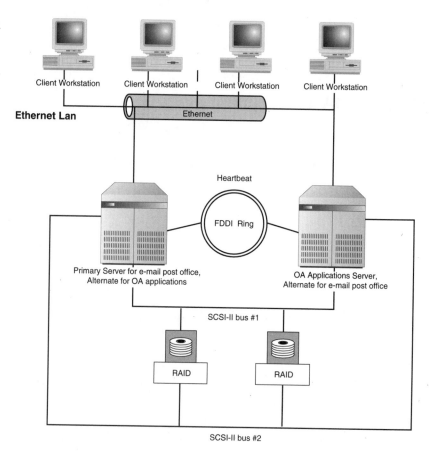

A dynamic load-balancing cluster can also provide the users of these applications with high availability through fail-over support. This type of cluster is illustrated in Figure 13.8.

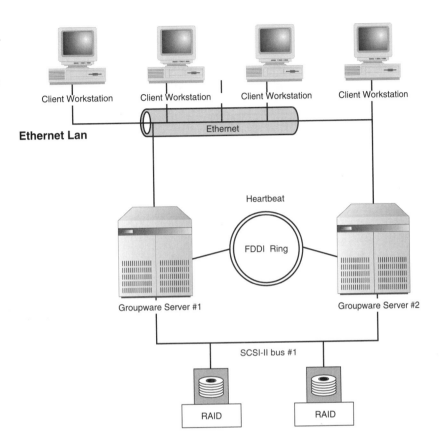

Figure 13.8.
Shared disk, dynamic load balancing, and fail-over support enhance the performance of server-based applications.

Client Workstation   Client Workstation   Client Workstation   Client Workstation

Ethernet Lan   Ethernet

Heartbeat

FDDI Ring

Groupware Server #1   Groupware Server #2

SCSI-II bus #1

RAID   RAID

13.6. Summary

NT clusters have the potential to deliver significant business value. The key to unlocking this value lies in objectively understanding the abilities and limitations of this technology. Once you have successfully separated hype and fiction (frequently found in marketing "literature") from technical reality, you can begin looking for ways to match the cluster's configuration and topology to the resource and processing requirements of its application.

As was demonstrated throughout this book, clusters can be wonderfully amorphous. Topologically speaking, there is no single right or wrong way to build them. Functionally speaking, the right way to build a cluster is any way that works to the clustered application's advantage. The examples presented throughout this chapter are intended to provoke thought. They are not intended as the solution to your clustering needs.

Remember, simply building a cluster won't necessarily impart any competitive advantages to your firm. Competitive advantages, like strong steel, must be forged. It is up to you to design a cluster that provides strength in the areas needed most by the applications that it will support. Thus, each cluster should be carefully crafted to fit those applications.

Chapter

14

Understanding and Utilizing the SCSI Hardware Interface

Throughout this book, SCSI has been frequently mentioned as the one of the predominant technologies used to interconnect devices to a server cluster. SCSI is the most viable means of interconnecting servers to one another so that both servers in a cluster can access a set of shared nothing, or partitioned data model, devices located on the SCSI bus.

Having many advantages over other hardware interfaces, the rapidly evolving SCSI interfacing technology has been embraced by Microsoft as one of the primary means of interconnecting servers via its Cluster Server. Of the three connections that can exist within a cluster, the SCSI connection is the most important.

Although two other cluster connections also exist (the *cluster interconnect* and *LAN connection*), this chapter will focus on the fundamentals of SCSI implementation and functions in a cluster, as well as provide a discussion of physical SCSI connections, SCSI technology speeds, and the limitations associated with the hardware interface. This chapter will also discuss setting up SCSI devices in Windows NT and general configurations for server clustering.

14.1. SCSI's Role in Clustering

In any cluster there are three predominant connections that can exist. The first is the *cluster interconnect*, which enables the servers to communicate and keep tabs on one another. The cluster interconnect is any communications link that Windows NT can support and utilize to determine the availability of a server or subsystem. The cluster interconnect normally uses a networking connection, typically Ethernet, through the use of network interface cards inserted into the servers.

The second major connection in the cluster is the LAN, which is the link between the cluster and its users. This connection, too, is established using one or more network interface cards.

In addition to these two cluster connections, the most vital link between Microsoft Cluster Servers, as well as the focus of this chapter, is the SCSI bus. The SCSI bus allows any range of devices, as well as the Cluster Servers, to be interconnected. Interconnecting allows storage area, typically via an array of drives, to be shared between servers in the cluster. Although each server has local drives, everything the servers share must reside on the SCSI bus.

> **NOTE** Keep in mind that although the devices on the SCSI bus are shared, the cluster is still a shared nothing cluster. This means that only one server may be actively using any given device at a time, even though both servers in the cluster have access to the device. The devices on the SCSI bus are shared in the sense that both servers have access to the devices, not in that both servers can access the device at the same time.

The SCSI bus is important not only to data storage, but it is also important to the fail-over capability of the cluster. However, before looking at the fail-over negotiation that occurs via the SCSI bus, you must first understand the fundamentals of SCSI technology, the physical connections involved, and the various types of SCSI implementations. In addition, it is important to acknowledge the speeds and limitations of various implementations because they can affect the efficiency and speed of the fail-over operations as well as data transfer.

14.1.1. SCSI Basics

Due to its capability to access large storage devices and allow access to many devices via a single bus, SCSI is a perfect solution for multitasking and multithreading environments such as Windows NT. When combined with the further requirements for Windows NT Cluster Server, SCSI is a logical choice for connecting devices to a cluster.

SCSI, pronounced *scuzzy*, is the acronym for Small Computer Systems Interface and is a standard for connecting peripherals, such as hard drives, CD-ROMs, and other devices, to a computer using a single, common bus. This is accomplished by chaining devices together, one after the other. The SCSI implementation also allows multiple hosts, or computers, to be connected to any given bus.

Composed of a set of standard commands and hardware specifications, SCSI can actually be divided into two separate sets of standards, SCSI-1 and SCSI-2. Realize that SCSI is a protocol that includes specifications for both hardware and command sets for devices.

From a hardware standpoint, the SCSI protocol is designed to provide an efficient peer-to-peer input and output bus with up to 16 devices (SCSI-2), including one or more host computers. SCSI-2 also includes specific command sets for CD-ROMs, magnetic and optical disks, printers, processors, tape drives, scanners, medium changers, and other communications devices. As a predecessor, SCSI-1 provides fewer commands, further limitations, and some compatibility problems.

Currently, the American National Standards Institute (ANSI) is working on a new revision, SCSI-3, which promises to further broaden the horizons for SCSI technology. Although many manufacturers claim SCSI-3 capability, you should realize that most are simply an applied modification of SCSI-2 for minor speed or functionality improvements. Once SCSI-3 is ratified and approved by ANSI, true SCSI-3 capability will be a real option.

14.1.2. The Evolution of SCSI

The SCSI protocol has rapidly advanced over the past two years, but it actually began around 1979. Shugart Associates, which eventually became Seagate

Understanding and Utilizing the SCSI Hardware Interface

Technology, developed a new drive interface that used a logical, rather than physical, addressing scheme.

Probably one of the first full-scale sweeps to the SCSI protocol was within Macintosh Apple machines. Designing the Macintosh as a closed system, engineers at Apple needed some means of expandability for the new and evolving system. With SCSI's single-bus/multiple-device construct, a system could remain closed (no internal expansion buses) and still give the user external expandability. Therefore, Apple was one of the first desktop companies to adopt and utilize the new SCSI technology.

Yet, PCs were much different. Because PCs were not a closed system, SCSI was not necessarily needed. PCs already had as many as six to eight additional slots where cards and other add-ons could be integrated. This is the primary reason SCSI was not instantly embraced by PC manufacturers.

Additionally, one of the biggest problems with early SCSI implementations on the PC was a lack of a real standard. The SCSI-1 standard predominantly defined parameters for the hardware connections. Early PC SCSI boards and devices, created by various manufacturers, had no end of incompatibilities. Drivers for one drive would work only with certain boards, and so on. Although the hardware was standardized, working with SCSI drivers, hardware, and other software was more of a black art than anything else.

Today, SCSI has matured far beyond the conflicts of the past. With the wide variety of speeds and capabilities of SCSI devices and controllers, almost any need can be met with SCSI as an option. SCSI will continue to be a viable option for all types of applications, including clustering.

14.1.3. SCSI versus Other Hardware Interfaces

Comparing SCSI to other hardware interfaces, such as IDE (Integrated Drive Electronics) or ATA (AT Attachment), reveals the real power of the SCSI protocol. In multitasking and multithreaded environments, as compared to IDE or ATA, SCSI is vitally important and needed.

Aside from the fact that SCSI drives support larger devices, the most important point to remember about SCSI, and a SCSI bus, is that multiple commands can be executed at a time. SCSI is a multithread-capable protocol, whereas IDE and ATA are not. Due to their construction and operation, IDE and ATA are single-threaded protocols. This means that they must accept, execute, and respond to each command before a new command may be issued.

For example, in an IDE environment, requests made to or from a device must be resolved before a new command may be executed. Once the processor has requested information from an IDE device or chain, it must wait for the device to execute the command before a new command may be issued. It also means that no commands may be sent to any other devices in the chain until the current transaction is complete. Due to this single-thread characteristic, the most expensive chip in the computer, the processor, spends a lot of time waiting on the IDE device to respond to commands.

However, SCSI devices do not work this way. With a SCSI bus the processor can send multiple commands to multiple devices on the bus without waiting for the command to be executed. This allows the processor to be busy with other tasks while the SCSI controller autonomously oversees execution of the commands on the SCSI bus and then replies to the processor at the appropriate time. In this respect, a SCSI bus can increase the speed of a machine by releasing the processor from the single-thread construct when I/O operations are being performed.

One other note about SCSI versus IDE or ATA is that SCSI can execute and respond to commands nonsequentially. This means that if commands are sent from the processor in a series, such as command A, command B, and so on, SCSI devices may reply in any sequence to the processor, depending on the readiness and speed of the devices to which those commands are sent. Commands do not have to be executed in a linear fashion, which allows devices to respond based on their own readiness and speed rather than the speed or readiness of other devices in the chain.

Alternatively, on an IDE chain, commands sent from the processor are required as a linear reflection of the progression in which they were sent. This also means that the speed of any device is dependent on the lower common denominator (device) in the chain. Not only does the processor have to wait, but other devices in the chain might have to as well.

The nonlinear capability of the SCSI bus increases machine speed by not only allowing multiple commands but also nonlinear execution and response, thereby making the I/O operations more efficient, particularly when multiple devices are involved. Due to these two factors, SCSI is the most applicable hardware interface for multitasking and multithreaded environments such as Window 95, Windows NT, and UNIX.

14.2. The Physical Connections

To fully understand SCSI technology, one needs to take a brief look at the physical connection of devices within the SCSI bus. Other technologies, such as IDE, ATA, and EIDE, are predominantly restricted to a certain number of devices (usually four) that are usually internal to the system unit of the computer. In addition, such devices are normally supported directly by the BIOS of the host computer.

Understanding and Utilizing
the SCSI Hardware Interface

However, due to the way SCSI is designed, a SCSI bus may include up to 16 devices that may reside internally or externally in relation to the system unit. SCSI support is provided via a SCSI BIOS chip rather than the computer's main BIOS program.

SCSI controllers that contain BIOS chips are also called *bus mastering controllers*, in that the card contains its own BIOS and autonomously maintains basic information about the devices connected to it. In addition, many computer manufacturers offer integrated system board support of SCSI, meaning that no additional interface cards are needed.

Within a SCSI bus, several physical features contribute to its operation and speed. Understanding SCSI operation requires an understanding of the three main parts of the SCSI bus:

- Host adapters, controllers, or initiators

- Cabling and connectors

- Devices and termination

Every SCSI bus contains at least a single host adapter, a single cable, an attached device, and two terminators. Figure 14.1(a) shows a basic configuration for a SCSI bus. Note that any number of devices (up to 16), including the host adapter, may be attached to a SCSI bus. In addition, multiple hosts may be attached to a SCSI bus so that multiple machines can share devices found on the bus itself (see Figure 14.1(b)). In the cluster environment, the latter is used to connect devices to cluster servers. Note also that multiple SCSI buses can be used for redundancy and device fail-over support. However, configurations cannot include "Y" configurations (see Figure 14.1(c)).

Within a SCSI bus, each device is connected to another device to create the SCSI chain. Devices are numbered, or addressed, logically from 0 to 7 (SCSI-1) or from 0 to 16 (SCSI-2). The SCSI address uniquely and logically identifies the device in the bus. During boot up, the SCSI controller identifies each device as a specific number in the SCSI bus and accesses it using the SCSI address identifier. However, devices may be rearranged or removed from the chain—device arrangement is unconstrained and not physically based.

Also, you should realize that devices can include items inside the system unit as well as outside the system unit. Typically, the controller card, which resides inside an expansion slot in the computer or in the system board, will start the chain, and a device will end the chain. Each end of the SCSI bus must also be terminated with a terminating resistor or termination power. Note that because devices can be inside or outside the computer, placement of the adapter card is arbitrary. The important point is that each end of the SCSI bus is terminated while the devices in between are not terminated.

Figure 14.1.

SCSI implementations must include at least a host adapter and a single device (a), but they can be made more complex with multiple adapters, devices, and hosts (b). Configurations cannot include Y-type scenarios (c).

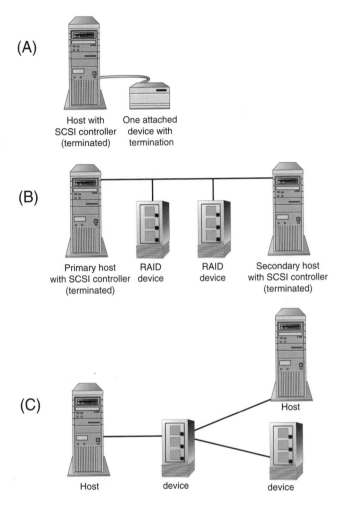

(A)

Host with
SCSI controller
(terminated)

One attached
device with
termination

(B)

Primary host
with SCSI controller
(terminated)

RAID
device

RAID
device

Secondary host
with SCSI controller
(terminated)

(C)

Host

Host

device

device

Each of the physical parts of the SCSI bus directly contributes to the overall efficiency and effectiveness of devices attached to the SCSI bus, regardless of the complexity of the configuration. The following sections further describe the important aspects of each feature and how they contribute to the SCSI bus.

14.2.1. Host Adapters

The host adapter, sometimes called a *controller* or *initiator*, is a card that is normally inserted into expansion slots found within the computer. Using a PCI slot, the SCSI controller is inserted into the computer to allow any range of devices to be connected to the system. In the Windows NT cluster, a SCSI bus with multiple initiators (controllers) is used to provide the storage component.

Yet, many of today's newer systems include a SCSI controller directly on the system board. The advantage of an integrated SCSI controller is that it does not consume one of the PC's expansion slots. With computers used in cluster configurations, PCI-type slots are a valuable commodity. Most cluster servers will require at least one, if not two, PCI network cards. In addition, two SCSI controllers will also be needed in each system.

The optimum configuration for cluster implementations utilizes two SCSI controllers—one integrated controller on the system board and one inserted into an expansion slot. Note that two PCI-based controllers may be used if a system based on EIDE or IDE is being used. Yet, the optimum system will be completely SCSI-based (see the following note).

> **NOTE**   Looking forward to Phase II of Microsoft's Cluster Server product, future expandability can be partially dependent on the number of expansion slots consumed by various interface cards. As more servers are interconnected within the cluster, it becomes important to use as many integrated interfaces as possible. Therefore, it is suggested that investments in server computers focus on integrated SCSI throughout the entire system.

Two of the most important points to remember about using multiple SCSI controllers is that they should be from the same manufacturer and that only one can be the bus master for a given machine.

The first point is quite obvious. With any application needing two SCSI controllers, controller boards from the same manufacturer will almost always work together with very few configuration problems. In addition, Microsoft has released a list of SCSI controllers that have been successfully tested on a shared SCSI bus. These are listed at the end of this chapter. It is suggested that SCSI controllers intended for use in a single machine be from the same manufacturer.

As previously mentioned, the BIOS of the SCSI controller masters or controls the bus and maintains the devices attached to the controller. When multiple controllers are used in a single system, only one controller can have its BIOS activated. Two controllers may not have BIOS enabled at the same time in the system. Most cards allow for configuration (turning BIOS on or off) via software, whereas others use a series of jumpers. Nonetheless, within a two–controller system, one controller is a bus master and the other provides the machine as a device on the secondary bus, as shown in Figure 14.2.

In Figure 14.2, you see two servers that each have two controller cards. In addition, two SCSI buses exist as labeled. Card A in the primary server masters or controls SCSI bus I. Card B, also in the primary server, simply provides the primary server as a device on SCSI bus II. In the secondary server, two SCSI cards are used to provide mastering for SCSI bus II via card D and the secondary server as a device on SCSI bus I via card C.

Figure 14.2.

In a two-controller configuration, only one card can master. The other provides the system to the secondary bus as a device.

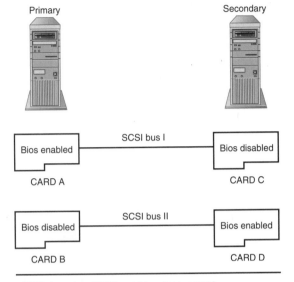

CARD A masters SCSI bus I (via primary server)
CARD B provides primary server as a device on SCSI bus II
CARD C masters SCSI bus II (via secondary server)
CARD D provides primary server as a device on SCSI bus I

> **NOTE** One last comment concerning SCSI controllers is that there are various classifications of SCSI-2 cards. Terms such as fast, wide, ultra, and so on are various modifications of the basic SCSI capability and will be covered later in section 14.3, "Types of SCSI Implementation." These various classifications do affect the performance of the SCSI card and should be understood before making purchases.

14.2.2. Cabling and Connectors

When dealing with cabling issues in SCSI buses, two important issues arise: the type of cable (and connectors) and the length of the cable. The type of cable can affect your physical ability to interconnect devices, due to a cable being of one type or another. In addition, there is a wide variety of connectors that can be used on those cables. Knowing whether you need a DB50, Centronics, or Mini DB50 becomes important when acquiring the necessary cables.

More important than cable type, the length of the cable can adversely affect the quality of the signals running through the cable. The SCSI protocol gives specific cable length measurements for both the overall bus length and individual segments of the SCSI chain. Most often, these cable length specifications become more important as the quality and speed of the SCSI controllers increase. However, to maximize SCSI performance, cable length specifications should always be adhered to.

Types of Connectors

In general, there are five different types of external SCSI connectors, ignoring the obvious differences between male and female connections. For internal connectors, there are two different types of connectors. These connectors can then be further subdivided into connectors for single-ended or differential SCSI (explained in the next section).

The most common connections on modern PCs are the High Density 50-Pin connectors and the High Density 68-Pin connectors, as shown in Figure 14.3. In most clustering environments, these are the cables you'll be working with. However, some devices might have other types of older connectors.

Figure 14.3.

The most commonly used SCSI connectors.

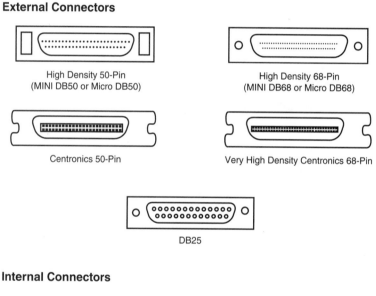

External Connectors

High Density 50-Pin
(MINI DB50 or Micro DB50)

High Density 68-Pin
(MINI DB68 or Micro DB68)

Centronics 50-Pin

Very High Density Centronics 68-Pin

DB25

Internal Connectors

Standard 50-Pin

High Density 68-Pin

Types of Cables

Although SCSI cables vary in quality based on manufacturer and price, there are generally two types of SCSI cables. First there is the older, 50-pin-based cables called *normal* or *single-ended SCSI*. Normal SCSI cables allow a single wire in the cable to be assigned to each signal that needs to be sent from device to device. For every signal there is a wire to carry it.

Second, for differential SCSI, which uses 68 pins (or wires) for each signal, there
exist two wires to carry each signal. The first cable in differential SCSI carries the
same signal as a single-ended SCSI cable. However, the second differential cable
carries the inversion of the first cable. Thus, the controller or device is able to
derive the differential or difference between the two signals, allowing for higher
quality signals and greater cable lengths (see "Cable Lengths," later).

NOTE One special note about purchasing cabling for SCSI devices. Many
cable manufacturers are selling "SCSI-2" cables that do not conform
to the real SCSI-2 specification. The SCSI-2 standard specifies that cables should
maintain an impedance of 90 to 132 ohms. Many manufacturers sell cables as SCSI-2
simply because they have high density connectors, not based on impedance specifications. Cabling that doesn't maintain its impedance can cause major performance
problems. Buy high quality, brand name SCSI cabling. As the speed and quality of your
SCSI bus increases, it becomes more important to purchase high-quality SCSI cabling.

WARNING Differential devices and cables are incompatible with single-ended
devices and cables and vice versa, due to physical differences in
connectors. Ensure that the devices and cables you order or purchase are the correct
ones for your bus. You can acquire single-ended to differential converters so that you
may attain longer cable lengths.

Differential SCSI cables are typically used with the fastest of SCSI controllers and
devices. Older controllers that are narrow (8-bit buses) use the normal SCSI
cables. In the clustering scenario, where speed is of the utmost importance,
differential SCSI is predominant. The most important note regarding cable type is
to buy good cables (ones that maintain the SCSI-2 specification of an impedance
of 90 to 132 ohms) with the proper cable type (normal or differential) and proper
connectors.

Cable Lengths

As important as cable type is cable lengths. The SCSI specification provides
information not only on the total length of the SCSI bus, but also on the spacing
or lengths between devices.

In general, the specifications state that "stubs" or devices in the chain should not
be any closer than .3 meters (12 inches) apart. However, the closeness of devices
varies, depending on the speed of the bus.

For example, with a SCSI-1 bus, the distance between devices doesn't matter
much. But when you are dealing with a Fast20 SCSI bus, which is discussed a
little later, this distance becomes very important.

Aside from device spacing, the important point to remember with SCSI buses is that overall length of the bus is vitally important. Determining the maximum length of your bus is dependent on the speed of the fastest device in your chain. When you are dealing with SCSI bus lengths, there is a relationship between speed (not width) and chain length. Table 14.1 shows the speeds of SCSI buses in MHz and maximum cable lengths, depending on whether you are using single-ended or differential connections.

Table 14.1. Specifications for total SCSI bus length based on fastest device speed.

Speed of Fastest Device	Maximum Single-ended Length	Maximum Differential Length
5 MHz (SCSI-1)	6 meters	25 meters
10 MHz (SCSI-2 Fast)	3 meters	25 meters
20 MHz (Ultra or Fast20)	1.5 meters	25 meters

Keep in mind that Table 14.1 assumes you know or can find out the speed of your fastest device. Often times, documentation can tell you what the device speed is. Some adapters come with a software utility that can provide this information.

You should realize that bus speed is negotiated by the controller at boot up and is set to the slowest speed of all the devices on the bus. Fast devices, such as 20 MHz, connected to a slow card, 10 MHz, will yield a bus speed of 10 MHz. Alternatively, the same is true with a fast card and slow devices.

NOTE   As you continue reading, keep in mind that cable length is based on fastest device speed, not on the width (number of bits transferred).

Synchronous versus Asynchronous Communication

Among the discussion of cable types and lengths, it seems appropriate that one other factor of SCSI communication be mentioned. In the SCSI environment, no matter if you are talking about SCSI-1, SCSI-2, or SCSI-3, communication can occur synchronously or asynchronously. The reason that this is important is because, when you are dealing with longer cables, synchronous communication is faster.

Asynchronous communication requires that a device answer a command before a new command is issued to a device. Much like the discussion of single and multithread capability earlier in this chapter, asynchronous communication requires a response from a device before more data is sent. In short bus length situations, this is not a factor. However, as cables get longer, this constant need to reply can become a hindrance to performance.

Yet, when synchronous communication is used, this is not the case. In synchronous mode, a device does not have to respond to the sending device before more data is sent. Therefore, as cables get longer, this ability to not respond over the given distance allows faster performance and less intercommunication between devices on a longer bus.

14.2.3. Devices and Termination

The last important feature of the SCSI bus is the devices connected to the bus. As you have read, the SCSI bus must be terminated at the beginning device and the ending device in the bus. Devices in the middle of the SCSI bus must have termination removed or turned off.

> **NOTE**   One thing that people typically forget is that if you put an adapter card in the middle of a SCSI chain, do not forget to disable termination on the card. Most adapter cards come from the manufacturer with termination enabled. The SCSI bus must only be terminated on the ends of the chain, not in the middle. Although most cluster applications of SCSI will have a card on each end of the bus, if the adapter is in the middle of the bus, remember to disable termination on the card.

When analyzing termination, you must realize that there are two types of SCSI bus termination: active and passive. Passive termination, which was the original SCSI-1 method, generally requires that a small connector be attached to the beginning and ending devices. The small connector contains a group of resistors that dampens reflected signals from the ends of the bus, thus removing signals that have reached their destination. Typically, passive termination is associated with SCSI-1 buses, but it's also useful for shorter SCSI buses.

The second type of termination is active termination, which has one or more voltage regulators that produce the termination voltage. Often active termination is provided via a switch on a device, rather than a physical connector that is attached to the bus connection. Many newer devices have an on, off, and auto switch state that can alleviate the need to be concerned about termination.

Active termination is best for applications in which bus lengths are longer. Active termination provides for a less noisy bus by reducing signal noise on the bus. Additionally, active termination improves the overall termination process by providing regulated termination voltage and reducing the current drawn from the termination power line within the bus.

> **NOTE**   Almost all SCSI-2 buses utilize active termination. Active termination is most applicable to clustering configurations.

14.3. Types of SCSI Implementation

Although there are many acronyms and terms that are associated SCSI and SCSI implementations, the important features apply to SCSI-2. Terms such as fast, wide, and ultra require an understanding of the main differences between SCSI-1 and SCSI-2, as well as an understanding of the proposed features that might be found in SCSI-3 implementations once it is ratified and accepted by ANSI.

The following sections focus on the differences between SCSI-1, SCSI-2, and up-and-coming SCSI-3, as well as terms such as fast, wide, and ultra SCSI.

14.3.1. SCSI-1 and SCSI-2

The predominant difference between SCSI-1 and SCSI-2 is that SCSI-2 provides a wealth of enhancements and speed/performance increases over SCSI-1. Due to the increasingly wide variety of devices and adapters focusing on SCSI-2, SCSI-1 usage is almost nonexistent, except in support of legacy devices and software. The predominance of cards being distributed are SCSI-2 cards because of the greater performance demands required for today's computers, networks, and applications.

SCSI-2 provides a wide variety of improvements over SCSI-1 in both hardware and command-set specifications. Many of the restrictive parameters associated with SCSI-1, such as single initiators (adapter cards), were eliminated. In addition, several options were added to further enhance the SCSI interface protocol. These include, but are not limited to, the following:

- Wide SCSI
- Fast SCSI
- High-density connectors
- Improved termination

In addition to hardware enhancements, command sets for various devices connected to the SCSI bus were also established. By dividing command sets up by device type, SCSI could more adequately fill the need for a wide range of devices that users connect. The various command sets that were added to SCSI include the following:

- CD-ROMs
- Scanner devices

- Optical memory devices

- Medium changer devices

- Communications devices

Although all these changes, additions, and modifications have extended the use and application of SCSI, three have the most significance in the clustering environment. Whenever you are dealing with SCSI for clustering, three terms will be inevitably mentioned: Wide SCSI, Fast SCSI, and Ultra SCSI. The next section describes the affect that these SCSI types have on the bus and communication.

14.3.2. Wide, Fast, and Ultra SCSI

The first of these SCSI implementations, Wide SCSI, uses an extra cable (or a 68-pin P cable) to send data 16-bits or 32-bits wide. Narrow SCSI, or normal SCSI, sends data 8-bits wide. Wide SCSI allows for double or even quadruple speed transfers over the SCSI bus. However, you must realize that no single drive reaches speeds of 16 bits or 32 bits. Yet, when several drives are connected using Wide SCSI, the additional bus width allows for faster data transfer.

Note that even on a Wide SCSI bus, some operations, such as arbitration, commands, status, and messages, are still 8-bit. It is the physical data being transferred that utilizes the 16-bit or 32-bit enhancement. Nonetheless, significant speed increases are noticeable when comparing Wide SCSI to Narrow SCSI.

> **NOTE** As previously mentioned, keep in mind that the bus width (Wide SCSI) doesn't change the maximum allowable cable lengths for the SCSI bus. The bus width is independent of bus length or speed. Bus length is dependent on the fastest device in the bus.

The second SCSI performance enhancement, Fast SCSI, allows for faster timing on the SCSI bus. Basically, a Fast SCSI connection is capable of 10-MHz speeds instead of 5-MHz speeds, assuming device arbitration determines all devices on the bus are capable of 10 MHz. If the controller card determines that there is a slow device on the bus, the speed of the slower device is used. However, on an 8-bit (narrow) SCSI bus, using Fast SCSI allows a theoretical speed of 10 MHz. Again, no individual device can probably hit 5 MHz, yet it does allow devices to run at speeds greater than the typical 5-MHz threshold.

When analyzing Fast SCSI, you must also acknowledge that the issue of synchronous and asynchronous communication modes also affects the amount of speed attainable via Fast SCSI. In the previous paragraph, synchronous communication was assumed.

Realize that SCSI-1 allowed asynchronous transfers up to 1.5 MBps and synchronous transfers up to 5.0 MBps. With SCSI-2 enhancements, Fast SCSI yields asynchronous transfers up to 3.0 MBps and synchronous transfers up to 10 MBps. Although Fast SCSI is typically associated with 10 MHz, realize that it is typically equated to devices that can attain synchronous transfers of greater than 5 MBps.

The last SCSI enhancement under discussion is Ultra SCSI. Ultra SCSI is a method that enables extremely fast data transfer rates over a SCSI bus. Typically, Ultra SCSI data transfer rates extend to 20 MBps. This alone is quite impressive; however, when Ultra SCSI is combined with Wide SCSI, data transfer rates can be extended to 40 MBps.

With the wide variety of SCSI combinations, realize that there are many more SCSI performance and speed enhancements on their way, such as Ultra-2 SCSI and Wide Ultra-2, as well as Ultra-3 and Wide Ultra-3. Although we still have yet to see them implemented, they will undoubtedly affect networking environments where many large storage devices are used together. Table 14.2 shows the various SCSI combinations as well as their relationships to other technologies such as EIDE, IEEE 1394 (Firewire), and Universal Serial Bus (USB).

Table 14.2. Speeds of common and proposed hardware interfaces.

Hardware Interface	Burst Data Transfer Rate
EIDE (Fast ATA)	1.1–1.6 MBps
Narrow SCSI	1.5 asynchronous / 5 synchronous
Wide SCSI	3 asynchronous / 10 synchronous
Fast SCSI	10 MBps
Universal Serial Bus (USB)	12 MBps
Fast/Wide SCSI	20 MBps
Ultra SCSI	20 MBps
Wide/Ultra SCSI	40 MBps
★Ultra-2 SCSI	40 MBps
★Wide Ultra-2 SCSI	80 MBps
★Ultra-3 SCSI	Greater than 80 MBps
★Wide Ultra-3 SCSI	Greater than 160 MBps

Hardware Interface	Burst Data Transfer Rate
IEEE 1394 (Firewire)	100 to 400 MBps
★IEEE 1394B	1.6 gigabytes per second (maximum)
★Currently under development	

14.3.3. SCSI-3

Most of the discussion and selling of "SCSI-3" devices is based on the fact that certain devices or controllers use the SCSI-3 cable specification (68-pin cable) that allows for complete 16-bit communication. Yet, SCSI-3 has not been ratified as yet, so beyond the fact that a device comes with a different cable, no other part of the device is truly "SCSI-3."

The current state of SCSI-3 is that the entire SCSI-2 standard has been divided into small groups, with the hopes that standardization will come quicker. SCSI-3 is more a group of standards than a single specification. There are actually 11 groups of standards, many of which are based on the command sets that evolved from SCSI-1 to SCSI-2. Nonetheless, the SCSI-3 group of standards has yet to be finalized, so conjecture or fortune telling about what it will include and what the devices will look like or how they will perform is uncertain.

14.4. SCSI and the Fail-over Operation

As you have read, in any cluster there are three predominant connections that can exist between the servers in the cluster: the cluster interconnect, the LAN connection, and the SCSI bus. The cluster interconnect is the primary means of communication between the servers. However, all three of these connections are important to the fail-over operation.

Assuming that the secondary server cannot communicate to the primary server through the cluster interconnect, it must then determine if the primary server is malfunctioning. To do this, it utilizes the LAN connection.

Realize that the LAN connection is used as a secondary polling mechanism, not just for user connection. If the server doesn't receive a response from the cluster interconnect—acknowledging that everything is okay—it can and will use the LAN connection as a backup cluster interconnect. This allows the server to determine if the server, or the cluster interconnect, is faulty. If the server still receives no acknowledgment from the primary server through the LAN connection, it then uses its third means of checking on the primary server—the SCSI bus.

Throughout this chapter, you have been looking at SCSI technology from the standpoint of storage. Indeed, this is the primary function of the SCSI bus—that is, the storage component. Yet, the SCSI bus is not only important from an I/O vantage. It is also important to the fail-over capability of the cluster.

As a third means of checking for the failure of a server, Cluster Server also uses the SCSI bus as a means of polling, assuming communication via the cluster interconnect and the LAN has failed. Using an indirect technique, the Cluster Server is able to determine if the primary server should be taken offline. To understand how this works, you must understand how the servers access the shared drives within the cluster environment.

Shared drives on the SCSI bus are managed by a bus arbitration scheme called *multi-initiator SCSI*. An initiator, as you have read, is simply a SCSI controller card, one of which is located inside each server (thus called multi-initiator).

Before a data transfer occurs across the SCSI bus, the controller tells the SCSI bus which drive or device it wants to access. If the other controller in the cluster is not accessing the device, the requesting controller locks the target for the duration of the transfer and then releases it.

Yet, in this target locking process, the initiator (controller) with the higher SCSI ID has priority to the targets on the SCSI bus. If an initiator with higher priority needs to access a target, the initiator with the lower SCSI ID must relinquish the target. It is this logical priority that is the basis for determining the working order of the primary server.

For example, assuming the primary server has the higher SCSI ID, the secondary server can check the status of the primary server by accessing the storage device on the SCSI bus and locking it out. If the primary server is in working order, at some point it will force the secondary server to relinquish control of the storage device, thereby signifying that it is in working order. If, over a period of time, no attempt is made by the primary server to access the storage device, the secondary server can assume that the primary server is malfunctioning.

14.5. SCSI and Windows NT

One of the nice things about Windows NT is that it directly supports a wide range of SCSI controllers as well as devices connected to a SCSI bus. Keep in mind that there are specific devices that have been tested (and are recommended) for use with Windows Cluster Server. Nonetheless, setting up SCSI devices in Windows NT is pretty easy.

Initial versions of Windows NT have a specific setup program for adding SCSI adapter drivers to the OS. However, with Windows NT 4.0, the OS automatically detects the adapter and adds drivers as appropriate. Additionally, Windows NT will add device-specific drivers. Yet, you may also choose to manually install controller or device drivers.

Selecting the SCSI adapter applet from the Control Panel menu option in the Start menu allows you to view the SCSI controllers that exist in a system, as well as the devices connected to each controller. (See Figure 14.4.)

Figure 14.4.

The SCSI adapter applet allows you to view the SCSI controllers and attached SCSI devices.

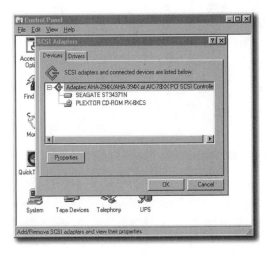

As shown in Figures 14.5 and 14.6, selecting the controller (or a device) and clicking the Properties button brings up additional information about the driver or controller.

Figure 14.5.

Viewing the properties of a SCSI adapter.

14.5.1. Configuring SCSI Devices in NT

Although SCSI will support a wide range of devices, the predominant devices attached in the cluster environment are individual hard disks as well as RAID (Redundant Array of Inexpensive [Independent] Disks) devices. Setting up these devices is relatively easy. However, there are three factors of which you must be

Understanding and Utilizing the SCSI Hardware Interface

aware. Two of these "set-up notes" concern the SCSI adapter. The other note relates to hard drives or disk arrays that are connected to the SCSI bus.

Figure 14.6.

Viewing the properties of a SCSI device.

Because most cluster servers include two SCSI controllers within the system, you must ensure that both controllers are addressed within the system with different BIOS addresses. Typically, if you purchase two controllers to be inserted into a system, they will be set to the default manufacturer BIOS and Port addresses. You might need to add or remove jumpers on one of the SCSI controllers so that the two cards use different BIOS and Port addresses. Depending on the manufacturer, address configuration might be performed using a software configuration program rather than physical jumpers. Even if you are using an integrated controller and one to be inserted into a PCI slot, you must check the BIOS and Port addresses of the two controllers. It is likely if the controllers are from the same manufacturer that they will be set to the same address.

The second note concerns a setting called Boot Time SCSI Reset on the adapter card. As you read earlier, only one SCSI card can have its BIOS enabled within a given system. As discussed, you usually utilize a configuration program to disable the BIOS on one of two cards so that they can operate in the same system.

This configuration program should also allow you to turn off the Boot Time SCSI Reset. This reset allows the computer to reset the devices on the SCSI bus upon restart. This reset interrupts anything else that is going on with the device. However, resetting the SCSI bus in a multi-initiator environment can be detrimental and inefficient.

For example, imagine that a fail-over has occurred and the primary server has been taken offline. The secondary server, while taking control of all system functions, decides to try to restart the primary server. If the primary server's SCSI card has Boot Time SCSI Reset enabled, it will disrupt the secondary server's operations by resetting the disks or arrays attached to the SCSI bus. Note that the

Boot Time SCSI Reset option should be disabled on all of the SCSI cards in the cluster configuration. This option is applicable to single initiator environments only.

The final note concerning clustering devices is that all hard disks or arrays used with Cluster Server must be formatted to NTFS (NT File System). In addition, Microsoft strongly recommends that each disk have only one partition because logical partitions cannot be independently failed-over.

14.5.2. Troubleshooting SCSI Buses

Probably the hardest part of using a SCSI bus is getting it to operate for the first time. Once it is up and running, maintenance is easy.

If you are having difficulty with a SCSI bus, start by checking all of the physical items involved with the bus. The following list contains common problems that can usually be resolved by just "checking it out." If you are having problems with a machine locking up during boot-up, make sure of the following:

- The BIOS is disabled on one of the cards in a multi-initiator environment. Having two cards in the same system, both with BIOS enabled, will usually cause the machine to lock up during boot-up.

- The SCSI cards you are using in your system do not use the same BIOS or Port addresses. Additionally, make sure the SCSI cards do not use the BIOS or Port address assigned to another device or card in the system.

- The SCSI cards you are using in your system do not use the same IRQ (interrupts) or DMA channels. Additionally, make sure the SCSI cards do not use the IRQ (interrupts) or DMA channels assigned to another device or card in the system.

Assuming your machine boots up into Windows NT, you've made it past the first hurdle. However, if you have problems with any particular device in the chain or with data transfers in general, make sure of the following:

- You check all connectors very carefully and ensure that they are securely fastened to one another.

- All the cables being used are high-quality cables. Poor quality cables can result in any range of undesirable results.

- Each device uses a unique SCSI ID number. If two devices have the same ID, the second device in the chain will not be accessible (that is, the first device to access the SCSI ID number will be accessible, the second will not).

- Cable length specifications are followed. Typically, exceeding the cable length specifications will result in unexpected behavior in devices toward the end of the SCSI chain. Problems may be exhibited as decreased performance.

- All devices in the SCSI chain are either differential or single ended. If a single to differential converter is used, single-ended devices should be attached to the end of the bus.

- Termination occurs at both ends of the SCSI bus. Additionally, make sure termination is not occurring anywhere between the two ends of the SCSI bus. Termination in the middle of a bus causes all devices from the termination point to be inaccessible.

- For longer cable lengths, ensure that active termination is used.

14.5.3. RAID Devices

As you have read, RAID is an acronym for Redundant Array of Inexpensive Disks. Other sources state it as Redundant Array of Independent Disks. Nonetheless, the premise is the same. Interconnect a series of smaller, and cheaper, drives to create a single storage unit rather attempting to create a single extremely large drive (which is very expensive). Although a RAID is composed of several hard disks, it is viewed and used as a single unit.

Developed by a team of individuals at UC-Berkley, RAID actually is more than a single defined construct. In the general sense, it is always composed of several disks. However, RAID devices can be classified into six different categories, depending on functionality and price. These categories include the following:

- RAID Level 0 is a RAID classification that uses data striping but provides for no redundancy among the drives. At Level 0, data is divided across drives (striping), which results in extremely high throughput. Although throughput is good, because no redundancy is available, failure of a single drive renders the entire RAID useless. Generally RAID Level 0 is used for any application that requires very high speed storage, such as digital video work or other speed-dependent tasks.

- RAID Level 1 uses the multiple drives to provide redundancy by duplicating all the data from one drive to another drive, which is called *mirroring*. As an entry-level device, RAID-1 does provide redundancy; however, the speed of the device is only slightly higher than a single drive.

Additionally, because two drives are used for the same data, the cost per megabyte of data is quite high. Typically, RAID Level 1 is used for small file servers where redundancy is required and fast random writes are important.

- RAID Level 2 is a special classification that provides for error correction for drives that do not support it. Yet, because all SCSI drives include error correction, Level 2 has very little use with SCSI drives.

- RAID Level 3 utilizes data striping at the byte level across multiple drives. Parity information is stored on a single drive and requires hardware support for efficiency.

- RAID Level 4 utilizes data striping at the block level across multiple drives. Akin to Level 3, Level 4 stores parity information on a single drive. Note that because only one drive stores the redundant data, the cost per megabyte of a Level 4 RAID is quite low. Generally, applications that require lower-cost redundancy with high-speed reads are applicable to RAID Level 4. RAID Level 4 is often used with larger file servers.

- RAID Level 5 is similar to Level 4, but it distributes parity among all the drives in the RAID. Generally the performance of RAID 5 is used with database servers, due to small, random input and output functions. RAID Level 5 is the most applicable level for clustering environments.

Understanding and Utilizing
the SCSI Hardware Interface

14.5.4. Microsoft Tested and Suggested Controllers

The following SCSI controller cards were supplied by the Microsoft Cluster Server documentation as cards that have been successfully tested on multi-initiator bus. The following cards are recommended for use in a Cluster Server cluster:

- Adaptec AHA-2940/U/UW

- Adaptec AHA-2944/W/U/W

- Adaptec AHA-3940/W/UW/UWD

- Adaptec AHA-3944/W/UW/UWD

- BusLogic BT-948

- BusLogic BT-958

- BusLogic BT-958D

> **NOTE** Microsoft also noted that the "boot-time reset operation" for the SCSI bus may be disabled using the configuration utilities. Adaptec's configuration utility allows SCSI BIOS parameters to be changed via software. Remember that the "boot-time reset operation" should be disabled so that, if the primary server comes back online after a fail-over, it will not reset or restart the SCSI devices attached to the SCSI bus.
>
> In addition, recent Adaptec products come with version 1.2*x* of the setup program, which will not allow disabling of bus resets. Adaptec has provided a fix for versions 1.2 and 1.25. According to Adaptec, version 1.1 should not be used for the Adaptec 2940 because the BIOS cannot be modified. Version 1.1 can be used for the Adapted 2940/U/UW.
>
> Microsoft also notes that BusLogic controllers on one node sometimes fail during bus scan if the other node in the cluster is using a device. Restarting the failed computer will usually fix this problem. BusLogic is testing a solution for this issue.

14.5.5. Microsoft Tested and Suggested Devices

The following SCSI devices were supplied by the Microsoft Cluster Server documentation as devices that have been successfully tested on a multi-initiator bus. The following devices are recommended for use in a Cluster Server cluster:

- Clarion RAID storage subsystem (and slot)
- Hewlett-Packard Auto RAID storage subsystem (with new firmware)
- Maxtor LXT340S (firmware revision 6.75)
- Micropolis 4221-09MZ Q4D HT02 SN CQ RA
- Micropolis 4221-09 1128RA28RA SN CQ RA
- Micropolis 3245-19MZ Q4D HT02 SN CQ RA
- Seagate ST31051W 0526 SN CQ W16
- Seagate ST31055W 0528 SN CQ W16
- Seagate ST32550W 0021 SN CQ W16 LC
- Seagate ST32550N 0012 SN CQ LC
- Seagate ST32550N 0014 SN CQ LC
- Seagate ST15150W 0023 SN CQ W16 LC
- Seagate ST31055N 0316 SN CQ

14.6. Summary

Throughout this chapter, you have taken a brief look at SCSI technology and the various types and implementations of it. Keep in mind that the main problems that occur with SCSI usually happen when the guidelines and limitations are breached. Be sure to adhere to the cabling and termination requirements as well as other logical constructs, such as only having a single BIOS enabled. These are frequently the cause of deficient SCSI buses, as are incompatible SCSI boards in multi-initiator systems.

Understanding and Utilizing
the SCSI Hardware Interface

Appendix

A

Technical Glossary

ADS (Active Directory Service)   An advanced directory service designed to facilitate the scaling of intranets. All networked resources are catalogued as objects into a central directory. This centralization makes all networked resources much easier to manage and access. The user is relieved of the burden of finding resources: They are all in the active directory of ADS.

API (Application Programming Interface)   A standardized software interface that an application program uses to access lower-level services.

availability   The readiness and capability of a computer system to accept and process requests.

CAN (cluster area network)   The networking that is used exclusively to interconnect clustered nodes is best described as a cluster area network.

ccNUMA (Cache Coherent Nonuniform Memory Access)   A direct memory access methodology that enables computers to access the memory of another computer without having to traverse either machine's I/O bus.

CISC (Complex Instruction Set Computer)   A microprocessor architecture that prefers a robust instruction set to the speed with which individual instructions can be executed. CISC instructions do not execute as quickly as instructions in a RISC architecture, but each instruction accomplishes more work than a RISC instruction.

cluster   A loosely coupled set of computers that function as a single computer. Clusters take a seemingly infinite variety of topologies, each tailored to extract a different combination of benefits from the distributed redundancy of the cluster's resources.

cluster-aware   Software that can recognize and access cluster services. To benefit fully from being clustered, operating systems and application software must be capable of recognizing and accessing cluster services through cluster APIs.

Cluster Server   Formerly known as *Wolfpack*. This is Microsoft's cluster management product. Initial releases of Cluster Server will be limited to fail-over service in a two-node cluster. In time, Cluster Server will support up to sixteen nodes, providing them with fail-over service as well as dynamic load balancing.

DLM (distributed lock manager)   An essential technique for controlling the modification of data in databases that are shared across multiple CPUs.

DSS (Decision Support System)   An application type that features CPU-intensive data analysis and modeling of business situations. The nature of a DSS is highly dynamic and not repetitive, thus queries must be ad hoc. DSS, unlike simple report generation, requires some abstraction of data. For example, time series and trends are legitimate objects of a DSS modeling exercise. These types of data do not exist naturally in an OLTP database and must be built for the DSS. The goal of a DSS is to test the appropriateness of decisions before actually making them. In this manner, DSS is used to facilitate the management of a business by leveraging the lessons of the past (as recorded in the data).

dynamic load balancing   A cluster's capability to automatically and spontaneously shift processing responsibilities to lesser utilized nodes in a cluster.

EIS (Executive Information System)   A highly specialized form of application that abstracts data, much like a DSS, but the queries tend to be less repetitive. The goal of an EIS is to inform executive management of the status of a business operation. Consequently, EIS queries tend to be more predictable and repetitive.

fail-back   The restoration of resource ownership to its primary node. This is the opposite of a fail-over and can occur either automatically or manually.

fail-over   The term used to describe the migration of clustered resources to other nodes. Major or minor failures can result in involuntary fail-overs. Preventive maintenance and other system activities might also be facilitated through a voluntary fail-over of active resources to other cluster nodes.

GUI (graphical user interface)   A visually oriented environment used by many operating systems, such as the Microsoft Windows family of products, that enables the user to access resources with a pointing device.

intercluster   Anything that occurs between two or more clusters.

internodal   Anything that occurs between two or more nodes within a single cluster.

intracluster   Anything that is confined to a cluster.

intranodal   Anything that occurs within a single node.

MBps (megabytes per second)   A metric of throughput, expressed in millions of bytes per second.

Mbps (megabits per second)   A metric of throughput, expressed in bits per second.

MPP (Massively Parallel Processor)   A unique multiprocessing architecture. As with any multiprocessing architecture, an MPP can support up to thousands of CPUs. What distinguishes an MPP, however, is that each CPU has its own memory and copies of the application and operating system. This enables the overall architecture to be massively scalable.

node   A computer system logically linked with other computer systems to form a cluster.

NORMA (No Remote Memory Access)   This I/O model is the conventional form of memory access with which most people are familiar. NORMA requires that all requests for access to memory must originate locally and pass through the local I/O bus. This enables all requests to be satisfied in a uniform time period.

NUMA (Nonuniform Memory Access)   A hybridized I/O model. This model still requires requests for memory access to pass through the I/O bus, but this is enforced in a nonuniform manner: memory can be accessed locally (on the same board) or nonlocally (on remote nodes). An external switching mechanism enables remote hosts (other cluster nodes) to directly address and access the memory resources of any host. Memory that is locally resident can be accessed much faster than external, remote memory.

OA (Office Automation)   A class of applications that supports general office activities. OA includes word processing, spreadsheet, electronic mail, and presentation development applications.

OLTP (Online Transaction Processing)   An application type that features real-time updating of databases to reflect ongoing data events or transactions. OLTP has historically been the mission critical application type of businesses and has been used to log the details of commercial activities.

parallelism   The redundant overlapping of processing capabilities, I/O, or memory, or all of these. Parallelism comes in two main varieties: internal and external. A cluster exhibits external parallelism. Internal parallelism can take the form of either a massively parallel processor, or a symmetrical multiprocessor.

quorum resource   Microsoft's Cluster Server uses a unique resource, known as the *quorum*, to ensure that failures do not split a cluster into two competing halves. Only the nodes that either own, or can see, the quorum resource remain active and in service.

RAID (Redundant Array of Inexpensive Disks)   RAID started out as a simple idea for developing auto-recovering, fault-tolerant, large logical disk drives from small, inexpensive drives. The multiple drives are housed in a common chassis. Data is written redundantly to multiple drives, thereby providing protection from the loss of a disk drive. When a drive is lost, and then replaced, the surviving RAID devices will automatically detect the broken file system and reconstruct. The rapidity with which this recovery is effected depends on the level of protection implemented. There are now seven separate levels of RAID support: RAID-0 through RAID-6. The first five were originally defined RAID-1 through RAID-5 at the University of California at Berkeley. These levels represent different combinations of cost and protection from failure. RAID-0 and RAID-6 are products of the marketplace.

RAID-0 (Redundant Array of Inexpensive Disks, Level 0)   Data is striped across multiple disks, without any error correction or redundancy.

RAID-1 (Redundant Array of Inexpensive Disks, Level 1)   Data is mirrored. One drive serves as the operational drive, with "live" contents. The second drive is an online backup of the first drive that is automatically updated: Every write operation performed on the first disk is automatically duplicated on the second.

RAID-2 (Redundant Array of Inexpensive Disks, Level 2)   A more robust implementation of RAID-0 that includes error checking and correcting codes (ECC). Data is striped across multiple disks along with the ECCs. This facilitates recovery from damaged data.

RAID-3 (Redundant Array of Inexpensive Disks, Level 3)   RAID-3 stripes data, in bytes, across multiple disks. One disk is used exclusively to record parity data.

RAID-4 (Redundant Array of Inexpensive Disks, Level 4)   Stripes data, in blocks, not bytes, across multiple disks. One disk is exclusively reserved for the recording of parity data.

RAID-5 (Redundant Array of Inexpensive Disks, Level 5)   This level of support is the most commonly used of the seven variants. Like RAID-4, it stripes data, in blocks, across multiple disks. The difference is that RAID-5 writes its parity data across multiple disks.

RAID-6 (Redundant Array of Inexpensive Disks, Level 6)   Provides all of the functions of RAID-5, but also implements redundant disk controllers, cabinet fans, and buses.

It is important to note that RAID is not a formal standard. Consequently, there is tremendous disparity between the levels of support provided at any given RAID level, across vendor products.

reliability   In a computer system, reliability is a step beyond mere availability. It means that the system is also ready and able to accept and process requests. However, reliability also requires the system to process each request without failure.

resource   Anything that can be shared by nodes in a cluster. Examples are physical devices, data, application software, IP addresses, and so on.

RISC (Reduced Instruction Set Computer)   A microprocessor architecture that features a relatively small set of simple instructions that execute more quickly, but perform less work, than a CISC instruction. Historically, RISC computers have been reserved for computationally intensive applications.

SAN (System Area Network)   Tandem Systems, Inc. uses the term *System Area Network* to describe its ServerNet technology. This term can also be used to describe the extension of memory access channels to remote machines in lieu of traditional I/O-based networking.

scalability   A measure of the efficiency with which linear expansion can occur on any given platform. It refers to the ratio of realized performance improvement to linear expansion of capacity.

Technical Glossary

SCI (Scalable Coherent Interface)   Recently standardized by the IEEE/ANSI standards numbered 1596-1992. It uses the NUMA I/O model and is designed to provide a scalable interconnect technology for cluster nodes.

SCSI (Small Computer Systems Interface—pronounced *scuzzy*)   A hardware interface used to interconnect hosts and peripheral devices. SCSI has been extended into multiple specifications. These specifications can support anywhere from 7 peripherals up to 15, and data rates from 5MBps to 40 MBps.

SCSI-1   The original small computer systems interface, this was more of a concept than a product, and was quickly superseded by SCSI-2.

SCSI-2   The first standardized form of SCSI, this specification featured an 8-bit bus that supported a total of 8 devices (including the adapter card) and had a data rate of 5 MBps. Single-ended cabling is limited to 19.7 feet. Differential cabling can extend to 25 meters.

> **Fast SCSI-2**   An improvement over SCSI-2 that increased the data rate to 10 MBps. Maximum supported single-ended cable length decreased to 9.8 feet.

> **Fast Wide SCSI-2**   A further improvement in the SCSI-2 specification that featured a 16-bit bus. This enables 16 devices (including the adapter card) to be interconnected, with a data rate that can range from 10 MBps to 20 MBps.

> **8-bit Ultra SCSI-3**   A new variant based on an 8-bit bus. The improvement came in a 20 MBps data rate for the 8 devices. Maximum length of single-ended cables depends on the number of devices. 9.8 feet can be used for 4 or fewer devices, otherwise the cable must be no greater than 4.9 feet.

> **16-bit Ultra SCSI-3**   The 16-bit version of the SCSI-3 specification features a 16-bit bus, with commensurate number of devices, and a 20- to 40-MBps data rate. The same cable length limitations for the 8-bit version apply.

ServerNet   The trade name used by Tandem Computers, Inc. for a semi-internal "network" specifically designed for interconnecting cluster nodes. Because it is semi-internal, Tandem calls it a System Area Network (SAN). It features the NUMA I/O model, and is designed to be the foundation for scalable clustering.

shared disk   A cluster whose nodes share common external disk resources. Shared disk clusters are relatively inexpensive to construct and operate, but suffer from a distinct lack of scalability.

shared nothing   As the name implies, shared nothing clusters are constructed of fully separate and redundant computer systems. No physical resources are shared.

SMP (symmetric multiprocessor)   A computer system whose architecture features multiple CPUs that share memory, I/O, and other system resources. To qualify as symmetric, each CPU's available resources must be identical. Thus, any resources that are available to individual CPUs (like the private memory featured in an MPP) renders the architecture asymmetric.

static load balancing   A technique used to manually distribute processing responsibilities between a cluster's nodes.

striping   A technique that simultaneously writes redundantly to multiple disks with a single write instruction. This is the foundation for the various RAID technologies.

system   Microsoft has elected to use the term *system* to describe individual nodes within a cluster.

uniprocessor   A computer system with a single CPU.

VAXCluster   The first real cluster product, introduced by Digital Equipment Company (DEC) in 1982. The VAXCluster offered more economical computing by uncoupling the input/output (I/O) devices from any single CPU. Instead, all CPUs could access the devices and their contents via a star topology bus and coupling device.

VIA (Virtual Interface Architecture)   VIA is an architecture—not a product—that has been proposed and supported by a wide variety of hardware manufacturers. The goal of this architecture is to make low-end clusters of x86 servers scalable enough to become competition for mid-range (and even mainframe) computers.

VLM (Very Large Memory)   The NT 5.0 Server Enterprise Edition will integrate support for 64-bit memory addressing. This concept, known as VLM, will allow up to 32 gigabytes (GB) of memory to be directly addressed. Operating systems that only use a 32-bit memory addressing scheme are mathematically limited to a maximum of 4 GB of RAM.

Wintel   The combination of Microsoft Windows and Intel x86 is commonly referred to as the *Wintel* platform.

Wolfpack   The Microsoft code name for the alpha and beta releases of its Cluster Server product.

Index

E-F

EIS (Executive Information Systems), 240-242
Enlist protocol (Communications Manager), 129
ESCON (Enterprise Server CONnectivity), 226-227
Ethernet
10-Mbps, 223-224
100-Mbps, 224
full duplex technology, 156
Event Manager, 130-131
external storage devices, developing clusters, 155-156

fail-back timing parameter, 127
fail-backs, 90, 126
fail-over clusters, 9-10, 22
shared disk, 19, 23-27
CANs, 25-26
load balancing, 24
non-load balancing, 25
scalability, 27
size, 26-27
shared nothing, 19, 28-34
load balancing, 31
non-load balancing, 33
topologies, 29-31
see also fail-overs
fail-over timing parameter, 126
Fail-over/Resource Manager, 131-132
fail-overs, 71-73
activating alternate resources, 87

application state replication, 89
automatic complete, 92-93
automatic partial, 92
data replication, 88-89
detecting failures, 73-75
identifying alternative resources, 85-86
identifying stricken resources, 76-78
manual complete, 91-92
manual partial, 90-91
networks, 229-230
notifications, 79
applications, 87-88
inferential, 80-84
order, 88
policies, 126-127
resource deactivation, 84-85
resuming applications, 89-90
scenarios, 73
SCSI, 267-268
sequencing, 93-95
see also fail-over clusters
FailbackWindowEnd property (resource groups), 126
FailbackWindowStart property (resource groups), 126
Fast Ethernet (100-Mbps), 224
Fast SCSI, 265
FDDI, 225
Fibre Channel, 227-228
file synchronization, 106
file systems, NTFS, 101-102
full duplex technology, 156
future of networking, 202

G-H

gathering requirements (cluster development), 143-144
Global Update Manager, 132
groups, *see* **resource groups**

heartbeats, 74
history
clustering, 3-4
networking, 201-202
SCSI, 253-254
host adapters (SCSI), 257-258
Microsoft suggested, 273-274
hot standby machines, 21-22
hybridization, 64-65

I

I/O, 43-45
ccNUMA, 44
NORMA, 43
NUMA, 43-44
VLM, 106
IDE (Integrated Drive Electronics), 254
versus SCSI, 254-255
identifying alternative resources (fail-over), 85-86
implementing clusters, 147
incremental synchronization, 106
inferential notifications, 79-84
initiators, *see* **host adapters**

A VIACOM SERVICE

The Information SuperLibrary™

Bookstore   Search   What's New   Reference   Software   Newsletter   Company Overviews

Yellow Pages   Internet Starter Kit   HTML Workshop   Win a Free T-Shirt!   Macmillan Computer Publishing   Site Map   Talk to Us

CHECK OUT THE BOOKS IN THIS LIBRARY.

You'll find thousands of shareware files and over 1600 computer books designed for both technowizards and technophobes. You can browse through 700 sample chapters, get the latest news on the Net, and find just about anything using our

We're open 24 hours a day, 365 days a year.

You don't need a card.

We don't charge fines.

And you can be as **LOUD** as you want.

Deploying Windows NT 4.0 in the Enterprise

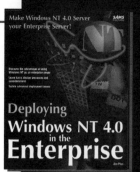

Jim Plas

Windows NT is quickly becoming a recognized contender in the enterprise software arena. This indispensable guide specifically addresses NT as an enterprise server, and covers topics ranging from LANs and WANs to multi-platform networks, as well as providing comprehensive coverage of server standardization, workstation standards, alternative clients, SNA connectivity, advanced trust relationships, and the challenges that are particular to large systems using the newest technologies. Covers Version 4

Price: $55.00 USA/$77.95 CAN   *User level: Accomplished–Expert*
ISBN: 0-672-31038-4   *500 pages*

Windows NT 4 Administrator's Survival Guide

Rick Sant'Angelo

This is the only survival guide an NT network administrator needs. Written by best-selling author Rick Sant'Angelo, this concise, easy-to-use guide provides all the information users need to successfully implement and maintain a Windows NT 4 Server. You'll find a reference guide to third-party products, logon scripts programming, technical terms, and commonly used NT utilities, along with tips and notes from the author on improving performance and saving money when implementing your Windows NT Server. Covers Version 4

Price: $49.99 USA/$70.95 CAN   *User level: Accomplished–Expert*
ISBN: 0-672-31008-2   *900 pages*

Windows NT Troubleshooting and Configuration

Robert Reinstein, et al.

Written for system administrators, this book shows you how to use Windows NT with the other components of the BackOffice suite. It includes coverage of NT design, system management, Registry modification and management, troubleshooting, Internet support, and security issues. You'll learn how to use NT with BackOffice and as a Web server with Internet Information Server and Microsoft's other Internet tools. It also contains a complete troubleshooting section outlining known problems and their solutions. Covers NT 4.0 and BackOffice

Price: $59.99 USA/$84.95 CAN
ISBN: 0-672-30941-6

User level: Accomplished–Expert
1,200 pages

Windows NT 4 Workstation Unleashed, Second Edition

Paul Cassel, Mike Sheehy & Sean Mathias, et al.

Written for those network administrators and power users whose corporations choose the NT Workstation as the corporate desktop platform, this Professional Reference Edition provides accurate information in an understandable, comprehensive format. You'll find over 500 pages of new material and expanded coverage, including 14 new chapters and a reference section containing seven new appendixes.

Price: $49.99 US/$70.95 CAN
ISBN: 0-672-31081-3

User level: Accomplished–Expert
1,200 pages

Add to Your Sams Library Today with the Best Books for Programming, Operating Systems, and New Technologies

The easiest way to order is to pick up the phone and call

1-800-428-5331

between 9:00 a.m. and 5:00 p.m. EST.
For faster service please have your credit card available.

ISBN	Quantity	Description of Item	Unit Cost	Total Cost
0-672-31038-4		Deploying Windows NT 4.0 in the Enterprise	$55.00	
0-672-31008-2		Windows NT 4 Administrator's Survival Guide (book/CD-ROM)	$49.99	
0-672-30941-6		Windows NT Troubleshooting and Configuration (book/CD-ROM)	$59.99	
0-672-31081-3		Windows NT 4 Workstation Unleashed, Second Edition	$49.99	
		Shipping and Handling: See information below.		
		TOTAL		

Shipping and Handling: $4.00 for the first book, and $1.75 for each additional book. If you need to have it NOW, we can ship product to you in 24 hours for an additional charge of approximately $18.00, and you will receive your item overnight or in two days. Overseas shipping and handling adds $2.00 per book. Prices subject to change. Call for availability and pricing information on latest editions.

201 W. 103rd Street, Indianapolis, Indiana 46290

1-800-428-5331 — Orders   1-800-835-3202 — FAX   1-800-858-7674 — Customer Service

Book ISBN 0-672-31135-6

MACMILLAN COMPUTER PUBLISHING USA

A VIACOM COMPANY

Support:

If you need assistance with the information in this book or with a CD/disk accompanying the book, please access the Knowledge Base on our Web site at **http://www.superlibrary.com/general/support**. Our most Frequently Asked Questions are answered there. If you do not find the answer to your questions on our Web site, you may contact Macmillan Technical Support **(317) 581-3833** or e-mail us at **support@mcp.com**.